Writing
BASEBALL

Writing BASEBALL

Edited by

JERRY KLINKOWITZ

UNIVERSITY OF ILLINOIS PRESS

Urbana and Chicago

Manufactured in the United States of America
1 2 3 4 5 C P 5 4 3 2 1

This book is printed on acid-free paper.

Library of Congress Cataloging-in-Publication Data

Writing baseball / edited by Jerry Klinkowitz.
    p. cm.
   Includes bibliographical references.
   ISBN 0-252-01820-6 (alk. paper). — ISBN 0-252-06192-6 (pbk. :
alk. paper)
    1. Baseball. I. Klinkowitz, Jerome.
GV862.5.W75 1991
796.357 — dc20   90-22474
                                                      CIP

CONTENTS

PREFACE   vii

INTRODUCTION   1
JERRY KLINKOWITZ

PROLOGUE
The Creation Myths of Cooperstown   23
STEPHEN JAY GOULD

I. KIDS

From *Florry of Washington Heights*   STEVE KATZ   37
The Aerodynamics of an Irishman   BARRY GIFFORD   48
Dreams of a Jewish Batboy   GERALD ROSEN   50
From *Brushes with Greatness:* Willie Mays   PAUL AUSTER   58
How I Got My Nickname   W. P. KINSELLA   60
Why I Hate Baseball   MICHAEL STEPHENS   70

II. MINORS

From *What's a Nice Harvard Boy Like You Doing in the Bushes?*
   RICK WOLFF   81
From *Short Season*   JERRY KLINKOWITZ   88
Triumphant Return   RICK WOLFF   103

III. SCOUTS

From *Dollar Sign on the Muscle*   KEVIN KERRANE   111
Clearing the Decks   PETER PASCARELLI   116
Free Agency for World Leaders   GERALD ROSEN   121

IV. PLAYERS

From *Foul Ball!*   ALISON GORDON   127
Time Loves a Haircut   BILL CARDOSO   143
Understanding Alvarado   MAX APPLE   147
From *High Inside*   DANIELLE GAGNON TORREZ   159
From *The Seventh Babe*   JEROME CHARYN   162

V. PROFESSORS

From *The Warsaw Sparks*   GARY GILDNER   173
Earl Wasserman, Johns Hopkins, Baseball and Me
   ERIC SOLOMON   181

VI. FANS

From *Blue Highways*   WILLIAM LEAST HEAT MOON   193
Three New Twins Join Club in Spring   GARRISON KEILLOR   195
From *The Dodgers Move West*   NEIL J. SULLIVAN   199
Confessions from Left Field   RAYMOND MUNGO   202

PREFACE

A FEW YEARS AGO, when presenting a Modern Language Association Convention paper on sports literature, I had to correct moderator Robert Newman's introduction: rather than speaking as a professor of English at the University of Northern Iowa and author of *Literary Disruptions*, I hoped to be received as a minor-league baseball executive. Back then the proudest line on my vita was "Executive Director, Waterloo Indians, Midwest League affiliate of the Cleveland Indians." The franchise I help operate has since changed labels, becoming the Waterloo Diamonds, one of the San Diego Padres' Class A farm clubs. But I'm still thrilled to be executive director, and it is my work in that capacity, rather than strictly as a teacher and scholar, that stands behind this book, the selections of which are quite different from those usually picked by literary critics.

Robert Newman of Texas A&M University deserves my thanks for getting me going on sports *literature*; as for *sports* literature, I'm in debt to former Cleveland Indians officials Dan O'Brien (now with the California Angels) and Bob Quinn (presently in Cincinnati by way of the Yankees), Cleveland's current assistant scouting director Phil Thomas, and San Diego Padres director of player development Tom Romenesko for giving me so much of their time to discuss how baseball functions both on and off the field. During the seventy-game home season of a minor-league club, many visitors pass through the park in various capacities—scouting their own or the home team, meeting clients for whom they are now agents, or as part of promotions—and I am similarly grateful to Tal Smith, the late Paul Richards, Pat Dobson, Ed Charles, Don Buford, Manny Sanguillen, Bob Feller, and Max Patkin for letting me take advantage of their open time between afternoon workouts and the evening's game. Our own managers and coaches shared hours of talk, especially Gomer Hodges, Steve Swisher, Chuck Stobbs, Glenn Adams, Brian Allard, Lenny Randle (posed in our card set blowing a bunted ball over the foul line), Jaime Moreno, and Mark Littell. Don Kruse, sports writer for the Waterloo *Courier*, taught me how to use a press pass in the dugouts, locker rooms, press boxes, media lounges, and around the batting cages at Fenway, Wrigley, Comiskey, and Milwaukee County Stadium. A number of professors across the country suggested materials for this book, including Jeff Copeland, Jim Martin, Kevin Kerrane, Don Blau, Bob Morace, Jim Holt, and Jerry Rosen, but all have close connections to the game as former professional players, umpires, scouts, baseball journalists, or front-office types.

Few English departments can boast a former NFL lineman or NBA forward on their faculties, but almost every one — including the Instytut Filologii Angielskiej at Warsaw University in Poland, as Gary Gildner's story in this volume shows — has a faculty member related at least tangentially to professional baseball. That relationship may well be one subtext this collection explores.

JERRY KLINKOWITZ
Waterloo Professional Baseball, Inc.

INTRODUCTION

Jerry Klinkowitz

Writing baseball—that's a phrase Roland Barthes would have savored had he been raised in Bayonne, New Jersey, rather than in Bayonne, France. As even American students of language would say today, there's something in the act described that makes one wonder whether it is a transitive or intransitive operation. Writing baseball, in these terms, is more like writing fiction than writing a letter, an address, or a set of instructions: it looks not to an object but to its own action. There is something in the nature of baseball that makes writing the subject (and surely talking it) something theorists have long thought was impossible; it lets one act purely reflexively while still having a universally recognizable object on the table when one's done. That's why "writing baseball" rather than "writing *about* baseball" is not only the technically correct term but also the one people in the street use to describe that act, just as they do for their more immediately linguistic business—that pop song's title, after all, was not "Talking about Baseball," nor did the activity it described come out as anything other than "talkin' baseball."

There are many reasons why the specific nature of baseball lends itself to such ideally intransitive activity, including the way it is played, managed, administered (even scouted), watched, and remembered. But foremost is its affinity with the play of language itself. Like all games, it is a system whose narrowly defined grammar is exercised within an equally restrictive syntax to generate an infinite realm of possibilities—infinite, yet absolutely understandable because everyone playing and watching is presumed to know the rules. To say it this way is to speak more like someone from France than New Jersey, but it is a reminder that like so many games seen by international visitors, any baseball Roland Barthes may have witnessed during his brief

1

residency at Middlebury College (during that same summer Warren Spahn, Lew Burdette, Joe Adcock, Eddie Mathews, and Hank Aaron were helping the Milwaukee Braves win their first pennant) would have been undecipherable given an ignorance of its form. Yet what baseball players say and what baseball writers write is translatable even in conceptual play, and it is this special affinity for language as a system—beyond dialect and idiom, more toward the essential nature of communication itself—that is the first great distinguishing point in baseball's fundamentally *writable* nature.

Consider the famous aphorisms of Yogi Berra: "Nobody goes there anymore—it's too crowded"; "Left field in this park is terrible—it gets late early out there"; "It's not over 'til it's over." These are not stupid mistakes, or even malapropisms a superior listener turns into wit or insight, but linguistic collisions that by virtue of their structural contradictions signal a higher level of meaning—and they are screamingly funny at the same time, precisely because they articulate a truth for which no one else had found just the right words. Baseball responds not by laughing off Berra as an idiot but by treasuring him as its *idiot savant*. Likewise for his manager, Casey Stengel, who earned the title of "the old professor" for his way with language and the peculiar nature of truths behind it, producing, for example, such gems as turning to a dugout bench on which just one forlorn player languished and announcing "One of you guys is going to Kansas City!" and telling the press he'd learned his lesson after being fired by the Yankees because of his age by saying "I'll never make the mistake of being seventy again."

Nor is it just a few linguistic superstars like Berra and Stengel who make baseball the language game. No matter what the situation, there always seems a way for any player to make linguistic capital of what transpires on and off the field. So much of the action is verbal anyway, from those long conversations on the mound to the words exchanged by batter and umpire concerning the strike zone. Lefty Gomez, facing Bob Feller's almost unhittable fastball, once let the first two whistle by without taking the bat off his shoulder; when Feller's third pitch was called a strike as well, Gomez turned to the ump and cautioned, "That last one sounded a little low." In the same batter's box a generation later, hitter Lou Piniella was more emphatic. "Where was that last one at?" When the umpire advised him not to end a sentence with a preposition, Piniella complied: "Okay, where was that last one at, you asshole." Off the field, where real life can dominate with its problems and inevitabilities, baseball people are equally noteworthy for their way with words, such as pitcher Bob Welch's explanation for finally undertaking the hard battle against alcoholism ("I got sick and tired of feeling sick and tired") and executive Branch Rickey's sad appraisal of what it is like to be a man growing very old ("First you forget names, then you forget faces; first you forget to zip your pants, then you forget to unzip them").

The tradition of naively colorful baseball language dates back to Ring Lardner's *You Know Me, Al,* parts of which first appeared in 1914, but even in a new age when most players sign out of or after college, minor-league general managers have master's degrees in sports administration, the American League president is a nationally eminent cardiologist, and a Dante scholar and former President of Yale could and did become Commissioner of Baseball, the game's notoriety for linguistic playfulness continues, now being recognized for brilliance rather than just low comedy. There are still malapropisms beat writers savor, such as Oil Can Boyd's disclaimer as he left the Red Sox for Toronto, "I thought I was a household product in Boston," but there are also ways players tease those same writers, as when the Blue Jays' Mike Flanagan discounted the 88-mile-per-hour fastball of Boston's Mike Boddicker: "That's only 83 Canadian." Asked how his team, down 0 to 2 to the Oakland A's in the 1989 World Series, would be influenced by the massive earthquake that devastated parts of the Bay area and northern California, one San Francisco Giants pitcher responded, "I guess you can say the momentum has shifted"—a possibly callous statement, whose humor lies in one of the banalities of sports journalism being turned against a writer so thoughtless to present such a question. Yet even in a day when postgame interviews take on the qualities of a cutting contest plenty of room remains for promptings of poetic philosophy, from Bart Giamatti's analyses of the game's ritual properties to George Plimpton's consideration of why so much time is wasted on the mound: "The pitcher is happiest with his arm idle. He prefers to dawdle in the present, knowing that as soon as he starts his windup he delivers himself to the uncertainty of the future."

The artfulness in these examples of "talkin' baseball" derives from structural play, all the way from Berra's transcendence of opposites (avoided/crowded, late/early, not over/over) to Plimpton's conflation of two different measures of the future (next pitch/next year). Branch Rickey fashions parallels with parallels, whereas Oil Can Boyd, by substituting "household product" for "household name," implies (perhaps subconsciously) a once-brilliant career going down the drain (unplugged no doubt by another household product become a household name, "Drāno"). Such quotes are appreciated by writers and sought after by fans. A regular part of each paper's sports section for December 31 is a list of the year's best one liners, and during game time a baseball pressbox is awash with running commentary—not from the broadcast crews partitioned off in their glass booths but from the beat and wire service writers, columnists, and sports editors transforming everything they see into a metanarrative on the nature of the game and their roles in it. In Milwaukee, Robin Yount lofts a long one that's likely to clear the center-field fence, which a dozen writers serenade with a clucking chorus of "back-back-back-back-back-back-back . . . " until the ball's safely out of the park. Next inning, a visitor not from the working press walks through, stops to watch a Brewer pitcher yield a bases-loaded double, and kicks the wastebasket while lamenting "Come *on*, Bosio!" Pure fan reaction, spontaneous and unexceptional, except it comes from the team's owner, Bud Selig. In Boston, Mrs. Yawkey and Johnny Pesky gab about the old days while the press corps, disregarding rookie Sam Horn's debut with two home runs, totes up the day's more significant action, how many writers visiting manager Dick Williams insulted before the game. At Wrigley, competing fielding averages are kept and studied exegetically—not of the Cubs versus the Giants but of the *Tribune* versus the *Sun-Times* writers' dexterity in copping free Cokes and burgers from the courtesy window. Creatures of structure create their own, players and writers alike, and from it evolves the verbal nature of this great American game.

For some, that nature is elevated into myth, the natural being fashioned to purpose, being made intentional, meaningful, even divine—in other words, made human. Such is the strategy behind the prose of Bart Giamatti and George Plimpton and the fiction of Bernard Malamud (*The Natural*). But because baseball is itself a human invention, and because it flaunts such obvious conventionality in every action, other writers have seen fit to either parody that myth-making, such as novelists Robert Coover and Philip Roth in *The Universal Baseball Association, Inc./J. Henry Waugh, Prop.* and *The Great American Novel*, respectively, or to move directly to the game itself for an appreciation of its self-apparent factors of reaction, as happens in the commentaries of Roger Angell and Thomas Boswell and the fiction of Jerome Charyn, Max Apple, and Gerald Rosen.

This attraction to the unadorned game is what most aptly character-izes baseball writing of recent years. If there are mythmaking properties, these writers say, let them emerge naturally from the materials rather than be imposed from without (or, as Coover so cleverly satirizes, from above, where his cardtable-game-playing creator projects a sense of character that in the end becomes a destiny he himself cannot control). After all, myths are formed to explain the inexplicable, to bring order to an otherwise disorderly world, to fill in gaps beyond the knowledge or comprehension of any mere mortal. In baseball, none of these is the case. Its physics are explicable: tools are weighted in half ounces, running speeds clocked in fractions of a second, and pitches timed by radar, the scientific device that won mankind's greatest and most terrible war now used by junior high school coaches and even sandlot scouts. Its conduct is orderly, framed by rules codified in subsections down to three decimal points. Most importantly, virtually everything is known. Professor Stephen Jay Gould is fond of reminding myth-makers that in one of his own hard sciences, paleontology, the nature of an object is assumed from evidential knowledge of as little as one half of one percent of its being, whereas in baseball one has the benefit of complete statistical records for almost everything that hap-pened in the history of the game—except for its creation, which fans insist be mythified rather than explained away in an evolutionary manner.

Just as baseball, with its 100 percent evidentiary presence, becomes the ideal science, so too do its properties allow it to serve as the perfect fiction. As Stephen Jay Gould sees scientific problems solved, so can any literary theorist find properties in writing baseball that not only resolve decades-long debates but produce a style of literature previous definitions had ruled impossible. Ever since Samuel Beckett inaugu-rated literary postmodernism by declaring that the best writing should not be about something but rather be that something itself, critics have struggled with a seemingly contrary factor in the nature of writing's components: that unlike daubs of paint, shapes of material, or notes of music—which allow items of painting, sculpture, and music, respectively, to be as abstract and self-referential as their creators want them to be—words by their nature refer to things outside themselves. Thus not only essays but novels and short stories are committed ultimately to reflecting a world outside themselves, regardless of their writers' intentions, because their basic building blocks are words, and words refer. To get around this limitation Beckett and a long line of his successors have tried various ways of overriding, diffusing, or destroying the referentiality of language in their works, from compositions built on mathematical permutations to mechanical cut-ups, typographic displays, self-conscious sunderings of tradition, unconventional use of literary conventions, and the elaborate Chinese box effect of narratives about an author writing a narrative about an author writing a narrative about.... Yet in every case they find themselves hard up against those original limitations of language and the writer's struggle with them: words refer, and the fictive characters and situations supposedly created by them are readable in the same way as are the doings of persons in the real world.

The implications for genre are even more profound. On the one hand, there is supposed to be the greatest distinction possible between a story in the newspaper and a story written by a fictionist, a distinction based on the dichotomies of reality and imagination, fact and fancy, life and art. Yet on the page both look the same. Theorists have striven to distinguish between a sentence written by the historian Taine—"The Marquis went out at 5 o'clock"—and the very same sentence Paul Valéry cited as being just the quintessential requirement for fiction that he could not bear to write and that thus kept him a poet. For all the theoretical distinctions, readers (and especially the poets among them) either cannot tell the difference or do not employ it in a practical way once they have settled down with the work.

When writing baseball (and reading it), these factors change, and with those changes the intrinsic limitations are removed. Consider Paul Valéry's fate had he wished to write a baseball novel. He would not have had to go about the embarrassing business of inventing a character who could both be interesting enough to merit existence yet also conform to history's comparative test. The game of baseball would have already done that for him, supplying such a thing as a first baseman, another such as a shortstop, and so forth. Valéry would not have to justify who and why they are, because the game itself describes their positions, their roles, and even characteristics sufficient to stock the most detailed novel of manners (the first baseman being properly big and strong to hit with power, tall enough to field errant throws, and perhaps left-handed—the better to tag a runner or cut him down going to second base; the shortstop being small, quick, nimble, and always right-handed so that double plays remain possible). Not only is there no need here to make up (and consequently bear the responsibility for) characters, but the field for their action is already in place. The hitter proceeds not into the great unknown (which would have to be invented and better be good), but down to first base. There is no need to impose an order on otherwise chaotic existence, for that has already been done by the rules committee, setting out the bases at right angles and 90 feet apart. Most crucially, there is not only no need to suspend disbelief, but the narrative can proceed within a suspension already undertaken: there is no reason to say "once upon a time," for that time has been established and set aside by Abner Doubleday or someone like him. Yet neither is there a requirement of fidelity to structures in the real world, for baseball is not a natural phenomenon but is as "made-up" as the most outrageous fiction.

Writing baseball lets an author both have the cake and eat it, too. The subject is at once invented (as a game) and real (by virtue of its history and of its observable nature once underway). In terms of language, the writer's words need not suffer for being referential, because in this format they do not refer to something but are that something itself: a game of ball. Even those awkward and ultimately unworkable distinctions of genre are transformed into simple contrasts of subject level; when Chicago *Tribune* beat writer Fred Mitchell writes his story about the Cubs' eleven-inning 7 to 6 loss to the Giants, and novelist Jerome Charyn follows his third baseman's exploits in a game against the Yankees, they are using the same tools—now less of a problem for genre theorists because in each case their subjects are imaginative inventions.

Not that all writers have taken advantage of this happy coincidence. The worst baseball journalism, just like the most embarrassing fiction on the subject, ignores the rare treasure of this middle ground to ape the excesses of the other—thus the now fortunately outdated sports writing that extolls the happenings of baseball as if they are indistinguishable in the march of time from the conquests of Napoleon or the long progress of geological ages and the equally discredited style of fiction writing that cannot allow baseball on the page without claiming it as a metaphor or symbol for youth, hope, sex, motherhood, fatherhood, brotherly love, uxorial hostility, and ultimately life itself. In our present age of writing baseball both the journalists and fictionists have shared an appreciation for baseball as a thing in itself. It provides the structure for their work at a time when structures and not content are considered the only palpable substance.

Readers and writers, of course, know the difference between a reportorial account in the Chicago *Tribune* and a Garrison Keillor story in *The New Yorker,* but with the theoretical hassles to such understanding removed, these same readers and writers share the opportunity of taking the act of writing baseball to new extremes of pleasurability. Part of such work's quality comes from personal admiration and envy: writers in the press boxes at Wrigley and Fenway wish they could trade places with writers at Yaddo and the McDowell Colony, and vice versa. It is therefore no accident that the best baseball reporting adopts the conventions of fiction, such as characterization, development by dialogue, informing images, and attentiveness to the sound of language, whereas baseball fiction shifts away from overbearing metaphors and symbols toward a visceral feel for the game's rhythms and movements. As these differently credentialed writers admire each other's work, they draw on each other's best respective elements of composition; and though a baseball game at Wrigley on June 13, 1986, differs from a baseball game in Jerome Charyn's imagination, each is still a baseball game, a correspondence that makes sense both on the abstract level of theory and on the practical level of writing produced.

Sentences from all-star catchers and World Series managers twisting through apparent contradictions, colliding at the caesura, and coming to rest as telling aphorisms catalogued with those of Abe Lincoln, Mark Twain, and Will Rogers; paragraphs from sports writers crafted with the care of Flaubert and sparkling with the epiphanic insight of James Joyce; short stories and novels that roll from the pen like a drag bunt down the line, or that rocket toward their conclusions like that line drive off the Staten Island Scot's bat—these are the perfect games played now and then in the world of writing baseball.

As the pieces selected for this volume show, writing baseball is a talent that extends to all aspects of the game. Because it is first of all a childhood game, men and women who have grown up to fashion talents with a writer's tools are often drawn back to baseball as a way of doing with words, phrases, and ideas what they used to do with bat, glove, and ball. In terms of subject, writing baseball puts them back in the box as kids—bunting no better than they did in 1950, but now with the linguistic talent to capture that imperfectly physical act in artistically refined language.

This is just what happens in the climactic scene to Steve Katz's *Florry of Washington Heights,* where the narrator—after suffering the threats of a rival gang for the novel's length—helps resolve matters by taking a central part in the baseball game that concludes the action.

Katz's personal role as author parallels the story told by his fifteen-year-old protagonist, Swanny Swanson, for as Swanny uses baseball to structure a life otherwise confused by the ravages of postpubescent but still preadult relationships between and among the sexes, Katz takes Swanny's memoir as a vehicle for moving beyond the antirealistic strategies of his previous fiction. The rival gang, the Fanwoods, is a figuration of the kid's wide-ranging fears—of leaving the shelter of his neighborhood, of dealing with girls, of high school, of graduating to face the draft and the risk of getting killed in Korea. Plus the Fanwoods are trouble enough themselves, and in melding these two natures of threat Katz manages to write a novel that is imaginatively unfettered but realistically pertinent at the same time. The neighborhood's baseball team is present from the first pages and figures both as a locus for action (as the kids organize, practice, and fend off threats) and as an index to Swanny Swanson's character (he wears number 15 in reference to his model, the quietly strong Tommy Henrich, nicknamed among the Yankees as "Old Reliable"—another reminder of baseball's ready-made structure). Yet just as baseball is not "about" anything other than itself, Swanny's experience with his team isn't a metaphor for his adolescence or a symbol of his self-sacrificing triumph in the beleaguered circumstances of growing up in a borderline-rough Manhattan neighborhood just across the river from the Bronx. Instead, Katz uses it as an enabling structure for his own narrative, the rhythms of which parallel but do not specifically repeat Swanny's storytelling.

The same rhythms distinguish Barry Gifford's "The Aerodynamics of an Irishman," an example of otherwise nonfictional writing taking on the qualities of fictive prose. Published independently, it matches the style of interpolations used to measure Gifford's more historically related sports memoir, *The Neighborhood of Baseball*, where short commentaries on the ongoing fates of the Chicago Cubs are interleaved with memories of Gifford's family and friends from the surrounding Lakeview district of Chicago. It is an example of how writing baseball transcends the definitive limits of genre, using history and imagination in equal parts to evoke a moment on the page.

A similar interweaving of fact and fiction creates the special texture of writing in Gerald Rosen's novel *Growing Up Bronx*, Paul Auster's recollection of meeting Willie Mays, and W. P. Kinsella's transfictional "How I Got My Nickname." Mays takes an important part in all three selections, just as he did in the lives of younger fans back in the early 1950s—not just as a phenomenal player but as a sensitive young man not that far removed from the uncertainties of adolescence himself (and needing the surrogate parenting of manager Leo Durocher to make that transition from kid to superstar).

In Rosen's book, Mays is part of a story within a story that itself serves as one of the novel's key episodes. For this collection Rosen has reached back into his original manuscript where the scene runs several pages instead of just a few, but the structural import remains the same: as a narrator-protagonist (much like Steve Katz's in *Florry of Washington Heights*) struggles to shape his unfolding life, he encounters something that is at once made-up and therefore already structured: baseball. Then, within that fabricated structure, he brushes shoulders with a character historically real, whose existence is verified by its celebrity nature in the papers, on the radio, and on TV, allowing himself not just a measure of his own stature (which is of course frighteningly small) but an intimation of how he has taken his own first step out into the playing field of what will become his public life. The same generating factor is implied in Paul Auster's page written for the book edited by Russell Banks, Michael Ondaatje, and David Young, *Brushes with Greatness: Chance Encounters with Celebrities,* where meeting the famous center fielder prompts not only this text but all others in Auster's canon.

Characters like Mays and Durocher are just that: personalities in literature as well as life whose presence inspires a writer's voice. Durocher's own *Nice Guys Finish Last* is distinguished by the colorful and controversial manager's voice as much as by any of its historical details; with coauthor Ed Linn's help Leo the Lip reminds readers that the most interesting thing about him was not simply his run-ins with players and owners but how he expressed himself in those dealings. It is this verbal presence that stands behind Kinsella's short story, in which a high school kid steps out onto the field at the 1951 Polo Grounds and, with Leo's encouragement, takes a leading role with the team. The imaginative source for this narrative performance, in which manager and players behave both within and outside of character, may well be Durocher's remark to owner Horace Stoneham, recorded in *Nice Guy's Finish Last,* appraising the beefy, flat-footed club Leo had been hired to run: "Horace, you're throwing your money away when you pay me. A little boy can manage this team. All you do is make out the lineup and hope you get enough home runs."

Durocher's tenure with the Giants, of course, proved to be anything but that simple, inspiring a style that Kinsella is able to adopt as a readymade but also play with by having the sharp-tongued manager talk about literary artifice as well as baseball, the narrative itself being generated by combining the two chief factors in the kid's life to date: a library of the classics (his father is a professor) and a mania for pro ball as it's seen during family trips to Chicago and St. Louis plus at minor-league parks closer to home in Iowa.

Though these initial selections are more winsome than fearsome, Leo Durocher would be the first to say that it isn't always pretty, either in baseball or in the game of growing up. In Michael Stephens's *Season at Coole*, a novel structured by a writer's personality emerging from a darkly comic and madly chaotic family life, baseball is one of the siblings' options, complementing others such as alcohol, drugs, psychosis, and grand larceny (in addition to the just as controversial choices of painting or literature). With eight brothers and sisters, the protagonist has a wide range of possibilities for suggesting ways out of childhood's confinements and exploring parallels among this diversity. Stephens is by no means the first to play with the affinities shared by the artistically creative and physically destructive lives, but locating professional baseball as a third endeavor and relating it to the other two is something as new as the Mets pitcher Dwight Gooden's assignment for substance-abuse rehabilitation to the same institution famous for curing novelist John Cheever. In a decades-later reprise to *Season at Coole*, Stephens explores just these issues in "Why I Hate Baseball," an example of writing that can talk about fictive worlds and the real one in the same breath, for so are they joined by the structures of our culture when it comes to this central sport.

Another style of complexity results when the focus in writing baseball shifts from the major to the minor leagues. Just like those startling modifications of familiar names—the Clinton Giants, the Cedar Rapids Reds, the Kenosha Twins—farm clubs are real things and counterfeits at the same time. They share many aspects of big-league play but operate by a system all their own, which for many famous players lingers as a bad-dream apprenticeship best forgotten. Yet recent years have found writers (with filmmakers close behind them) drawn to these specific aspects. Because minor leaguers even at the lowest rung are still professionals in the same organizations that pay multimillions to Kevin Mitchell, Eric Davis, and Kent Hrbek, the reality of existing on one seventh of the meal money and five thousandths of the contracted salary is something that crosses the line into absurdity. Especially when the time and space gap can be as tiny as a ten-second call from a big club's general manager: "Swindell: report to Cleveland," a transaction I witnessed myself (and that had happened before when Von Hayes went straight from our A-ball club to Cleveland, and Kent Hrbek, Gary Gaetti, and Jim Eisenreich jumped almost as directly from the Twins' cellar dwellers in our league to the starting lineup in Minnesota).

Factors such as these generate a body of minor-league literature with an energy all its own. Selected here are three varieties from my own experience at this level of professional baseball. A passage from Rick Wolff's *What's a Nice Harvard Boy Like You Doing in the Bushes?* is the first, an account of a college student's experiment with his own life of fiction, taking off for two years to pursue a career at second base in the Detroit Tigers' organization. At the time, Detroit had its better A club at Clinton, Iowa, and so after a good start with the rookie team at Anderson, South Carolina, Wolff found himself playing in the Mid-west League (where I've worked for the past decade as an executive director of what was first the Cleveland Indians' and is now the San Diego Padres' affiliate in Waterloo). Though major-league baseball has changed radically in the last twenty years, the minors seem timeless: Wolff's 1970s are identical to the 1980s I worked with the Waterloo Indians and the 1990s I've begun with the Waterloo Diamonds (the Padres like farm clubs to have their own names). Though I hadn't read the *Harvard Boy* book when writing my own minor-league stories, the two volumes compare on a level that transcends both time and genre, as each is a direct product not of authorial attitudes but of the material's own rhythms and nuances, especially as those factors derive from the game itself.

A trio of vignettes from my *Short Season* suggests the nature of the book, which cannot be a conventional novel because the variables in a minor-league season make it virtually impossible to have a consistently central character and a coherently developing theme, given all the roster changes and the classification's emphasis on learning and evaluating rather than just winning. But neither is it a collection of independent short stories, for the short season from mid-April to late August does have the same integrity of structure one finds at any level of baseball: three-out innings, nine-inning games, series with other teams, homestands, road trips, and the seasonal progress through the subtle varieties of spring and then summer in the upper Midwest.

Because baseball itself is both real and made-up, there is even a debate as to whether such writing is essentially fiction or reportage.

Novelists and short-story writers who tackle the subject are forever questioned about what difference exists between the games in their minds and games on the field, while reporters and columnists often hear complaints (from players, management, and fans) that their work is so idiosyncratic and prejudicial that it becomes a whole reality apart from what's transpiring down on the diamond. Such habits carry over into baseball broadcasting, where you can tune a silent TV to network coverage of a Cubs game while listening to Harry Caray do the radio account and get the impression of experiencing two entirely different ball games. To complete the Borgesian cycle, players on occasion tailor their performance to the media's eye: not for nothing did Gary Carter win the nickname "Camera," for he was reputed to know the Game of the Week director's angles as well as what pitches to call for an opposing hitter.

Short Season itself risked being implicated in this process and making its mark in baseball history. Robert Creamer of Sports Illustrated wanted to publish "Five Bad Hands and the Wild Mouse Folds" as an article rather than as the short story I was honestly calling it; when I insisted that I could not provide the "verification" he wanted because no such action had ever happened, a group of players on that year's real team intervened and offered to do on the next road trip just what my story had projected. Luckily, I was able to talk them out of it, eager as they were to please and to help solve such knotty problems of literary theory.

As fiction, the vignettes knit together in Short Season avoid the more conventional restraints of fictive narrative in that they plot the progress of an invented minor-league team's annual campaign without any impositions of meaning: what images and metaphors there are result from the game's own phenomenology, especially as it reaches from the field to the many supporting factors in running such an operation. Perhaps that is why "Five Bad Hands" read like fact to Bob Creamer, although the lesson here is that just as fiction can be truer than life, writing baseball in postmodern times challenges one to avoid the pontifications and easy invocations of humanistic ideals that spoil the game.

Thus Rick Wolff's Harvard Boy and my Short Season hope to be bookends to a style of creative action that shares major affinities on the field and on the page. But like the radio says, there is always "the rest of the story," and for that Wolff files his "Triumphant Return." When the paperback rights for Short Season were sold, the top bid came from

him—in the fifteen years since Rick had played in the Midwest League
he'd given up professional baseball, returned to Harvard, gone on to
law school, and begun a career in publishing that had made him
director of sports books for Macmillan. Now he was calling in not just
with a proposal to do a Collier-Macmillan edition but with the asser-
tion that *Short Season* was virtually the biography of a year in his life.
As the paperback went through production and promotion, Rick
found himself once again making the transition into a life of fiction. I
joked that the current crop of teams passing through our ballpark all
looked pretty weak at second base and that if he was thinking of
getting back in the game, now was the time. He took it seriously, and
within the month had a contract to play with the South Bend White
Sox, where the average teammate was hardly more than half his age.
There is a fine tradition of writers practicing the "New Journalism" of
Tom Wolfe, Dan Wakefield, and Hunter S. Thompson—rather than
trying to describe an event from the outside, they put themselves at
the event's center and write autobiographically. Yet Wolff's experience,
accompanied as it was with an assignment from *Sports Illustrated*, is
something beyond Donald Hall's spring training workout with the
Pirates in *Playing Around* and George Plimpton's pre-exhibition-game
contest of pitching to squads of all-star National and American leaguers
in *Out of My League* for the same reason that effaces so many distinctions of genre in these selections for *Writing Baseball*: taking the field at
South Bend for three games in an actual Midwest League season, Rick
Wolff can be a real second baseman without having to stop being a real
writer, and vice versa, because of baseball's nature in general and
because of his specific experience in both professions.

From the test bed of the minor leagues *Writing Baseball* moves to
the level at which baseball becomes a deadly serious business: "the
bigs," as nearly everyone involved calls them, where players sign $23
million contracts, franchises change hands for over $100 million, and
television and other subsidiary rights approach billions. Yet the charm
of the game and the appeal of writing baseball is that many of the
same factors working for kids and for the minors still operate way up
here. Though the financial figures are astronomical, they are generated
by a game, and not just metaphorically. Business people will talk about
the stock market and so forth as "a game," "a racket," or "a circus,"
but business on Wall Street is not conducted in anything near the
style described by the contributors to Terry Pluto and Jeffrey Neuman's
A Baseball Winter, nor can it match in novelistic richness the real-

life world of scouting Kevin Kerrane explores in *Dollar Sign on the Muscle.*

Take Hugh Alexander: Kerrane catches this legendary one-handed scout at spring training, whereas Peter Pascarelli tracks him through the trading season between the World Series and the major-league meetings that form a crucial part of baseball's off-season life. Scouting, trades, contract holdouts, free agent signings, the amateur draft — these business details, analogous in financial impact to corporate transactions studied in a newspaper's business section, often debated with the seriousness accorded to political developments in the editorial columns, and even snapped up as eagerly and anxiously as front-page events, take on exceptional color and liveliness in the sports pages. The reason is a combination of readerly interest and writerly style, but at the root is the nature of baseball, which offers all the data of real life yet remains by definition and in essence a game, no matter how many George Steinbrenners and Marge Schotts try to enforce business ideals, management principles, and bottom-line accountability.

The gamesmanship of writing baseball is a style that can be transferred intact, as Gerald Rosen's "Free Agency for World Leaders" shows. Kids trade baseball cards in the same style as major league general managers swap players, and perhaps (as a beer commercial showed it several years ago) vice versa. Rotisserie League Baseball, a deft combination of fantastic control over some very real historical and actuarial data, builds on the same concept. All Rosen has to do to translate world affairs into the language of sports commentary is to grab some superstar names from the political news on page one and run them through the paces used to measure the doings of baseball players up for trades or free agency — and in the process reveal insights about political events worthy of the freshest column by Flora Lewis or David Broder. The tradition is an honorable one, with borrowings from the opposite direction by George Will that readers can expect whenever the fortunes of political conservativism look as bleak as a Chicago Cubs season gone bad by the end of May.

What about the players and their game on the field? Though there have been attempts to follow such action inning by inning and even pitch by pitch, such writing has never been as satisfactory as that which expands or contracts the action. In terms of art, it suggests the difference between constructing a scene with convincing dialogue and leaving the tape recorder on during dinner. In writing *Short Season* I found that there was so much else to deal with that I never got around to describing an entire game until the very last section (of twenty-eight). Before that, there were things to contract, such as a ten-day road trip into a few key scenes, and at least one instance to radically expand, which involved devoting 2,000 words to what happens within the interval between two pitches to a batter.

For *Writing Baseball,* the selections on players find authors drawn to elements of structure. Alison Gordon, who served as a beat reporter for the newly born Toronto Blue Jays, emphasizes how her subjects fit into the larger picture. The opening chapter of her *Foul Ball!* is multilinear, sketching with one line how individuals are fitting into the team and with another how this new entity called an "expansion franchise" has become part of a grander sweep of events that includes older clubs (Boston, New York, Detroit, Chicago) and their historic ballparks, all of which comes together to form a "dream game" taking place simultaneously across the continent. Such sweeping range becomes even greater for Bill Cardoso, who draws on the expansive properties of both time and space when looking up former player Bernie Carbo in a Detroit barbershop. For Max Apple, structure is found in the way baseball's rituals can be transposed to whatever else you want, a reversal of the older tradition that imposes ritual and romance on the game (such as Bernard Malamud did in *The Natural* to the delight of older and crustier English professors everywhere, as Eric Solomon recalls in the "Professors" section that follows "Players").

Wives have a unique perspective on their player-husbands' lives, and Danielle Gagnon Torrez uses hers to construct a complex portrait of the game in *High Inside,* the penultimate pages of which are excerpted here. Throughout the book she has played the fortunes of Mike Torrez's sports career (including the quotidian politics in the business of baseball) with the fate of their marriage, each of which starts with great promise, struggles with adversity, flourishes for a time, and then declines. With women writing baseball, both language and perspective become critically important. Note here how Danielle can sympathize with her soon-to-be-ex-husband's generosity in favoring a poor, anonymous kid with an autograph and some empowering attention from a superstar yet also doubt that such a touch-from-the-gods can be a good example for facing life. Would she want her own son raised this way, on either end of the exchange? Yet it is as a baseball wife that she's been empowered to write — not as subserviently and as reverently as the author of *The Babe and I,* who appears both on the title page and in copyright as "Mrs. Babe Ruth" (can one imagine reading *The Bell Jar* by Mrs. Ted Hughes, and either *Boston Adventure* or *A View of My Own* by Mrs. Robert Lowell?), but neither as celebrity-bound as the women profiled in Jeanne Parr's *The Superwives: Life with the Giant Jocks.* Holding the pen in one's own name is the key, a subtext that informs nonfiction and fiction alike: in *Home Games* coauthor Bobbie Bouton responds as much to her former husband Jim's *Ball Four* as to their unwritten life together, whereas the protagonist of Barbara Gregorich's *She's on First* strikes back against a prejudicial establishment that has blocked her playing career by becoming an author herself and literally rewriting the sexual codes that structure baseball. No major work has yet appeared by a player's mother, but the opening line of Alison Gordon's *Foul Ball!* setting the stage for a late-night charter flight home remains one that few other beat writers might construe: "Baseball players, like children, are at their most appealing when they are asleep."

The closest a truly postmodern writer has taken writing baseball to the cradle-to-grave mythology is Jerome Charyn, whose *The Seventh Babe* gathers almost all the structural elements just described and uses them to conclude a moving story of veteran major leaguers, banned from baseball since their raw youth in the 1920s and surviving as unlikely barnstormers in the Negro Leagues, now playing on in even more marginal circumstances half a century later. Like Malamud at his modernistically mythical best, there is more than a strong hint of immortality here. Is the plot itself unbelievable? Yes, but only when recounted in the language of ordinary events. When the text is produced by writing baseball, an activity in which the suspension of disbelief has already been suspended, in which readers need not pretend to believe (and hence really not) the results can be magical.

Then come the professors: Gary Gildner, Fulbrighting at Warsaw University, where he fields a Polish team that could stay in a game at Warsaw, Indiana, if ever so tested, plus Eric Solomon, who finds in baseball a breath of fresh air amid the stuffiness of an early 1960s English department. Solomon's experience anticipates the day when those monumental professorial egos and snobbishly restrictive hiring policies would vanish so thoroughly that it would not be unusual for a former pitcher and present-day scholar of baseball scouting to be a full professor of English and American studies at the University of Delaware (Kevin Kerrane) or for a former New York Giants batboy to hold similar rank and distinction at Sonoma State (Gerald Rosen). And the fact that Gildner's most highly praised achievement during his Fulbright would not be a concordance to Joseph Conrad but a narrative about his Polskiej baseball team is the final proof that Eric Solomon's hopes have triumphed, especially as Gildner's book was published by a major university press.

And finally the fans, who because the spectacle is ultimately for them always get the last word. Here all questions of genre fly completely to the winds. A representative section from William Least Heat Moon's *Blue Highways* demands that familiar but still self-contradictory label: nonfiction novel. "Three New Twins Join Club in Spring" reads like the title of a most insipidly routine piece of sports news; instead, it is a bona fide short story by Garrison Keillor, published as such in *The New Yorker* and gathered with his other fiction in *We Are Still Married*. And to prevent these collections from concluding without acknowledging once again that not everything is going to be pretty, note how the language of public administration and urban policy is transformed by baseball in Neil J. Sullivan's Oxford University Press study, *The Dodgers Move West*, and how even the most devoted fan in the stands—Raymond Mungo—knows that the hallowed rituals embraced by "take me out to the ball game" can be turned inside out.

The voice of the fans, like all these examples of writing baseball, is something distinctive. It permeates American culture and is one of the most revealing things about us as a people. When a blues singer such as Little Milton wants to convey how bad he feels, he claims he feels just like a ball game on a rainy day. When a person in any walk of life talks about a new development in his or her life by saying "it's a whole new ball game," the game in mind is almost certainly baseball, just as baseball's own realities have taken on service in other sports, such as basketball's court-long pass being called a "baseball throw" and football's second-string quarterbacks carrying the label of "relief pitcher." And although almost everything today is signed, the earliest and still most common piece of any sport's equipment to bear autographs is the baseball. I have one signed for me by Bob Feller on a Hall of Fame tour and another by Greg Swindell about an hour before he pitched his first professional game. Maybe you have ones signed for you by Willie Mays and Orel Hershiser, or signed for your grandfather by Babe Ruth. For sure, neither of us will ever throw them away.

WORKS CITED

Apple, Max. "Understanding Alvarado." *New American Review* no. 22 (February 1975): 258–72; collected in *The Oranging of America*, 79–94. New York: Grossman, 1976.

Auster, Paul. "Willie Mays." In *Brushes with Greatness: An Anthology of Chance Encounters with Celebrities*, edited by Russell Banks, Michael Ondaatje, and David Young, 97. Vancouver: Big Bang Books, 1989.

Bouton, Bobbie, and Nancy Marshall. *Home Games: Two Baseball Wives Speak Out*. New York: St. Martin's/Marek, 1983.

Bouton, Jim. *Ball Four*. Cleveland: World, 1970.

Cardoso, Bill. "Time Loves a Haircut." *Harper's*, April 1987, 68–69.

Charyn, Jerome. *The Seventh Babe*. New York: Arbor House, 1979.

Coover, Robert. *The Universal Baseball Association, Inc./J. Henry Waugh, Prop.* New York: Random House, 1968.

Durocher, Leo, with Ed Linn. *Nice Guys Finish Last*. New York: Simon and Schuster, 1975.

Gifford, Barry. "The Aerodynamics of an Irishman." In *The Temple of Baseball*, edited by Richard Grossinger, 94–95. Berkeley: North Atlantic Books, 1985.

——. *The Neighborhood of Baseball*, 2d ed., revised and expanded. San Francisco: Creative Arts, 1985.

Gildner, Gary. *The Warsaw Sparks*. Iowa City: University of Iowa Press, 1990.

Gordon, Alison. *Foul Ball!* Toronto: McClelland & Stewart, 1984.

Gould, Stephen Jay. "The Creation Myths of Cooperstown." *Natural History*, November 1989, 14, 16, 18, 20, 22, 24.

Gregorich, Barbara. *She's on First*. Chicago: Contemporary Books, 1987.

Hall, Donald. *Playing Around*. Boston: Little, Brown, 1974.

Heat Moon, William Least. *Blue Highways*. Boston: Little, Brown, 1982.

Katz, Steve. *Florry of Washington Heights*. Los Angeles: Sun & Moon, 1987.

Keillor, Garrison. "Three New Twins Join Club in Spring," *The New Yorker*, February 22, 1988, 32–33; collected in *We Are Still Married*, 7–10. New York: Viking, 1989.

Kerrane, Kevin. *Dollar Sign on the Muscle: The World of Baseball Scouting*, 2d ed., revised. New York: Simon and Schuster, 1989.

Kinsella, W. P. "How I Got My Nickname." *Spitball*, March 1982, 11–19; collected in *The Thrill of the Grass*, 49–59. New York: Penguin, 1984.

Klinkowitz, Jerry. *Short Season and Other Stories*. Baltimore: Johns Hopkins University Press, 1988.

Lardner, Ring. *You Know Me, Al*. New York: Scribner's, 1925.

Malamud, Bernard. *The Natural*. New York: Farrar, Straus, 1952.

Mungo, Raymond. "Confessions from Left Field." *Smoke Signals*, September 1984, 14.

Parr, Jeanne. *The Superwives: Life with the Giant Jocks*. New York: Coward, McCann & Geoghegan, 1976.

Pascarelli, Peter. "Clearing the Decks." In *A Baseball Winter: The Off-Season Life of the Summer Game*, edited by Terry Pluto and Jeffrey Neuman, 15–20. New York: Macmillan, 1986.

Plimpton, George. *Out of My League*. New York: Harper & Row, 1961.

Rosen, Gerald. "Free Agency for World Leaders." *San Francisco Chronicle/This World*, January 24, 1988, 3.

——. *Growing Up Bronx*. Berkeley: North Atlantic Books, 1984.

Roth, Philip. *The Great American Novel*. New York: Holt, Rinehart & Winston, 1973.

Ruth, Mrs. Babe [Claire Hodgson Ruth], with Bill Slocum. *The Babe and I*. Englewood Cliffs, N.J.: Prentice-Hall, 1959.

Solomon, Eric. "Earl Wasserman, Johns Hopkins, Baseball and Me." *Johns Hopkins Magazine*, April 1984, 10, 12–16.

Stephens, Michael. *Season at Coole*. New York: Dutton, 1972.

Sullivan, Neil J. *The Dodgers Move West*. New York: Oxford University Press, 1987.

Torrez, Danielle Gagnon. *High Inside: Memoirs of a Baseball Wife*. New York: Putnam's, 1983.

Wolff, Rick. "Triumphant Return." *Sports Illustrated*, August 21, 1989, 6, 10, 12.

——. *What's a Nice Harvard Boy Like You Doing in the Bushes?* Englewood Cliffs, N.J.: Prentice-Hall, 1975.

PROLOGUE

The Creation Myths of Cooperstown
Or Why the Cardiff Giants Are an Unbeatable and Appropriately Named Team

Stephen Jay Gould

Y̶OU MAY EITHER LOOK upon the bright side and say that hope springs eternal or, taking the cynic's part, you may mark P. T. Barnum as an astute psychologist for his proclamation that suckers are born every minute. The end result is the same: you can, Honest Abe notwithstanding, fool most of the people all of the time. How else to explain the long and continuing compendium of hoaxes—from the medieval shroud of Turin to Edwardian Piltdown Man to an ultramodern array of flying saucers and astral powers—eagerly embraced for their consonance with our hopes or their resonance with our fears?

Some hoaxes make a sufficient mark upon history that their products acquire the very status initially claimed by fakery—legitimacy (although as an object of human or folkloric, rather than natural, history. I once held the bones of Piltdown Man and felt that I was handling an important item of Western culture).

The Cardiff Giant, the best American entry for the title of paleontological hoax turned into cultural history, now lies on display in a shed behind a barn at the Farmer's Museum in Cooperstown, New York. This gypsum man, more than ten feet tall, was "discovered" by workmen digging a well on a farm near Cardiff, New York, in October 1869. Eagerly embraced by a gullible public, and ardently displayed by its creators at fifty cents a pop, the Cardiff Giant caused quite a brouhaha around Syracuse, and then nationally, for the few months of its active life between exhumation and exposure.

The Cardiff Giant was the brainchild of George Hull, a cigar manufacturer (and general rogue) from Binghamton, New York. He quarried a large block of gypsum from Fort Dodge, Iowa, and shipped

With permission from *Natural History,* November 1989; copyright the American Museum of Natural History, 1989.

it to Chicago, where two marble cutters fashioned the rough likeness of a naked man. Hull made some crude and minimal attempts to give his statue an aged appearance. He chipped off the carved hair and beard because experts told him that such items would not petrify. He drove darning needles into a wooden block and hammered the statue, hoping to simulate skin pores. Finally, he dumped a gallon of sulfuric acid all over his creation to simulate extended erosion. Hull then shipped his giant in a large box back to Cardiff.

Hull, as an accomplished rogue, sensed that his story could not hold for long and, in that venerable and alliterative motto, got out while the getting was good. He sold a three-quarter interest in the Cardiff Giant to a consortium of highly respectable businessmen, including two former mayors of Syracuse. These men raised the statue from its original pit on November 5 and carted it off to Syracuse for display.

The hoax held on for a few more weeks, and Cardiff Giant fever swept the land. Debate raged in newspapers and broadsheets between those who viewed the giant as a petrified fossil and those who regarded it as a statue wrought by an unknown and wondrous prehistoric race. But Hull had left too many tracks—at the gypsum quarries in Fort Dodge, at the carver's studio in Chicago, along the roadways to Cardiff (several people remembered seeing an awfully large box passing on a cart just days before the supposed discovery). By December, Hull was ready to recant, but held his tongue a while longer. Three months later, the two Chicago sculptors came forward, and the Cardiff Giant's brief rendezvous with fame and fortune ended.

The common analogy of the Cardiff Giant with Piltdown Man works only to a point (both were frauds passed off as human fossils) and fails in one crucial respect. Piltdown was cleverly wrought and fooled professionals for forty years, while the Cardiff Giant was preposterous from the start. How could a man turn to solid gypsum, while preserving all his soft anatomy, from cheeks to toes to penis? Geologists and paleontologists never accepted Hull's statue. O. C. Marsh, later to achieve great fame as a discoverer of dinosaurs, echoed a professional consensus in his unambiguous pronouncement: "It is of very recent origin and a decided humbug."

Why, then, was the Cardiff Giant so popular, inspiring a wave of interest and discussion as high as any tide in the affairs of men during its short time in the sun? If the fraud had been well executed, we might attribute this great concern to the dexterity of the hoaxers (just as we grant grudging attention to a few of the most accomplished art fakers for their skills as copyists). But since the Cardiff Giant was so crudely done, we can only attribute its fame to the deep issue, the raw nerve, touched by the subject of its fakery — human origins. Link an absurd concoction to a noble and mysterious subject and you may prevail, at least for a while. My opening reference to P. T. Barnum was not meant sarcastically; he was one of the great practical psychologists of the nineteenth century — and his motto applies with special force to the Cardiff Giant: "No humbug is great without truth at bottom." (Barnum made a copy of the Cardiff Giant and exhibited it in New York City. His mastery of hype and publicity assured that his model far outdrew the "real" fake when the original went on display at a rival establishment in the same city.)

For some reason (to be explored, but not resolved, in this essay), we are powerfully drawn to the subject of beginnings. We yearn to know about origins, and we readily construct myths when we do not have data (or we suppress data in favor of legend when a truth strikes us as too commonplace). The hankering after an origin myth has always been especially strong for the closest subject of all — the human race. But we extend the same psychic need to our accomplishments and institutions — and we have origin myths and stories for the beginning of hunting, of language, of art, of kindness, of war, of boxing, bowties, and brassieres. Most of us know that the Great Seal of the United States pictures an eagle holding a ribbon reading *e pluribus unum*. Fewer would recognize the motto on the other side (check it out on the back of a dollar bill): *annuit coeptis* — "he smiles on our beginnings."

Cooperstown may house the Cardiff Giant, but the fame of this small village in central New York does not rest upon its celebrated namesake, author James Fenimore, or its lovely Lake Otsego or the Farmer's Museum. Cooperstown is "on the map" by virtue of a different origin myth — one more parochial, but no less powerful, for many Americans, than the tales of human beginnings that gave life to the Cardiff Giant. Cooperstown is the sacred founding place in the official myth about the origin of baseball.

Origin myths, since they are so powerful, can engender enormous practical problems. Abner Doubleday, as we shall soon see, most emphatically did not invent baseball at Cooperstown in 1839 as the official tale proclaims; in fact, no one invented baseball at any moment or in any spot. Nonetheless, this creation myth made Cooperstown the official home of baseball, and the Hall of Fame, with its associated museum and library, set its roots in this small village, inconveniently located near nothing in the way of airports or accommodations. We all revel in bucolic imagery on the field of dreams, but what a hassle when tens of thousands line the roads, restaurants, and port-a-potties during the annual Hall of Fame weekend, when new members are enshrined and two major league teams arrive to play an exhibition game at Abner Doubleday Field, a sweet little 10,000-seater in the middle of town. Put your compass point at Cooperstown, make your radius at Albany — and you'd better reserve a year in advance if you want any accommodation within the enormous resulting circle.

After a lifetime of curiosity, I finally got the opportunity to witness this annual version of forty students in a telephone booth or twenty circus clowns in a Volkswagen. Since Yaz (former Boston star Carl Yastrzemski to the uninitiated) was slated to receive baseball's Nobel in 1989, and his old team was playing in the Hall of Fame game, and since I'm a transplanted Bostonian (although still a New Yorker and not-so-secret Yankee fan at heart), Tom Heitz, chief of the wonderful baseball library at the Hall of Fame, kindly invited me to join the sardines in this most lovely of all cans.

The silliest and most tendentious of baseball writing tries to wrest profundity from the spectacle of grown men hitting a ball with a stick by suggesting linkages between the sport and deep issues of morality, parenthood, history, lost innocence, gentleness, and so on, seemingly *ad infinitum*. (The effort reeks of silliness because baseball is profound all by itself and needs no excuses; people who don't know this are not fans and are therefore unreachable anyway.) When people ask me how baseball imitates life, I can only respond with what the more genteel newspapers used to call a "barnyard epithet," but now, with growing bravery, usually render as "bullbleep." Nonetheless, baseball is a major item of our culture, and it does have a long and interesting history. Any item or institution with these two properties must generate a set of myths and stories (perhaps even some truths) about its beginnings. And the subject of beginnings is the bread and butter of this column on evolution in the broadest sense. I shall make no woolly analogies between baseball and life; this is an essay on the origins of baseball, with some musings on why beginnings of all sorts hold such fascination for us. (I thank Tom Heitz not only for the invitation to Cooperstown at its yearly acme but also for drawing the contrast between creation and evolution stories of baseball, and for supplying much useful information from his unparalleled storehouse.)

Stories about beginnings come in only two basic modes. An entity either has an explicit point of origin, a specific time and place of creation, or else it evolves and has no definable moment of entry into the world. Baseball provides an interesting example of this contrast because we know the answer and can judge received wisdom by the two chief criteria, often opposed, of external fact and internal hope. Baseball evolved from a plethora of previous stick-and-ball games. It has no true Cooperstown and no Doubleday. Yet we seem to prefer the alternative model of origin by a moment of creation—for then we can have heroes and sacred places. By contrasting the myth of Coopers-town with the fact of evolution, we can learn something about our cultural practices and their frequent disrespect for truth.

The official story about the beginning of baseball is a creation myth, and a review of the reasons and circumstances of its fabrication may give us insight into the cultural appeal of stories in this mode. A. G. Spalding, baseball's first great pitcher during his early career, later founded the sporting goods company that still bears his name and became one of the great commercial moguls of America's gilded age. As publisher of the annual *Spalding's Official Base Ball Guide,* he held maximal power in shaping both public and institutional opinion on all facets of baseball and its history. As the sport grew in popularity, and the pattern of two stable major leagues coalesced early in our century, Spalding and others felt the need for clarification (or merely for codification) of opinion on the hitherto unrecorded origins of an activity that truly merited its common designation as America's "national pastime."

In 1907, Spalding set up a blue-ribbon committee to investigate and resolve the origins of baseball. The committee, chaired by A. G. Mills and including several prominent businessmen and two senators who had also served as presidents of the National League, took much testimony but found no smoking gun for a beginning. Then, in July 1907, Spalding himself transmitted to the committee a letter from an Abner Graves, then a mining engineer in Denver, who reported that Abner Doubleday had, in 1839, interrupted a marbles game behind the tailor's shop in Cooperstown, New York, to draw a diagram of a baseball field, explain the rules of the game, and designate the activity by its modern name of "base ball" (then spelled as two words).

Such "evidence" scarcely inspired universal confidence, but the commission came up with nothing better—and the Doubleday myth, as we shall soon see, was eminently functional. Therefore, in 1908, the

Mills Commission reported its two chief findings: first, "that base ball had its origins in the United States"; and second, "that the first scheme for playing it, according to the best evidence available to date, was devised by Abner Doubleday, at Cooperstown, New York, in 1839." This "best evidence" consisted only of "a circumstantial statement by a reputable gentleman"—namely Graves's testimony as reported by Spalding himself.

When cited evidence is so laughably insufficient, one must seek motivations other than concern for truth value. The key to underlying reasons stands in the first conclusion of Mills's committee: hoopla and patriotism (cardboard version) decreed that a national pastime must have an indigenous origin. The idea that baseball had evolved from a wide variety of English stick-and-ball games—although true—did not suit the mythology of a phenomenon that had become so quintessentially American. In fact, Spalding had long been arguing, in an amiable fashion, with Henry Chadwick, another pioneer and entrepreneur of baseball's early years. Chadwick, born in England, had insisted for years that baseball had developed from the British stick-and-ball game called rounders; Spalding had vociferously advocated a purely American origin, citing the colonial game of "one old cat" as a distant precursor, but holding that baseball itself represented something so new and advanced that a pinpoint of origin—a creation myth—must be sought.

Chadwick considered the matter of no particular importance, arguing (with eminent justice) that an English origin did not "detract one iota from the merit of its now being unquestionably a thoroughly American field sport, and a game too, which is fully adapted to the American character." (I must say that I have grown quite fond of Mr. Chadwick, who certainly understood evolutionary change and its chief principle that historical origin need not match contemporary function.) Chadwick also viewed the committee's whitewash as a victory for his side. He labeled the Mills report as "a masterful piece of special pleading which lets my dear old friend Albert [Spalding] escape a bad defeat. The whole matter was a joke between Albert and myself."

We may accept the psychic need for an indigenous creation myth, but why Abner Doubleday, a man with no recorded tie to the game and who, in the words of Donald Honig, probably "didn't know a baseball from a kumquat"? I had wondered about this for years, but only ran into the answer serendipitously during a visit to Fort Sumter in the harbor of Charleston, South Carolina. There, an exhibit on the first skirmish of the Civil War points out that Abner Doubleday, as captain of the Union artillery, had personally sighted and given orders for firing the first responsive volley following the initial Confederate attack on the fort. Doubleday later commanded divisions at Antietam and Fredericksburg, became at least a minor hero at Gettysburg, and retired as a brevet major general. In fact, A. G. Mills, head of the commission, had served as part of an honor guard when Doubleday's body lay in state in New York City, following his death in 1893.

If you have to have an American hero, could anyone be better than the man who fired the first shot (in defense) of the Civil War? Needless to say, this point was not lost on the members of Mills's committee. Spalding, never one to mince words, wrote to the committee when submitting Graves's dubious testimony: "It certainly appeals to an American pride to have had the great national game of base ball created and named by a Major General in the United States Army." Mills then concluded in his report: "Perhaps in the years to come, in view of the hundreds of thousands of people who are devoted to base ball, and the millions who will be, Abner Doubleday's fame will rest evenly, if not quite as much, upon the fact that he was its inventor . . . as upon his brilliant and distinguished career as an officer in the Federal Army."

And so, spurred by a patently false creation myth, the Hall of Fame stands in the most incongruous and inappropriate locale of a charming little town in central New York. Incongruous and inappropriate, but somehow wonderful. Who needs another museum in the cultural maelstroms (and summer doldrums) of New York, Boston, or Washington? Why not a major museum in a beautiful and bucolic setting? And what could be more fitting than the spatial conjunction of two great American origin myths — the Cardiff Giant and the Doubleday Fable? Thus, I too am quite content to treat the myth gently, while honesty requires 'fessing up. The exhibit on Doubleday in the Hall of Fame Museum sets just the right tone in its caption: "In the hearts of those who love baseball, he is remembered as the lad in the pasture where the game was invented. Only cynics would need to know more." Only in the hearts; not in the minds.

Baseball evolved. Since the evidence is so clear (as epitomized below), we must ask why these facts have been so little appreciated for so long, and why a creation myth like the Doubleday story ever gained a foothold. Two major reasons have conspired: first, the positive block of our attraction to creation stories; second, the negative impediment of unfamiliar sources outside the usual purview of historians. English stick-and-ball games of the nineteenth century can be roughly classified into two categories along social lines. The upper and educated classes played cricket, and the history of this sport is copiously documented because the literati write about their own interests, and because the activities of men in power are well recorded (and constitute virtually all of history, in the schoolboy version). But the ordinary pastimes of rural and urban working people can be well nigh invisible in conventional sources of explicit commentary. Working people played a different kind of stick-and-ball game, existing in various forms and designated by many names, including "rounders" in western England, "feeder" in London, and "base ball" in southern England. For a large number of reasons, forming the essential difference between cricket and baseball, cricket matches can last up to several days (a batsman, for example, need not run after he hits the ball and need not expose himself to the possibility of being put out every time he makes contact). The leisure time of working people does not come in such generous gobs, and the lower-class stick-and-ball games could not run more than a few hours.

Several years ago, at the Victoria and Albert Museum in London, I learned an important lesson from an excellent exhibit on the late nineteenth century history of the British music hall. This is my favorite period (Darwin's century, after all), and I consider myself tolerably well informed on cultural trends of the time. I can sing any line from any of the Gilbert and Sullivan operas (a largely middle-class entertainment), and I know the general drift of high cultural interests in literature and music. But here was a whole world of entertainment for millions, a world with its heroes, its stars, its top forty songs, its gaudy theaters — and I knew nothing, absolutely nothing, about it. I felt chagrined, but my ignorance had an explanation beyond personal insensitivity (and the exhibit had been mounted explicitly to counteract the selective invisibility of certain important trends in history). The music hall was the chief entertainment of Victorian working classes, and the history of working people is often invisible in conventional written sources. It must be rescued and reconstituted from different sorts of data; in this case, from posters, playbills, theater accounts, persistence of some songs in the oral tradition (most were never published as sheet music), recollections of old-timers who knew the person who knew the person. . . .

The early history of baseball — the stick-and-ball game of working people — presents the same problem of conventional invisibility — and the same promise of rescue by exploration of unusual sources. Work continues and intensifies as the history of sport becomes more and more academically respectable, but the broad outlines (and much fascinating detail) are now well established. As the upper classes played a codified and well-documented cricket, working people played a largely unrecorded and much more diversified set of stick-and-ball games ancestral to baseball. Many sources, including primers and boys' manuals, depict games recognizable as precursors to baseball well into the early eighteenth century. Occasional references even spill over into high culture. In *Northanger Abbey,* written at the close of the eighteenth century, Jane Austen remarks: "It was not very wonderful that Catherine . . . should prefer cricket, base ball, riding on horseback, and running about the country, at the age of fourteen, to books." As this quotation illustrates, the name of the game is no more Doubleday's than the form of play.

These ancestral styles of baseball came to America with early settlers and were clearly well established by colonial times. But they were driven ever further underground by Puritan proscriptions of sport for adults. They survived largely as children's games and suffered the double invisibility of location among the poor and the young. But two major reasons brought these games into wider repute and led to a codification of standard forms quite close to modern baseball between the 1820s and the 1850s. First, a set of social reasons, from the decline of Puritanism to increased concern about health and hygiene in crowded cities, made sport an acceptable activity for adults. Second, middle-class and professional people began to take up these early forms of baseball, and with this upward social drift came teams, leagues, written rules, uniforms, stadiums, guidebooks: in short, all the paraphernalia of conventional history.

I am not arguing that these early games could be called baseball with a few trivial differences (evolution means substantial change, after all), but only that they stand in a complex lineage, better called a nexus, from which modern baseball emerged, eventually in a codified and canonical form. In those days before instant communication, every region had its own version, just as every set of outdoor steps in New York City generated a different form of stoopball in my youth, without threatening the basic identity of the game. These games, most commonly called town ball, differed from modern baseball in substantial ways. In the Massachusetts Game, a codification of the late 1850s drawn up by ballplayers in New England towns, four bases and three strikes identify the genus, but many specifics are strange by modern standards. The bases were made of wooden stakes projecting four feet from the ground. The batter (called the striker) stood between first and fourth base. Sides changed after a single out. One hundred runs (called tallies), not higher score after a specified number of innings, spelled victory. The field contained no foul lines, and balls hit in any direction were in play. Most importantly, runners were not tagged out but were retired by "plugging," that is, being hit with a thrown ball while running between bases. Consequently, since baseball has never been a game for masochists, balls were soft—little more than rags stuffed into leather covers—and could not be hit far. (Tom Heitz has put together a team of Cooperstown worthies to re-create town ball for interested parties and prospective opponents. Since few other groups are well schooled in this lost art, Tom's team hasn't been defeated in ages, if ever. "We are the New York Yankees of town ball," he told me. His team is called, quite appropriately in general but especially for this essay, the Cardiff Giants.)

Evolution is continual change, but not insensibly gradual transition; in any continuum, some points are always more interesting than others. The conventional nomination for most salient point in this particular continuum goes to Alexander Joy Cartwright, leader of a New York team that started to play in Lower Manhattan, eventually rented some changing rooms and a field in Hoboken (just a quick ferry ride across the Hudson), and finally drew up a set of rules in 1845, later known as the New York Game. Cartwright's version of town ball is much closer to modern baseball, and many clubs followed his rules—for standardization became ever more vital as the popularity of early baseball grew and opportunity for play between regions increased. In particular, Cartwright introduced two key innovations that shaped the disparate forms of town ball into a semblance of modern baseball. First, he eliminated plugging and introduced tagging in the modern sense; the ball could now be made harder, and hitting for distance became an option. Second, he introduced foul lines, again in the modern sense as his batter stood at a home plate and had to hit the ball within lines defined from home through first and third bases. The game could now become a spectator sport because areas close to the field but out of action could, for the first time, be set aside for onlookers.

The New York Game may be the highlight of a continuum, but it provides no origin myth for baseball. Cartwright's rules were followed in various forms of town ball. His New York Game still included many curiosities by modern standards (twenty-one runs, called aces, won the game, and balls caught on one bounce were outs). Moreover, our modern version is an amalgam of the New York Game plus other town ball traditions, not Cartwright's baby grown up by itself. Several features of the Massachusetts Game entered the modern version in preference to Cartwright's rules. Balls had to be caught on the fly in Boston, and pitchers threw overhand, not underhand as in the New York Game (and in professional baseball until the 1880s).

Scientists often lament that so few people understand Darwin and the principles of biological evolution. But the problem goes deeper. Too few people are comfortable with evolutionary modes of explanation in any form. I do not know why we tend to think so fuzzily in this area, but one reason must reside in our social and psychic attraction to creation myths in preference to evolutionary stories—for creation myths, as noted before, identify heroes and sacred places, while evolutionary stories provide no palpable, particular thing as a symbol for reverence, worship, or patriotism. Still, we must remember—and an intellectual's most persistent and nagging responsibility lies in making this simple point over and over again, however noxious and bothersome we render ourselves thereby—that truth and desire, fact and comfort, have no necessary, or even preferred, correlation (so rejoice when they do coincide).

To state the most obvious example in our current political turmoil. Human growth is a continuum, and no creation myth can define an instant for the origin of an individual life. Attempts by antiabortionists to designate the moment of fertilization as the beginning of personhood make no sense in scientific terms (and also violate a long history of social definitions that traditionally focused on the quickening, or detected movement, of the fetus in the womb). I will admit—indeed, I emphasized as a key argument of this essay—that not all points on a continuum are equal. Fertilization is a more interesting moment than most, but it no more provides a clean definition of origin than the most interesting moment of baseball's continuum—Cartwright's codification of the New York Game—defines the beginning of our national pastime. Baseball evolved and people grow; both are continua without definable points of origin. Probe too far back and you reach absurdity, for you will see Nolan Ryan on the hill when the first ape hit a bird with a stone; or you will define both masturbation and menstruation as murder—and who will then cast the first stone? Look for something in the middle, and you find nothing but continuity — always a meaning-ful "before," and always a more modern "after." (Please note that I am not stating an opinion on the vexatious question of abortion — an ethical issue that can only be decided in ethical terms. I only point out that one side has rooted its case in an argument from science that is not only entirely irrelevant to the proper realm of resolution but also happens to be flat-out false in trying to devise a creation myth within a continuum.)

And besides, why do we prefer creation myths to evolutionary stories? I find all the usual reasons hollow. Yes, heroes and shrines are all very well, but is there not grandeur in the sweep of continuity? Shall we revel in a story for all humanity that may include the sacred ball courts of the Aztecs, and perhaps, for all we know, a group of *Homo erectus* hitting rocks or skulls with a stick or a femur? Or shall we halt beside the mythical Abner Doubleday, standing behind the tailor's shop in Cooperstown, and say "behold the man" — thereby violating truth and, perhaps even worse, extinguishing both thought and wonder?

I

KIDS

From *Florry of Washington Heights*

Steve Katz

So you couldn't call it a war between the Bullets and the Fanwoods. It was just a skirmish. It didn't even last through the winter.
When it gets cold and the snow flies it's hard to think of fighting in the
streets. Winter is the most relentless aggressor. Hitler made his troops
go into Russia, and millions of Russians died, Jews and everyone, and
then the winter came on the steppes, and Hitler's armies died there.
They froze in Russia. Winter hit them like revenge, and that eventually
drove the Führer into his bunker and the rest of the Nazis to Argentina.
As crazy as Ryan might have seemed to us for wanting to fight, he
wasn't crazy enough to make his Fanwoods fight on some frozen streets.
Besides, everyone wore so many clothes in the winter that you couldn't
land a good shot, even with a sledgehammer. By the time spring came
around the whole mess seemed forgotten, part of the past.

Two big things happened around the block in April. One was that
President Truman stood up to General MacArthur, the madman who
wanted to invade China and kill a lot of Chinese people and a lot of
Americans on the way. So he fired him. That was on April 11. On
April 28 the other thing happened. The Bullets got their baseball
uniforms with *Zooky's Confectionery* in big purple letters on the back.
MacArthur made his stupid speech where he said, "Old soldiers never
die, they just fade away." Just as long as you get rid of them, I thought.
Everyone, especially Dufner, liked to make fun of that speech. "Old
gym teachers never die," he said once to Kutzer, who was persecuting
him. "They just eat rotten jockstraps."

As soon as the Bullets got their uniforms they put them on and

paraded down Ft. Washington. When Barney saw us he had a connip-
tion fit.

"I thought you were gonna let me sponsor you," he shouted, and
leaned so far out over his magazines to see all of us we thought he'd fall
onto the sidewalk. "I'm the one who's had to put up with you every
day."

"Barney, you told me you didn't want to," I said. "You said it was a
waste of money for you."

"Who said that? I never said such a thing. It's good publicity and
you can write it off your taxes. You should have asked me."

We all marched into Zooky's with the uniforms on and filled up the
whole store.

"What is it?" he asked.

"We've got the uniforms on, Zooky. With *Zooky's Confectionery* in
big purple."

"It looks good. It looks great," said Zooky, and he started bouncing
up and down on his side of the counter, like a kid.

"What looks good," said his wife, coming in from the little closet
kitchen in the rear. "What are all of you doing here? What are these
kids all doing here, these hoodlums? If this is a stickup I'll give you a
stickup. What is this, *Zooky's Confectionery,* a joke? Zooky, what have
they got on their shirts?"

"Mrs. Tits," Stames said, but luckily she didn't hear that. "In honor
of the best egg cream in Washington Heights, we've decided to put
your name on all our shirts."

"Yeah, and somewhere else too," said Frankie Dufner. "You want
to see where else?"

"What is this honor? You can die from some stinking honor," she
said. "Buy something, and then tell me about honor." She was smiling,
though, like she couldn't help it.

"Boys," said Zooky, "I feel great. You look great. You'll win all your
ball games in those uniforms."

We changed back into old clothes and went down to the river to
practice. The uniforms were only for league games. At that practice
Baldeen told us, or rather Sugarman, who was back in form, told us
from Baldeen's mouth, that our first preleague game was going to be
on May 3, afternoon, and it was going to be against the Fanwoods. The
silence was enormous. Fanwoods had maybe been in the back of our
minds, but nobody had talked or thought Fanwoods all winter, and we
knew we were going to high schools out of the neighborhood, and the

issue would disappear, so we were almost home free, and here they were right in our faces again because of stupid Baldeen.

"Why the Fanwoods?" I asked.

"You play baseball, you play hardball," Baldeen said himself, not trusting his deepest wisdom to the mouth of Sugarman.

"You've got tits for brains, Baldeen," said Stamatakis.

"Why the Fanwoods?" I asked Sugarman after practice. "There are a hundred teams we could play. Why can't we just forget about the Fanwoods?"

"Jack Ryan came to me himself. He spoke to Baldeen and asked for the game."

"So you just said okay?"

"They just want to play ball," Sugarman said. "Ryan seemed okay to me. I met his sister."

"Great," I said. "So did I."

"I like her," said Sugarman.

"You like the Irish girls, Sugarman," Dufner said. "Why don't you find yourself a nice Jewish girl?"

Suddenly for me the ghost of Florry O'Neill seemed to settle on this whole conversation and make all the jokes strange. Sugarman didn't seem to mind. He had passed through it. He was turning into one of those people who could suffer a lot, and then forget it. His was a healthy attitude. It was just me. I couldn't forget Florry O'Neill, and that colored boy locked up because of it, to sit in the electric chair.

"Didn't you and Baldeen ever think that what the Fanwoods want to do is get us all down there so they can jump us," Zoo said.

"It wasn't like that, Zoo," said Sugarman. "They want to play ball."

"Yeah," said Grossman. "Old Bullets never die. . . . "

"They just quit the Bullets," Dufner added. "I'm quitting the Bullets. This is it. I'm a lover, not a fighter."

"You're not even a lover, Dufner," said Stames. "I talked to Audrey Wolfe."

"Yeah," said Grossman.

"Sit on these and rotate," said Dufner, lifting both his middle fingers.

So on the afternoon of May 3 once again the Bullets had to face the Fanwoods. Baldeen and Sugarman talked us into it. If we didn't play in this game, we couldn't play in any of the league games. Everyone showed up. Fourteen Bullets. Myself I thought okay. Play a game for Florry O'Neill. We got there early and started warming up, some calisthenics, some wind sprints, batting practice, infield drill, fungoes to the outfield. We all stopped when we saw it, like it was our mutual nightmare, that cloud of black jackets coming at us down the path of the park at Riverside Drive. We slowly moved closer together. A few of them in the front carried their baseball bats. Hubby ran over to our duffel and pulled out all our bats and distributed them to the members of the infield. I leaned on the bat he gave me and thought, not this, Jesus, not this.

When they got closer we saw that maybe they had actually come to play ball. They had baseball mitts, and were pounding their fists into the pockets. They looked as mean as ever when they walked onto the field, but they had actually come to play ball. They did nothing friendly, but stared at us like Ezzard Charles looking at Jersey Joe Walcott before a fight. They didn't seem to want to swing those bats at anything but a baseball. Ryan looked at me at one point, with a certain look of recognition that comes from some deep place you hold in common. I remembered that look once when I went to a party on the Bowery with the client I mentioned before who was an artist. She has since become famous herself, and has already sold all the paintings she could ever possibly paint in her life. She's hiding out in New Mexico now. That party was in the loft of another artist who was becoming famous fast, and he was living with Eva Hesse. It was the first time I saw her after I found out who she had become; and she looked at me, and it was a look that saw me and saw a little kid at the same time, just as I saw it in her. The room was full of New York people, all grown up, all holding glasses of wine, some of them not even New Yorkers, but from the Midwest or California or Italy, and Eva looked at me and put a finger to her lips, as if asking me to keep it a secret between us, our childhood together in Washington Heights. Somehow that look of Eva's brought Florry O'Neill to my mind, and the look Ryan gave me before the game, as if to say whatever was is over, and this is the next step.

There weren't many ballplayers among the Fanwoods. You could tell from the way they warmed up. Our infield had begun to look real snappy, but they stumbled around looking like they were trying to invent the game all over again. It made us feel like pros watching them. This was a cinch. This would be a piece of cake.

"Maybe we better not beat 'em," said Stames.

"Nah," said Sugarman. "We'll beat 'em."

Baldeen was sitting on his haunches and scouting them. He signaled for Sugarman to come over and squat down next to him, and then had a long whisper in his ear. Sugarman came back over to us.

"They got a couple of guys. A pitcher and a catcher who Baldeen says are really good." He pointed at two guys warming up in the outfield. "The pitcher's name is Christopoulos. He pitches for G.W."

"He's a Greek," Stames said in disbelief.

"And the other guy, Stein, is his catcher."

"Stein?" several of us said in unison. It could have been a German name, but it was probably Jewish, and on the Fanwoods. I met a great guy named Sean Golden once, and he was Irish, and not even Jewish. The mayor of Dublin was Jewish for a while, too. And I found out later that Leopold Bloom, James Joyce's character, was supposed to be Jewish. So why not on the Fanwoods?

"He hits a long ball," Sugarman said.

"They're not even Fanwoods," said Mamoulian, "and they play high school ball."

"You want to tell them they can't play?" Sugarman said.

"What'll we do?" Mamoulian asked.

"We'll win," said Sugarman. "Schletzbaum is good. Stein has never faced him before, and they're both lefties."

"They always throw ringers in against us," Grossman said.

"That's 'cause we're good," said Sugarman. He turned to see Dufner walking across the field. "About time you got here, Dufner."

"I was waiting."

"Waiting for what?"

"To see if someone needed to call the police."

"Warm up, Dufner. The game's gonna start."

The game was more or less a pitcher's duel. I mean the outfielders could have gone to sleep, and I think Stames did once in right field. The only action was tossing the ball around the infield after Schletzbaum struck someone out. We didn't have a chance against this Christopolous either. He was so fast I'd still be waiting there for the pitch after it was in the catcher's mitt. And it was the first time we had ever really seen a sharp breaking curve. We were falling out of the batter's box until we realized what was going on.

We had two umpires. Baldeen called the game when the Fanwoods were at bat, and Ryan, who said he didn't like baseball, but played football for the body contact and bone breaking, called them when we were up. He was really fair as an umpire; in fact, he always gave us the benefit of the doubt if the pitch was close. Not that it made any difference. Everyone was striking out.

The game was supposed to go seven innings, and in the top of the sixth it was still 0-0. Schletzbaum had walked one in the second and one in the fourth, but the Fanwoods couldn't touch him, though Stein connected for a couple of line drives foul. For a kid who was so fast Christopoulos had great control. Nobody got on base until Zoo worked him for a walk in the third, and then stole second to cause some excitement, but there were two outs, and of course I struck out on a curveball that started in Connecticut and ended in South Jersey.

With one out in the sixth inning, Christopoulos connected for a clean single over second base. Bloustein, who had come to the team with Baldeen, and moved Zoo to left field, fielded the ball perfectly and held him on first. Schletzbaum struck out Kevin, who swung so hard that if he ever connected we'd say goodbye to the ball, or who-ever was in its way. Stein was up next, swinging three bats in the on-deck circle. As soon as he stepped into the batter's box you could feel something charge up. Something horrible for us was going to happen. I walked up to the pitcher's mound to talk to Schletzbaum. Sugarman came in from short.

"Why don't we just walk this guy?" I said.

Schletzbaum looked at me as if I'd insulted his father.

"What do you think, Freddy? He ought to walk him, right? That red-headed kid up next can't hit."

"He's pitching. He knows better than we do. Anyway that red-headed kid is a righty, and Stein is a lefty. With a left-handed pitcher you don't pass a lefty to get at a righty."

"Play ball," Baldeen shouted from behind the plate. Baseball sense. I couldn't believe it, it sounded so stupid. Baldeen was the umpire. I couldn't consult with him. "Play ball," he shouted again.

"I don't give intentional walks," Schletzbaum said. I couldn't believe it.

"That's part of baseball," I said.

"Not the way I play it."

The first two pitches to Stein were wide, so I figured maybe he'd walk him anyway. Stein swung at the next pitch and pulled the ball right at me like a bullet and I stuck up my glove and even jumped a little, but three minutes after it was gone behind me, fouled down the right field line, called by Baldeen, and even verified by Ryan. 2 and 1. Stein swung and missed at the next pitch. It was beautiful to watch him swing, even when he missed. His swing was even and fluid, and his whole body was into it, and he followed through; I mean, he was the meaning of "follow through," the bat way behind him, his left knee bent to the ground.

The next pitch was a ball to make it 3 and 2. He'll walk him, I thought, and relaxed. I sighed with relief when I saw the pitch going wide, but Stein wasn't going to let that happen. He stepped almost across the plate to swing at that pitch, and lofted one so far into center field, and so high that it was out of sight. I could hear Mel Allen in my mind shouting "going . . . going . . . ," and it was gone. Bloustein just watched it, and Zoo started after it, but stopped. Two days later it was probably still going. The score was two to zip. Schletzbaum struck out the next two, and we were up in the bottom of the sixth. And we were down 1, 2, 3 in the bottom of the sixth.

There was no more damage in top of the seventh, and we were up again with Hubby, Schletzbaum, and the top of the order with Zoo and then me, who batted second like Tommy Henrich, in the unlikely case that I was needed. Seven innings didn't seem to have tired Christopoulos at all. He struck Hubby out easily. Schletzbaum would have loved to get back at him, to be the first to hit him; but though he was a good pitcher he was no hitter at all. He stared down Christopoulos' face to intimidate him, but no luck; one foul tip, two balls, three strikes. He was out. Grossman had his catching gear tied up together. Hubby was collecting the bats to put them in the duffel. The Bullets were ready to go home.

"What do you expect?" Hubby said to me, as he watched Zoo step into the batter's box. "That guy pitches for George Washington."

"They probably paid him," Dufner said.

"Still we should have won this game," I said. "They weren't hitting Schletzbaum, except for Stein."

We shut up. Zoo for some reason still was in the middle of the game, working Christopoulos. Greek against Greek. Christopoulos had him 1 and 2, but Zoo kept fouling him off, just stuck out his bat and got a piece of the ball, and the count got to 3 and 2. I was half hoping he'd strike out, so I didn't have to make the last out of the game. Christopoulos looked impatient. He threw the last pitch wide, and Zoo trotted down to first base, bouncing up and shouting, "Come on, Swanny. Let's get 'em back."

Now the game depended on me. Strike-out Swanson. I hadn't seen the ball all day. Christopoulos looked at me as if the idea of pitching to me bored him, as if I might as well give it up. He wanted it over with right away, and that was why he got pissed when Ryan called the first pitch I waited out a ball. He kicked the dirt around the pitcher's mound. He might just throw me something I could hit, I thought. He looked angry, and just a little tired suddenly. I looked down at Baldeen, coaching at third. He rubbed his left hand across his chest. That was the bunt sign. I couldn't believe it. I called time and stepped out of the batter's box and looked at Baldeen again. The bunt sign, for sure. His left hand across his chest. Two out, we're down by two runs, and he wants me to bunt. I couldn't believe it. Aside from the fact that of all things I hated to do in baseball, bunting was the worst of them, this didn't even make sense as strategy. Bunt with two outs, down by two? Zoo had a long lead off first. "C'mon Swanny," he was shouting. He was in the game. The other Bullets had stood up, and were watching, a little excitement rising even among those who had given up. The game was not over, as they said, until the last out. The bunt sign was on me. Christopoulos wound up, and pitched, and the ball was by me before I had even half-heartedly squared away. Baldeen called time and signaled me to meet him halfway down the third-base line.

"Are you playing baseball, or is this 'go fish'?"

"I think I can hit him, Baldeen."

"The bunt sign is on," he said, and walked back behind third.

I hated it. And to square away and face head on someone with a fastball and a curve like Christopoulos, that was craziness.

"Swanny babes, let's go," shouted Hubby. "Just put it down somewhere. They can't see it anyway." Someone grabbed Hubby and gagged him, but the excitement was still there, like the game had just started. That's baseball, with nothing happening the excitement grows. The next pitch was so wide I didn't even bother to square away. I looked down to third. Bunt. Why? I had to do it. I was playing for a team. We had this manager, who was supposed to know the best strategies. Even though I thought this was stupid I had to do it. I squared away and the pitch came down right at me. Curve, I thought. I felt it touch my bat, and then this incredible shock, like all the doors had slammed around my head, and everyone was shouting, "Run, Swanny. Go babes. Great bunt, Swanny." Before I even knew what had happened I was safe on first base, and Zoo was sliding into third, safe, and there was this throbbing in my head I couldn't believe. I put my hand up to my face and could feel it swelling. I had hit that bunt with my eye. It was a foul ball in the rule books, but no one had seen it, including me. Now Stames was up, the winning run at the plate, and you could see Christopoulos was a little shook with two men on base, and Stein waving at the outfield to send them deep. It was Greek against Greek again. It was the Trojan War.

"C'mon Stames. C'mon babes. Hit for the big boobs." The Bullets were all up and jumping by the bench. Zoo took his lead off third, and I, with my head throbbing a ton, took my lead off first. The eye that had bunted the ball was closing up. I didn't understand how I'd stayed on my feet, getting hit like that. But I guess I'd proved it enough times: hit me in the head and I'm fine. Christopoulos looked like he wished he'd never come to this game, as if he'd like the whole scene to disappear. A train went by on the tracks beyond the fence, and he waited for it to pass. I heard a small plane flying up the river but I couldn't see it. The train was gone, and Christopoulos toed the rubber, and went into his full windup. He kicked high in the air, and came down with everything he had left behind that first pitch he threw at Stames. I didn't see what happened because I finally spotted that small plane flying under the bridge. That was amazing. That was illegal. I vaguely heard the crack of the bat, and then there was silence, so I thought it was probably a strike, but suddenly the whole Bullet team roared. That ball was gone. Stames had done it. Before I started to move he was almost down to first base. Zoo trotted home. I held a hand over my eye and touched every base. I didn't believe it. We had won the game and only I knew the quality of that victory. This was the second time we had beaten the Fanwoods and both times it was with some kind of bunt.

"You laid that one down, Swanny. Great bunt," Sugarman said, slapping me on the butt on his way to shake hands with Stames. "That's what kept us alive. That's baseball." I couldn't take it. I went off and leaned against the fence, holding my eye, my back to the Fanwoods. I turned only because I felt this weird silence behind me. There were all the Fanwoods gathered in a bunch behind third base, and the Bullets standing by the first base line, watching to see what they would do.

"Maybe it was a mistake to beat them," I heard Grossman say.

"It's never a mistake to win," said Sugarman.

Hubby spotted me. "Swanny. Look at Swanny. What happened to your eye?"

"Jesus." They all came closer to look at me.

"Which one of them hit you?" Stames asked.

"Christopoulos," I said. I couldn't help it. Even then I was a sick joker.

"That Greek. He isn't even a Fanwood," Stames clenched both fists.

So suddenly that we all jumped, this noise burst out of the Fanwoods. "Two four six eight / who do we appreciate / the Bullets the Bullets— yeeeaaahhhhh!"

That shocked us. Everyone was silent for a long minute. We were even embarrassed, because the etiquette of this situation was that the winning team cheered first. We hadn't even thought of it. We got into our little huddle and cheered, but I felt like it sounded weak by comparison.

The Fanwoods left the field first, and the Bullets followed. I never would have believed that everything could have ended so peacefully. I lagged behind, because I didn't really want them to see my eye. At a certain point there was Jack Ryan, watching some Chinese guys pulling crab traps out of the river.

"Swanson, come here," he shouted at me. "You think they really eat that shit, out of this slimy river?"

"They must," I said. "Maybe that's why they turn yellow." It was a nasty joke, and he liked it.

"Hey. You really used your head on that bunt," he said, and touched my swollen eye. He saw what happened, and he had been the ump, and he hadn't said anything.

"Why didn't you call it?" I asked.

"Listen, it wasn't my idea to get Christopoulos to pitch for us, or Stein. That was stupid. That was chickenshit. But I wanted to see if you guys could beat him. Big high school pitcher."

"Did you guys have to pay him to pitch for you?" That was me, Swanson, one too many questions.

"Baseball is a game," Ryan said. "No big thing."

"You never know," I said to him.

"I know you're still a punk," he said. "And you tell that little Jewboy, Sugarman, to lay off my sister." He raised a fist at me and left.

So there I was, Swanson, by the river, alone, swollen eye. I went over to where the Chinese guys were pulling out the crabs and squatted down by their straw baskets to watch. I could hear the crabs moving under the wet newspaper. One old man came over and touched my eye with his pinky and made a sucking sound.

"You eat these crabs?" I asked.

He pulled back the *Daily News* to show me.

"You eat these crabs?" I asked again.

He didn't understand me. "Two dollah," he said. "Mamma good."

If I'd had two dollars I would've bought them off him, just to scare my mother, and keep her from looking at my eye. I walked up to Haven Avenue by myself. All the Bullets were proud of that victory and thought it meant a great season for us in the Kiwanis. I was a little proud of it too; how it resolved things in a weird way, how I, pardon the bad joke, had used my head to bunt my way out of the traps of Washington Heights. Florry O'Neill, my love for you runs deep, deep as the river, that river of all our dreams that first astonished Henry Hudson. That game was a satisfaction. It gave all of us, especially the Bullets, a few months before they disappeared into high school, to live in Washington Heights, as if it was a place where you could live, like California, or Colorado.

The Aerodynamics of an Irishman

Barry Gifford

THERE WAS A MAN on our block named Rooney Sullavan who'd
often come walking down the street while the kids would be playing
ball in front of my house or Johnny McLaughlin's house. He would
always stop and ask if he'd ever shown us how he used to throw the
knuckleball back when he pitched for Kankakee in 1930.

"Plenty of times, Rooney," Billy Cunningham would say. "No
knuckles about it, right?" Tommy Ryan would say. "No knuckles about
it, right!" Rooney Sullavan would say. "Give it here and I'll show you."
One of us would reluctantly toss Rooney the ball and we'd step up so
he could demonstrate for the fortieth or fiftieth time how he held the
ball by his fingertips only, no knuckles about it.

"Don't know how it ever got the name knuckler," Rooney'd say. "I
call mine The Rooneyball." Then he'd tell one of us, usually Billy
because he had the catcher's glove, the old fat-heeled kind that didn't
bend unless somebody stepped on it, a big black mitt that Billy's dad
had handed down to him from *his* days at Kankakee or Rock Island or
someplace, to get sixty feet away so Rooney could see if he could "still
make it wrinkle."

Billy would pace off twelve squares of sidewalk, each square being
approximately five feet long, the length of one nine-year-old boy's
body stretched head to toe lying flat, squat down and stick his big
black glove out in front of his face. With his right hand he'd cover his
crotch in case the pitch got away and short-hopped off the cement
where he couldn't block it with the mitt. The knuckleball was unpre-
dictable, not even Rooney could tell what would happen to it once he
let it go.

"It's the air makes it hop," Rooney claimed. His leather jacket creaked as he bent, wound up, rotated his right arm like nobody'd done since Chief Bender, crossed his runny grey eyes and released the ball from the tips of his fingers. We watched as it sailed straight up at first then sort of floated on an invisible wave before plunging the last ten feet like a balloon that had been pierced by a dart.

Billy always went down on his knees, the back of his right hand stiffened over his crotch, and stuck out his gloved hand at the slowly whirling Rooneyball. Just before it got to Billy's mitt the ball would give out entirely and sink rapidly, inducing Billy to lean forward in order to catch it, only he couldn't because at the last instant it would make a final, sneaky hop before bouncing surprisingly hard off Billy's unprotected chest.

"*Just* like I told you," Rooney Sullavan would exclaim. "All it takes is plain old air."

Billy would come up with the ball in his upturned glove, his right hand rubbing the place on his chest where the pitch had hit. "You all right, son?" Rooney would ask, and Billy would nod. "Tough kid." Rooney'd say. "I'd like to stay out with you fellas all day, but I got responsibilities." Rooney would muss up Billy's hair with the hand that held the secret to The Rooneyball and walk away whistling "When Irish Eyes Are Smiling" or "My Wild Irish Rose." Rooney was about forty-five or fifty years old and lived with his mother in a bungalow at the corner. He worked nights for Wanzer Dairy, washing out returned milk bottles.

Tommy Ryan would grab the ball out of Billy's mitt and hold it by the tips of his fingers like Rooney Sullavan did, and Billy would go sit on the stoop in front of the closest house and rub his chest. "No way," Tommy would say, considering the prospect of his ever duplicating Rooney's feat. "There must be something he's not telling us."

Dreams of a Jewish Batboy

Gerald Rosen

For ONE DAY IN 1955, I served as visiting team batboy for the New York Giants at the Polo Grounds. I was given the job by my friend Bobby "Midge" Weinstein, who was the Giant's regular batboy. He had inherited the position from the previous batboy, who lived in his building and was a friend of Midge's older brother.

For me, a Jewish kid from the Bronx who used to cut Hebrew school to play stickball in the streets, it was a dream come true. My ancestors in Europe might have dreamed of becoming great Rabbis. I dreamed of playing major-league baseball.

Midge Weinstein had been the Giant's batboy during their miracle world championship year of 1954 and it was during that year that my own association with the Giants had begun. Sometimes, after school, when the Giants were on the road, Midge and I would cross to the Polo Grounds on the walking bridge which at that time joined Manhattan to the Bronx over the Harlem River. We would enter the clubhouse where we would sign baseballs for the veterans in hospitals. We each practiced our imitations of the players' signatures and we came to be quite good at these forgeries, specializing in about half the team apiece.

In a way, I guess you could say this was my first experience in fiction writing. After all, I was taking on the identity of other characters, imitating them, writing their words for them, and I had an audience who believed the words were true and, presumably, received a certain pleasure from reading my words if my craft was good enough. It seemed a harmless enough ruse to get close to the game I adored, and in some Jeremy Bentham utilitarian scheme of ethics, it probably did increase the total amount of happiness in the world.

It certainly increased my own happiness because after we signed our quota of baseballs for the day, Midge and I would venture out onto the beautifully cut, sweet grass of the vacant stadium where we would hit balls to each other. We were not allowed on the infield. The Polo Grounds' infield was reputed to be one of the finest in the majors and the groundskeepers protected it from intruders like ourselves as diligently as, a couple years later, we would find college fraternities protecting themselves from us because our parents were Jewish.

Nonetheless, we had no grass in our neighborhood, and thus playing on a major-league outfield in a great old stadium which seated 55,000 people was thrilling enough. Trotting out onto the field seemed like entering a kind of ritual space, a space which had contained history, a space which was often televised and thus seemed to open onto a higher level of reality than that of our daily lives. To a Bronx kid like myself, it uncovered a window to great American vistas of the imagination. I walked differently on the huge, beautifully kept field. I moved my mouth up and down unconsciously as if chewing an imaginary plug of tobacco. And I found especially fertile ground for my dreams out in center field. For center field at the Polo Grounds at that time was the home turf of Willie Mays.

Leon Trotsky said of the acerbic French novelist Ferdinand Celine that Celine entered great literature like a man entering his own house. This is a perfect description of the way Willie Mays had entered center field at the Polo Grounds. Today, with our suburban, all-purpose, uniform, astro-turfed stadiums, it is difficult to imagine there ever was a major-league park like the Polo Grounds. Shaped more like a running track than a circle, it seemed a more proper home for football than baseball. Only 257 feet down the right-field line, it stretched 483 feet to straight-away center field. Thus it had always been Paradise Found for pull hitters. But when Willie Mays arrived, the park suddenly felt like a gift of the Gods to baseball aficionados.

On the one hand, the dimensions of the park gave the center fielder an entire meadow, a veritable pasture in which to chase down long fly balls without the need to slow down or ever even think about running into a fence. It thus presented a kind of world without limits, a space in which the right person could uncompromisingly achieve the heights of his craft. The moment the young Willie Mays walked out there, we all knew he was that right person.

On the other hand, the field presented the danger that a single mistake by the center fielder on the simplest play would result in clearing the bases and giving the batter the equivalent of a home run. So everyone played cautiously in center field at the Polo Grounds. Everyone that is, except Willie Mays. With a man on first, for example, and a line drive single to center, Mays would sometimes come flying in and seem to run past the ball, and just when you thought to see it disappearing into the distance out by the bleachers, out by the Harlem River in fact, he would spear it with his bare right hand behind him and in the same motion drill a throw to third to catch the lead runner sliding in.

Mays was a kind of matador. Making his patented "breadbasket" catches of fly balls, his glove down at his waist where he could hardly see the ball, courting danger, coming teasingly close to tragedy and then finessing his way out of the predicament with daring and, most importantly, with style. In some respects, watching him play reminded one of watching Dizzy Gillespie in that same period, mamboing in front of his band while spewing out fusillades of perfect notes like a Spitfire's machine guns through that same trumpet whose bell would soon be twisted skywards, towards Mars. Neither man believed in the aesthetic that less is more.

Thus, I had no second thoughts about signing some names on a baseball, if it would allow me to play center field in the Polo Grounds when the Giants were out of town, where I could shag fly balls hit by Midge Weinstein and try to make breadbasket catches of my own and pretend I was Willie Mays. Like most teenagers, like most Americans in fact, I was an inveterate dreamer and I spent much of my life imagining myself committing great feats in front of the television camera which followed me around all the time in my imagination and made me feel real. In my own lifetime, I had seen the world change from a Marxian dialectic of bosses and workers to a new set of opposing classes—those who had been on TV and those who hadn't. To Paraphrase Rene Descartes, my basic philosophy about the world was: I am on TV, therefore I am.

But, if playing on the empty field was exhilarating, how much better would it be to be out there in front of tens of thousands of fans at a real game. To be part of the action. Out there in uniform. With the real players. And, *mirabile dictu,* as if that weren't thrilling enough, to be appearing on real television as well. On the same millions of glowing screens which had held Milton Berle and Howdy Doody and Hopalong Cassidy and Lassie. Me! Jerry Rosen. From the Bronx. Was it possible? I could hardly believe it. I could scarcely wait or sleep at night. My wildest dreams seemed on the Gillette stainless-steel edge of coming true.

On the day of the game I arrived at the park early and entered the visitors' club house. I went to my locker and changed into my Cincinnati Reds uniform. The Reds wore sleeveless uniforms in those days, designed perhaps to intimidate the other team by revealing Ted Kluszewski's tree-trunk arms. The lockers were not like the gray steel theft preventers which lined the walls in high school, but rather were open, wooden compartments, each about the size of a large phone booth with no door. There were none of the rugs on the floor or tape players or pastel walls that you would expect today, but rather a quiet wooden ambience, in which all the uniforms and equipment were hung and laid out neatly before the players arrived. It seemed a sensible, businesslike, rather old-fashioned environment.

Once on the field, I joined Midge, who showed me around and briefed me on my duties. The primary requisite for success for the batboy is not skill with handling towels and the like. It involves having a sense of the flow of the game. The best batboy, like the best umpire, was the one you didn't notice. Being a batboy conferred a large responsibility on a young person. You were out there on the field of play, even if usually in foul territory, and the play could easily slide off the field into your area, for example, on a foul pop-up or the overthrow of a base. You had to know enough about the game to anticipate the flow of play and to clear the bat out of the way or to remove yourself quickly in the other direction from the one in which the play would unfold.

As batting practice proceeded and the stands began to fill, I waved to my parents, who were filming me from the boxes, and I picked up my glove and, somewhat self-consciously, ambled out into the outfield. I ventured into center field. No one seemed to object, so I simply stood there, trying to look as nonchalant as possible. A man in a Giants' uniform trotted over to my right. He had large, strong shoulders, rounded like a bison, or a Brancusi. His number was 24. I swallowed as I realized it was Willie Mays.

What struck me, as I tried not to panic, as I wondered whether I, as batboy, belonged there at that moment, was how grounded he seemed to be. How *there*. And why not, I realize now. The Buddhists tell us imagination is the product of desire. Why should Willie Mays have desired to be any place else or any other person? Therefore why should he be living in his mind, like the rest of us alienated dreamers, as opposed to simply being there, at home, on the Earth, grounded like a secure electric power cable?

I was ill at ease. I was standing about fifteen feet to his left, still unsure of my franchise to be there. But as far as I could judge, he seemed to accept me, turning his gaze toward the plate, watching for a fly ball. I turned toward the plate too, and just at that moment, before I had any further time to think, a right-handed batter gently sliced a high fly ball over toward our left, toward right-center field. I moved instinctively as soon as the ball left the bat, watching it spin lazily in the air as I ran to catch up with it. As I drew even with it, I saw someone on my right, also chasing the ball. "I got it," I shouted, as I had done thousands of times on the concrete surface of the P.S. 104 schoolyard. The other fielder swerved easily away and I reached up and caught the ball and threw it, I hoped gracefully, back toward the pitcher's mound. As I looked over to my right, I saw Willie Mays turn and move away from me and start back toward his position in center field.

And suddenly, it occurred to me, what I had done. I, Jerry Rosen, Jewish teenager, of Nelson Avenue in the Bronx, had just waved off Willie Mays, arguably the best all-around baseball player who has ever lived, and I had caught a ball on his territory, center field at the Polo Grounds, a large section of Manhattan real estate which he *owned*, which in its glorious immensity seemed to have been built with some premonition of his arrival in mind, so he could display his amazing talents in front of millions of awe-struck spectators, and I had simply shouted, "I got it," and I had caught the ball beside him just like that.

I didn't know what to make of this. On the one hand I feared I was violating some sacred rule of batboys, some taboo which Midge had not told me about, and I was depriving Willy Mays of his chance to warm up for the games that afternoon. On the other hand, there was Willy, back to his position about fifteen feet over to my right, not complaining, acting as if I had merely done what I should have, called for a ball that was mine.

I felt somewhat uneasy for a moment, but then I began to feel as if I were glowing, as if I had been alleviated by moon gravity and somehow all the organs and tubes which filled my body had been magically transmuted into a diamondlike light. After all, I had caught the ball, hadn't I? Yes, easily. And gracefully, I was sure. Perhaps . . . perhaps I was better than I thought.

I lived with my bliss for a few moments, out there in my uniform, next to Willie Mays, and then, not wanting to take another ball away from him, I ambled away, toward an empty area in the outfield over near the left-field foul line, where I could relax in my sense of unambiguous belonging and show off my newfound talents to the thousands of fans who were filling the park.

No sooner had I set myself in my new position than the batter hit a high line drive in my direction. It came rapidly toward me and began hooking hard toward the line, toward my right. I moved quickly with it, over to the right and back, back toward the wall, moving fast, and before I had a chance to think, I reached across my body with my glove, leaped, and lunged toward the ball, grabbing it backhand, above my head, just as the ball and I together smashed into the thick, fifteen-foot high, dark green steel wall.

I was shaken, and vaguely hurt. I stayed down for a few seconds to gather myself together. Two players who were jogging past came over to check up on me, and I saw them smile as I not only untangled my limbs and rose from the ground but held the ball up in my glove to show the fans that I had held on to it. Again, this was an automatic gesture, one you would make if you had fallen in a stickball game on the cobblestones of 170th Street and wanted to show everyone you'd held on to the ball for the out, but here, in the Polo Grounds, I was suddenly startled to realize that hundreds of fans who were waiting for a batting practice home-run ball in the left-field stands, hundreds of fans were applauding. For me! In the Polo Grounds. Real fans.

And then, as I smiled and touched the bill of my hat lightly to acknowledge the applause, the truth struck me with the full unimpeded force of revelation: I was great! It was obvious. The fans knew what they were applauding for. This was no idle solipsistic fantasy. This was really happening. On the plane of actuality. As unbelievable as it seemed.

But after all, hadn't I, just last week, gotten a winning double in the ninth inning for our sandlot team, the Bronx Philtons, against the Paramounts on Frankie Frisch Field in the East Bronx? Granted, I was barely hitting .220 for the Philtons, and I hadn't even been good enough to make it as a substitute on our high school team, but I was sixteen, and leaving the reality principle behind was, to me, as easy as stepping over a chalk line of a sidewalk potsy game.

I was great. It had taken a great challenge to bring this out in me. The streets of the Bronx had not been a large enough arena. I had needed a major-league occasion to rise to my full stature in life. It was obvious.

And so, like Fyodor Dostoevski at the tables in Germany, putting

his railway tickets along with the last of the money he and his wife had
left in the world down on a particular roulette number which he knew,
he simply *knew* that the Gods had prepared for him, that they were
testing him with, that he could only miss out on if he didn't *believe*, if
he didn't believe in what was being told him at that very moment so
clearly by the Gods themselves, I looked toward the home plate and
saw that the regular Giant infield was at their positions except for the
shortstop, Alvin Dark. And I realized at once that this was that
opening that is provided by destiny perhaps once in a person's life.
The chance that only those with true faith and vision will take.

And almost before I knew it, sailing on the winds of hubris, like an
electron that jumps from one orbit to another without passing through
the space between, I found myself playing shortstop with the starting
infield of the New York Giants. On my right, at third base, was Henry
Thompson. On my left, at second, Daryl Spencer. Across the diamond
at first base, Whitey Lockman. And at shortstop, that kid from the
Bronx, that new rookie sensation the whole nation was talking about:
me.

The batter was right handed. I moved into position. Leaned forward.
My game face on, loose jaw, cool mean eyes, hands on my knees,
balanced, agile, and ready for whatever might come my way.

On the first pitch, the batter swung and hit a line drive screaming
right at me. Not *to* me, but *at* me. One of those line drives that are hit
with so much force they stay about two feet off the ground and don't
come down until they're way out in the outfield near the fence.

This particular line drive was rocketing along at such a swift pace it
somehow made real life seem like a film in slow motion. The ball set
out as if headed slightly to my left, but then it began to hook toward
the right. In fact, I quickly realized that it was coming directly at me.
And it seemed to be making a kind of horrible swooshing sound as it
approached.

In fact, as I fled toward my right to escape, the ball seemed to be
following me. Chasing me. Finally, after what seemed like minutes, I
made a desperate, terrified leap away from it, awkwardly raising my
legs up into the air at the last second as if trying to somehow leap over
an attacking wild boar, and the ball passed like an artillery shell just
under my legs, nearly sawing them off as I tumbled to the ground in a
disorganized heap.

When I finally summoned the nerve to look up, I saw the entire
Giants' starting infield, standing in their places and laughing good-

naturedly but uncontrollably. Laughing at me. Jerry Rosen from the Bronx.

I smiled along with them and after a few aeons, we all returned to the business at hand. But I knew I had received a quick education in about the interval of time it took one to reach over to turn on a light. For it had never occurred to me before that a baseball could be hit that hard. That it could travel that fast. Suddenly I understood exactly how a baseball can kill a man. Suddenly I, who had imagined every eye in the park on me after I had made that fine catch in left field, suddenly I felt miserable and cowardly and ashamed.

For I had been presented by the Gods with a sad truth which my friends might still, with some luck, be able to avoid for a few more years, or perhaps for a lifetime in fact. I knew that I couldn't catch a ball hit that hard ever — today, tomorrow, or if I practiced for twenty years.

I knew, with absolute certainty, that I was not going to be a major leaguer. I was not cut out to be a major leaguer. No amount of practice or dedication would have made the slightest difference. Major-league baseball was played on a level which I could never attain. It was simply beyond me. I could substitute for Alvin Dark with the pen, signing his name to baseballs in the clubhouse, but I could not substitute for him on the field at shortstop. Never.

The remainder of the day went quite well. I handled the batboy's chores with competence; I mingled with the players and got along with them easily enough; I even entered the sacred fraternity of "The Televised," when the Cincinnati trainer gave me a little cup of liquid to run onto the field to give to Ted Kluszewski for an eyewash as the game was stopped temporarily and the eyes of a great city focused on electronic images of Ted and myself, standing in the dusk just behind first base.

After the game was over, heading back home with my family in the warmth of our maroon 1947 Buick, I carried with me some precious objects. I had about four dollars which I was paid for the game. I had a new major-league baseball, courtesy of the Cincinnati Reds baseball club, the customary tip for a batboy. And I had a sheaf of memories which would stay with me for a lifetime.

What I did not have was the single most sustaining and compelling dream which had buoyed my life up to that moment.

From *Brushes with Greatness:* Willie Mays

Paul Auster

MY DEVOTION TO BASEBALL began during the 1954 World Series. I was seven years old and the New York Giants became my team. After their sweep of the heavily favored Cleveland Indians, it was only natural that I should have fallen in love with the men in the black-and-orange hats. Of all the players on that team, Willie Mays was the one I followed most passionately.

In the spring of 1955 I was invited to my first major-league game. Friends of my parents had box seats at the Polo Grounds, and six or seven of us went along to watch the Giants play the Milwaukee Braves. It was a warm May night, and if I don't remember much about the game, I do remember the overwhelming impression it made on me: the noise of the crowd, the flood lights shining on the green grass, the utter whiteness of the bases.

After the game my parents and their friends sat talking in their seats until the stadium had emptied out. In order to leave, we had to walk across the diamond to the center-field exit. In all other ballparks, the locker rooms are behind the dugouts, but in the Polo Grounds (an ancient structure that has since been torn down), the lockers were located in a little house that jutted out from the center-field wall. To my amazement, just as we approached the wall, I saw Willie Mays standing there in his street clothes. Trembling with awe, I approached my hero and forced some words out of my mouth, "Mr. Mays," I said, "could I please have your autograph?"

"Sure, kid, sure," he said. "You got a pencil?"

As it turned out, I didn't have a pencil. Nor did my parents. Nor did any of their friends. Willie Mays stood there watching me in silence as I asked one adult after another the same question, and when it became clear that no one in the group had anything to write with, he turned to me and shrugged. "Sorry, kid," he said. "Ain't got no pencil, can't give no autograph." And then he walked out of the stadium into the night.

I remember the tears that fell down my cheeks and how embarrassed I felt to be crying, but there was nothing I could do to stop myself.

Since that day, I have always carried a pencil with me. As I like to tell my son, that's why I became a writer.

How I Got My Nickname

W. P. Kinsella

For Brian Fawcett,
whose story "My Career with the Leafs"
inspired this story.

IN THE SUMMER OF 1951, the summer before I was to start Grade 12, my polled Hereford calf, Simon Bolivar, won Reserve Grand Champion at the Des Moines, All-Iowa Cattle Show and Summer Exposition. My family lived on a hobby-farm near Iowa City. My father, who taught classics at Coe College in Cedar Rapids, and in spite of that was still the world's number one baseball fan, said I deserved a reward—I also had a straight A average in Grade 11 and had published my first short story that spring. My father phoned his friend Robert Fitzgerald (Fitzgerald, an eminent translator, sometimes phoned my father late at night and they talked about various ways of interpreting the tougher parts of *The Iliad*) and two weeks later I found myself in Fitzgerald's spacious country home outside of New York City, sharing the lovely old house with the Fitzgeralds, their endless supply of children, and a young writer from Georgia named Flannery O'Connor. Miss O'Connor was charming, and humorous in an understated way, and I wish I had talked with her more. About the third day I was there I admitted to being a published writer and Miss O'Connor said "You must show me some of your stories." I never did. I was seventeen, overweight, diabetic, and bad-complexioned. I alternated between being terminally shy and obnoxiously brazen. I was nearly always shy around the Fitzgeralds and Miss O'Connor. I was also terribly homesick, which made me appear more silent and outlandish than I knew I was. I suspect I am the model for Enoch Emery, the odd, lonely country boy in Miss O'Connor's novel *Wise Blood*. But that is another story.

On a muggy August morning, the first day of a Giant home stand at the Polo Grounds, I prepared to travel into New York. I politely invited Miss O'Connor to accompany me, but she, even at that early date, had to avoid sunlight and often wore her wide-brimmed straw hat, even indoors. I set off much too early and, though terrified of the grimy city and shadows that seemed to lurk in every doorway, arrived at the Polo Grounds over two hours before game time. It was raining gently and I was one of about two dozen fans in the ballpark. A few players were lethargically playing catch, a coach was hitting fungoes to three players in right field. I kept edging my way down the rows of seats until I was right behind the Giants dugout.

The Giants were thirteen games behind the Dodgers and the pennant race appeared all but over. A weasel-faced batboy, probably some executive's nephew, I thought, noticed me staring wide-eyed at the players and the playing field. He curled his lip at me, then stuck out his tongue. He mouthed the words "Take a picture, it'll last longer," adding something at the end that I could only assume to be uncomplimentary.

Fired by the insult I suddenly mustered all my bravado and called out "Hey, Mr. Durocher?" Leo Durocher, the Giants manager, had been standing in the third base coach's box not looking at anything in particular. I was really impressed. That's the grand thing about baseball, I thought. Even a manager in a pennant race can take time to daydream. He didn't hear me. But the batboy did, and stuck out his tongue again.

I was overpowered by my surroundings. Though I'd seen a lot of major-league baseball I'd never been in the Polo Grounds before. The history of the place . . . "Hey, Mr. Durocher," I shouted.

Leo looked up at me with a baleful eye. He needed a shave, and the lines around the corners of his mouth looked like ruts.

"What is it, Kid?"

"Could I hit a few?" I asked hopefully, as if I was begging to stay up an extra half hour. "You know, take a little batting practice?"

"Sure, Kid. Why not?" and Leo smiled with one corner of his mouth. "We want all our fans to feel like part of the team."

From the box seat where I'd been standing, I climbed up on the roof of the dugout and Leo helped me down onto the field.

Leo looked down into the dugout. The rain was stopping. On the other side of the park a few of the Phillies were wandering onto the field. "Hey, George," said Leo, staring into the dugout, "throw the kid here a few pitches. Where are you from, son?"

It took me a few minutes to answer because I experienced this strange, lightheaded feeling, as if I had too much sun. "Near to Iowa City, Iowa," I managed to say in a small voice. Then "You're going to win the pennant, Mr. Durocher. I just know you are."

"Well, thanks, Kid," said Leo modestly, "we'll give it our best shot."

George was George Bamberger, a stocky rookie who had seen limited action. "Bring the kid a bat, Andy," Leo said to the batboy. The batboy curled his lip at me but slumped into the dugout, as Bamberger and Sal Yvars tossed the ball back and forth.

The batboy brought me a black bat. I was totally unprepared for how heavy it was. I lugged it to the plate and stepped into the right-hand batter's box. Bamberger delivered an easy, looping, batting-practice pitch. I drilled it back up the middle.

"Pretty good, Kid," I heard Durocher say.

Bamberger threw another easy one and I fouled it off. The third pitch was a little harder. I hammered it to left.

"Curve him," said Durocher.

He curved me. Even through my thick glasses the ball looked as big as a grapefruit, illuminated like a small moon. I whacked it and it hit the right-field wall on one bounce.

"You weren't supposed to hit that one," said Sal Yvars.

"You're pretty good, Kid," shouted Durocher from the third base box. "Give him your best stuff, George."

Over the next fifteen minutes I batted about .400 against George Bamberger, and Roger Bowman, including a home run into the left center-field stands. The players on the Giants bench were watching me with mild interest, often looking up from the books most of them were reading.

"I'm gonna put the infield out now," said Durocher. "I want you to run out some of your hits."

Boy, here I was batting against the real New York Giants. I wished I'd worn a new shirt instead of the horizontally striped red and white one I had on, which made me look heftier than I really was. Bowman threw a sidearm curve and I almost broke my back swinging at it. But he made the mistake of coming right back with the same pitch. I looped it behind third where it landed soft as a sponge, and trickled off toward the stands—I'd seen the play hundreds of times—a stand-up double. But when I was still twenty feet from second base Eddie Stanky was waiting with the ball. "Slide!" somebody yelled, but I just skidded to a stop, stepping out of the baseline to avoid the tag. Stanky whapped me anyway, a glove to the ribs that would have made Rocky Marciano or Ezzard Charles proud.

When I got my wind back Durocher was standing, hands on hips, staring down at me.

"Why the hell didn't you slide, Kid?"

"I can't," I said, a little indignantly. "I'm diabetic, I have to avoid stuff like that. If I cut myself, or even bruise badly, it takes forever to heal."

"Oh," said Durocher. "Well, I guess that's okay then."

"You shouldn't tag people so hard," I said to Stanky. "Somebody could get hurt."

"Sorry, Kid," said Stanky. I don't think he apologized very often. I noticed that his spikes were filed. But I found later that he knew a lot about F. Scott Fitzgerald. His favorite story was "Babylon Revisited" so that gave us a lot in common; I was a real Fitzgerald fan; Stanky and I became friends even though both he and Durocher argued against reading *The Great Gatsby* as an allegory.

"Where'd you learn your baseball?" an overweight coach who smelled strongly of snuff, and bourbon, said to me.

"I live near Iowa City, Iowa," I said in reply.

Everyone wore question marks on their faces. I saw I'd have to elaborate. "Iowa City is within driving distance of Chicago, St. Louis, Milwaukee, and there's minor-league ball in Cedar Rapids, Omaha, Kansas City. Why there's barely a weekend my dad and I don't go somewhere to watch professional baseball."

"Watch?" said Durocher.

"Well, we talk about it some too. My father is a real student of the game. Of course we only talk in Latin when we're on the road, it's a family custom."

"Latin?" said Durocher.

"Say something in Latin," said Whitey Lockman, who had wandered over from first base.

"The Etruscans have invaded all of Gaul," I said in Latin.

"Their fortress is on the banks of the river," said Bill Rigney, who had been filling in at third base.

"Velle est posse," I said.

"Where there's a will there's a way," translated Durocher.

"Drink Agri Cola . . ." I began.

"The farmer's drink," said Sal Yvars, slapping me on the back, but gently enough not to bruise me. I guess I looked a little surprised.

"Most of us are more than ballplayers," said Alvin Dark, who had joined us. "In fact the average player on this squad is fluent in three languages."

"*Watch?*" said Durocher, getting us back to baseball. "You *watch* a lot of baseball, but where do you play?"

"I've never played in my life," I replied. "But I have a photographic memory. I just watch how different players hold their bat, how they stand. I try to emulate Enos Slaughter and Joe DiMaggio."

"Can you field?" said Durocher.

"No."

"No?"

"I've always just watched the hitters. I've never paid much attention to the fielders."

He stared at me as if I had spoken to him in an unfamiliar foreign language.

"Everybody fields," he said. "What position do you play?"

"I've never played," I reiterated. "My health is not very good."

"Cripes," he said, addressing the sky. "You drop a second Ted Williams on me and he tells me he can't field." Then to Alvin Dark: "Hey, Darky, throw a few with the kid here. Get him warmed up."

In the dugout Durocher pulled a thin, black glove from an equipment bag and tossed it to me. I dropped it. The glove had no discernable padding in it. The balls Dark threw hit directly on my hand, when I caught them, which was about one out of three. "Ouch!" I cried. "Don't throw so hard."

"Sorry, Kid," said Alvin Dark and threw the next one a little easier. If I really heaved I could just get the ball back to him. I have always thrown like a non-athletic girl. I could feel my hand bloating inside the thin glove. After about ten pitches, I pulled my hand out. It looked as though it had been scalded.

"Don't go away, Kid," said Leo. "In fact why don't you sit in the dugout with me. What's your name anyway?"

"W. P. Kinsella," I said.

"Your friends call you W?"

"My father calls me William, and my mother . . ." but I let my voice trail off. I didn't think Leo Durocher would want to know my mother still called me Bunny.

"Jeez," said Durocher. "You need a nickname, Kid. Bad."

"I'll work on it," I said.

I sat right beside Leo Durocher all that stifling afternoon in the

Polo Grounds as the Giants swept a doubleheader from the Phils, the
start of a sixteen-game streak that was to lead to the October 3, 1951,
Miracle of Coogan's Bluff. I noticed right away that the Giants were all
avid readers. In fact, the *New York Times* Best Seller Lists, and the
Time and *Newsweek* lists of readable books and an occasional review
were taped to the walls of the dugout. When the Giants were in the
field I peeked at the covers of the books the players sometimes read
between innings. Willie Mays was reading *The Cruel Sea* by Nicholas
Monsarrat. Between innings Sal Maglie was deeply involved in Carson
McCullers's new novel *The Ballad of the Sad Cafe*. "I sure wish we
could get that Cousin Lyman to be our mascot," he said to me when he
saw me eyeing the bookjacket, referring to the hunchbacked dwarf
who was the main character in the novel. "We need something to
inspire us," he added. Alvin Dark slammed down his copy of *Requiem
for a Nun* and headed for the on-deck circle.

When the second game ended, a sweaty and sagging Leo Durocher
took me by the arm. "There's somebody I want you to meet, Kid," he
said. Horace Stoneham's office was furnished in wine-colored leather
sofas and overstuffed horsehair chairs. Stoneham sat behind an oak
desk as big as the dugout, enveloped in cigar smoke.

"I've got a young fellow here I think we should sign for the stretch
drive," Durocher said. "He can't field or run, but he's as pure a hitter
as I've ever seen. He'll make a hell of a pinch hitter."

"I suppose you'll want a bonus?" growled Stoneham.

"I do have something in mind," I said. Even Durocher was not
nearly so jovial as he had been. Both men stared coldly at me. Durocher
leaned over and whispered something to Stoneham.

"How about $6,000," Stoneham said.

"What I'd really like . . . " I began.

"Alright, $10,000, but not a penny more."

"Actually, I'd like to meet Bernard Malamud. I thought you could
maybe invite him down to the park. Maybe get him to sign a book for
me?" They both looked tremendously relieved.

"Bernie and me and this kid Salinger are having supper this evening,"
said Durocher. "Why don't you join us?"

"You mean J. D. Salinger?" I said.

"Jerry's a big Giant fan," he said. "The team Literary Society read
Catcher in the Rye last month. We had a panel discussion on it for eight
hours on the train to St. Louis."

Before I signed the contract I phoned my father.

"No reason you can't postpone your studies until the end of the season," he said. "It'll be good experience for you. You'll gather a lot of material you can write about later. Besides, baseball players are the real readers of America."

I got my first hit off Warren Spahn, a solid single up the middle. Durocher immediately replaced me with a pinch runner. I touched Ralph Branca for a double, the ball went over Duke Snider's head, hit the wall and bounced halfway back to the infield. Anyone else would have had an inside the park homer. I wheezed into second and was replaced. I got into 38 of the final 42 games. I hit 11 for 33, and was walked four times. And hit once. That was the second time I faced Warren Spahn. He threw a swishing curve that would have gone behind me if I hadn't backed into it. I slouched off toward first holding my ribs.

"You shouldn't throw at batters like that," I shouted, "someone could get seriously hurt. I'm diabetic, you know." I'd heard that Spahn was into medical texts and interested in both human and veterinary medicine.

"Sorry," he shouted back. "If I'd known I wouldn't have thrown at you. I've got some good linament in the clubhouse. Come see me after the game. By the way I hear you're trying to say that *The Great Gatsby* is an allegory."

"The way I see it, it is," I said. "You see the eyes of the optometrist on the billboard are really the eyes of God looking down on a fallen world . . . "

"Alright, alright," said the umpire, Beans Reardon, "let's get on with the game. By the way, Kid, I don't think it's an allegory either. A statement on the human condition, perhaps. But not an allegory."

The players wanted to give me some nickname other than "Kid." Someone suggested "Ducky" in honor of my running style. "Fats" said somebody else. I made a note to remove his bookmark between innings. Several other suggestions were downright obscene. Baseball players, in spite of their obsession with literature and the arts, often have a bawdy sense of humor.

"How about 'Moonlight,'" I suggested. I'd read about an old time player who stopped for a cup of coffee with the Giants half a century before, who had that nickname.

"What the hell for?" said Monty Irvin, who in spite of the nickname preferred to be called Monford or even by his second name Merrill. "You got to have a reason for a nickname. You got to earn it. Still, anything's better than W. P."

"It was only a suggestion," I said. I made a mental note not to tell Monford what I knew about *his* favorite author, Erskine Caldwell.

As it turned out I didn't earn a nickname until the day we won the pennant.

As every baseball fan knows the Giants went into the bottom of the ninth in the deciding game of the pennant playoff trailing the Dodgers 4-1.

"Don't worry," I said to Durocher, "everything's going to work out." If he heard me he didn't let on.

But was everything going to work out? And what part was I going to play in it? Even though I'd contributed to the Giants' amazing stretch drive, I didn't belong. Why am I here? I kept asking myself. I had some vague premonition that I was about to change history. I mean I wasn't a ballplayer. I was a writer. Here I was about to go into Grade 12 and I was already planning to do my master's thesis on F. Scott Fitzgerald.

I didn't have time to worry further as Alvin Dark singled. Don Mueller, in his excitement, had carried his copy of *The Mill on the Floss* out to the on-deck circle. He set the resin bag on top of it, stalked to the plate and singled, moving Dark to second.

I was flabbergasted when Durocher called Monford Irvin back and said to me "Get in there, Kid."

It was at that moment that I knew why I was there. I would indeed change history. One stroke of the bat and the score would be tied. I eyed the left-field stands as I nervously swung two bats to warm up. I was nervous but not scared. I never doubted my prowess for one moment. Years later Johnny Bench summed it up for both athletes and writers when he talked about a successful person having to have an *inner conceit.* It never occurred to me until days later that I might have hit into a double or triple play, thus ending it and *really* changing history.

When I did take my place in the batter's box, I pounded the plate and glared out at Don Newcombe. I wished that I shaved so I could give him a stubble-faced stare of contempt. He curved me and I let it go by for a ball. I fouled the next pitch high into the first base stands. A fastball was low. I fouled the next one outside third. I knew he didn't want to go to a full count: I crowded the plate a little looking for the fastball. He curved me. Nervy. But the curveball hung, sat out over the plate like a cantaloupe. I waited an extra millisecond before lambasting it. In that instant the ball broke in on my hands; it hit the bat right next to my right hand. It has been over thirty years but I still wake deep in the night, my hands vibrating, burning from Newcombe's pitch. The bat shattered into kindling. The ball flew in a polite loop as if it had been tossed by a five-year-old; it landed soft as a creampuff in Peewee Reese's glove. One out.

I slumped back to the bench.

"Tough luck, Kid," said Durocher, patting my shoulder. "There'll be other chances to be a hero."

"Thanks, Leo," I said.

Whitey Lockman doubled. Dark scored. Mueller hurt himself sliding into third. Rafael Noble went in to run for Mueller. Charlie Dressen replaced Newcombe with Ralph Branca. Bobby Thomson swung bats in the on-deck circle.

As soon as umpire Jorda called time-in, Durocher leapt to his feet, and before Bobby Thomson could take one step toward the plate, Durocher called him back.

"Don't do that!" I yelled, suddenly knowing why I was *really* there. But Durocher ignored me. He was beckoning with a big-knuckled finger to another reserve player, a big outfielder who was tearing up the American Association when they brought him up late in the year. He was 5 for 8 as a pinch hitter.

Durocher was already up the dugout steps heading toward the umpire to announce the change. The outfielder from the American Association was making his way down the dugout, hopping along over feet and ankles. He'd be at the top of the step by the time Durocher reached the umpire.

As he skipped by me, the last person between Bobby Thomson and immortality, I stuck out my foot. The outfielder from the American Association went down like he'd been poleaxed. He hit his face on the top step of the dugout, crying out loud enough to attract Durocher's attention.

The trainer hustled the damaged player to the clubhouse. Durocher waved Bobby Thomson to the batter's box. And the rest is history. After the victory celebration I announced my retirement, blaming it on a damaged wrist. I went back to Iowa and listened to the World Series on the radio.

All I have to show that I ever played in the major leagues is my one-line entry in *The Baseball Encyclopedia:*

W.P. KINSELLA Kinsella, William Patrick "Tripper" BR
TR 5'9" 185 lbs. B. Apr. 14, 1934
Onamata, Ia.

						HR							Pinch Hit	
	G	AB	H	2B	3B	HR	%	R	RBI	BB	SO	EA	BA	AB	H
1951 NY N	38	33	11	2	0	2	6.0	0	8	4	4	0	.333	33	11

I got my outright release in the mail the week after the World Series ended. Durocher had scrawled across the bottom: "Good luck, Kid. By the way, *The Great Gatsby* is *not* an allegory."

Why I Hate Baseball

Michael Stephens

At a memorial for my old friend and former teacher, the poet Joel Oppenheimer, I was reminded of my awkward relationship to one of his great loves, baseball.

Joel was in love with poetry, of course, and the history of the Civil War, but baseball probably took up as much time in his life as anything else. I simply had forgotten this until the memorial. In my mind, I thought of Joel in the context of his rabbinical beard and his poetic cadences from William Carlos Williams and the Bible, of Black Mountain College, his profession as a printer, and especially drinking, in his case, bourbon and the Lion's Head bar on Sheridan Square in New York, the time the late sixties.

Joel was *the* quintessential Mets' fan, and his nonfiction book *the wrong season* was his epic poem to that team. When I think of it now, my friendship with Joel over twenty-five years and my lack of interest in baseball was like a blindman befriending Matisse, like a deafman engaging Mozart, because I simply missed half of what this man was about. Yet I must add that the affinities for poetry and alcohol were binding enough to allow the friendship to prevail, even when Joel became abstinent from booze for the last eighteen years of his life.

To show how foreign I was to the lore of baseball, I missed Joel's point in his deathbed request to have nine friends speak at his memorial at St. Mark's Church in the Bowery. To me, the third of nine children, I only saw a familiar number from my childhood. (I never envisioned my own family as a baseball team but rather a basketball squad with a good bench.) The writer Brian Breger, the tenth man, was the Casey Stengel of the evening, introducing the lineup. I was the leadoff hitter, though as I say, in my ignorance, I thought I spoke first because I was the youngest of Joel's friends and maybe because I introduced him to his last wife Theresa over drinks after a play of mine.

Yet the parallels between the memorial and baseball were obvious to even the most cursory baseball fan. I was to walk or hit a single. The former Met star Ron Swoboda batted fourth, cleanup, clearing the bases with an oratorical home run, which was exactly what he did.

Prior to his death I hadn't spoken with Joel or seen him in quite some time. Yet I did call him a few days before he died, responding to a postcard he sent me, and he told me of his impending end from cancer and how I should come up to New Hampshire for a visit before he died. I explained that I was just a few days out of a rehab, and Joel seemed genuinely pleased that I finally stopped drinking. He was even more impressed that I had been to a place where Dwight Gooden went for his own treatment.

"John Cheever was there some time ago," I reminded him.

"Fuck Cheever," Joel said, "I knew something was wrong with Gooden's game before he went into the rehab."

After the memorial, I tried to figure out where baseball and I went wrong. I loved nearly all sports and played football and basketball in high school, was a fairly decent golfer as a teenager from working on a course as a caddy and greenskeeper; I was a good boxer, played paddleball well. As an adult, I ran, played basketball occasionally, and continued with paddleball in the park, rode a bicycle, jumped rope, and years ago used to play squash a few times a week. I still work out several times a week. On television, I watch football, basketball, and boxing. I had been to a handful of Mets games in recent years with either my wife and daughter or friends who went more regularly. But I realized I was more attracted to the physical details like the green grass on the field than the game itself, which bored me after a few innings.

As a kid, I saw the Dodgers play at Ebbets Field, had been to five or six Yankee games, and saw Willie Mays catch flyballs and hit home runs once or twice at the Polo Grounds. But unlike my childhood friends, I did not follow box scores in the newspaper, did not know the lineups of the home teams, had no baseball cards, and went to games more for the social outing than the sporting event. I never really cared who won.

Of course, my lack of interest in baseball is traceable to a source. He stood outside with me after the memorial at St. Mark's Church. He had parked his taxicab around the corner and came by to hear me speak. It was one of my older brothers, several of whom knew Joel from his drinking days at the Lion's Head.

When our nextdoor neighbor threw flyballs into the air, they disappeared into the clouds. I never was able to field them and my oldest brother Jimmy had no interest in the sport. My younger brothers were too little to be playing in the street. But my second oldest brother Peter never missed a chance to catch one of those humungously high balls.

Peter could have shown me how to catch the ball or how to bat or do anything on a baseball diamond, but he declined. Baseball was his territory.

None of us had rooms of our own, not even our own beds. There were that many children in the family. But each of us, outside the house, tried to find one thing to excell at. Jimmy, the class clown, had his humor, and his dancing ability, executed on Sunday night at the church dances in the school basement around the corner.

The other kids in the family were too young to have interests yet, but I had school and basketball. I was the best student in my class and I had the best jumpshot in the playground. But my way on the basketball court was nothing compared to Peter's on the baseball diamond.

He skipped the Little League farm and minor leagues and went right to the majors and then onto the All-Star Team that represented our town in the Little League World Series.

Jimmy wanted to be a priest when he grew up, Peter a professional baseball player. When I was still on the lean end of being a single-digit midget, the old man brought home 16-ounce boxing gloves for his older sons. I became Jimmy and Peter's sparring partner.

This simply meant that in a context of sport, my two older brothers were allowed to beat the crap out of me. I learned, if not to win, to slip punches, to bob and weave away from them. I learned the beauty and necessity of footwork, of moving side to side.

Jimmy went for my solar plexus; Peter was a headhunter. Usually when they tired of boxing, one of them smothered my head with a pillow.

"Let's kill Michael," Peter suggested, blond-haired, blue-eyed, an altar boy with an angel face.

"Let's," Jimmy said, stocky and with a brown-haired pompadour and bucked teeth. Peter pinned me and Jimmy applied the *coup de grace*.

"What color is he?" Peter asked.

"Too soon to tell," Jimmy said, "I just started applying the pressure."

I gasped and kicked. My legs were the strongest part of my body, and if I located one of their frames, I knew I could disable him for life.

"You have to hold the pillow on his face until he turns blue," Peter said.

"He's a little red in the face," Jimmy replied, pulling the pillow off momentarily, while, unbeknownst to these two young American sportsmen, I furtively sucked a resupply of air.

Jimmy and Peter, of course, were no slouches when it came to torture. They were aware that I probably stole air when The Great One checked my facial color, and so he applied the pillow harder.

"Is he green?" Peter asked.

"I thought you said he's supposed to turn blue," Jimmy shouted. "Make up your mind, will ya?"

It was good to get them fighting. They had their differences. If the feud grew strong enough, they might even forget about me and go at each other. Jimmy was stronger and tougher, Peter faster and sneakier. The big one was good in a quick thrashing, while Pete had stamina like a beast of burden, wearing down his opponents over the long haul.

"Green or blue, it don't matter."

Jimmy removed the pillow quickly and put it back before I could get air.

"He's red."

"Keep applying the pressure," Peter said. "He'll be a deadman before too long."

My lungs burst and I felt my head dry out like a grape evaporating into a raisin in the sun. My voice was muffled, I kicked wildly, hoping to make contact.

"Boys!" our mother called from downstairs. "What are you doing up there?"

"Nothing, mommy," Jimmy called, pressing hard with the pillow.

"Well, come downstairs for some peanut butter and jelly sandwiches."

They left.

I lay on the floor, sucking in air. Brain cells were gone, I knew, but at least I was alive.

That afternoon I tried out for Little League. I was hopeless, not fast enough, scared of the ball hitting me when I batted, flinching away from it when I was on the field. I was sent to the farm team immediately.

"He's Pete's brother, too," I heard the coach say, amazed that I was so terrible.

That evening I asked Peter to show me how to play baseball because I was desperate to learn. This was the Eisenhower era, and I felt un-American not being able to field or hit. Peter took me into the yard and then beyond the garage, its roof crushed in from a hurricane the year before.

He got me in a headlock and applied noogies liberally to my skull.

"I'm the baseball player in this family," he said, "get that into your thick skull, fatso. Nobody plays baseball but me in this family. Understand?"

"Understood."

"What?" he asked, rubbing his forearm across my neck with his headlock, giving me an Indian burn. "What?"

"Understoop," I muttered.

He let go.

"Under stoop," I said. "Under the stoop, up your ass, stupid," and he chased me down the block until he got bored, because if he wanted to, being the fastest kid in the neighborhood, he could have caught me within a couple of yards.

So Peter became the baseball legend in the family and I was the scholar and poet and basketball player. Jimmy was the body-puncher, Peter the headhunter, and I was the Rubber Man, slipping and sliding away from their punches.

All nine children had tough bodies for sports, but most chose not to use them. The one exception was my youngest brother Brendan, who like Peter was a great baseball player, even better than Peter, the house full of the kid's trophies.

Peter had learned to play ball from our next door neighbor, Connie, who had been a professional player himself, but Brendan learned from the master, his older brother Pete.

Yet our family was known for other things than baseball or basketball or scholastics or poetry. All of us were great drinkers, at first, and later seemed to get into trouble with alcohol and drugs and brawling, myself included.

Jimmy led the way, his clown act and dancing feet on the weekend second only to his way with his fists and boozing. Peter was a crazy drunk, not in trouble every time he drank, but drunk every time he got in trouble. Baseball disappeared from his life quickly after he discovered the bottle.

It's a shame, too, because he probably could have been a decent professional player at second base or shortstop. With my youngest brother Brendan, I don't know what got his mind from baseball, maybe his girlfriend, maybe boozing and drugs, it's hard to figure, because he was a great player, too.

My regular athletic days were over even before I finished high school. I just lost interest in team sports, didn't feel I fit in. I know I loved the regimen, getting and staying in shape, the after-school workouts and practices; they were second nature to me, my great love, something I've done through my adult life.

Of course, I was Mr. Goody-Goody in terms of my brothers and sisters' shenanigans. I was the first to go to college, the first to drop out of college. But I had my jobs, wrote my books, even went back to school years later, and eventually wound up teaching, too. I never included myself in this estimate of my family's talents, and how they squandered them. I seemed to be on track with what I wanted to do in life.

Then I collapsed, too. It happened on a June morning, New York City evilly humid and inhumanly hot, I just collapsed. Afterward, I thought of that Frank O'Hara poem about Lana Turner collapsing, how O'Hara said he had drunk too much and smoked too much but never actually collapsed. Like everyone else in my family, I had strength and courage and lots of guts in fights, I had incredible stamina and fortitude, a stubborn resilience, and a single-minded nature. But, like them, the booze got me, a magic greater than I was, a power bigger than any footwork and slipping-sliding I could lay on it. I wound up in an alcohol and drug rehab.

I thought I was in good company because this was the place where John Cheever started his recovery. But I was also aware — even before Joel mentioned it to me a few days before he died — that this was where Dwight Gooden, that fabulous ace for the Mets, had dried out and got clean, too.

That was perfect because, although I hated baseball, I had come to appreciate it for the first time, in spite of my brothers, watching Gooden pitch.

The Doc was in a league with super-athletes like Earl Monroe, Magic Johnson, Julius Irving, Kareem Abdul Jabbar, Jerry West, and Elgin Baylor. Funny, I could only think of basketball players when I thought of qualities beyond sport itself, a transcendence by virtue of physical grace.

Yet these great athletes were superseded in my mind by another class of athlete. Here I only thought of boxers: Muhammad Ali, Archie Moore, and Sugar Ray Robinson. Actually, I put Gooden there, with Ali and Robinson, when I realized I loved Archie, not for grace, but stamina and will, his ballet to potbellies and middle age.

So there I was on the East Side of Manhattan in an old theatrical mansion once owned by Billy Rose, rooming with alkies and druggies, a couple of them athletes, one even a professional basketball player. There weren't any literary types for this particular twenty-eight days of rehabilitation, a counselor told me. He also said that educationally, I was without peer, though that only made me feel a little dumber and lonelier.

That would change midway through my journey at the rehab. A huge, old Viennese gentleman checked in for "the cure," and he often roamed the halls with a fat book under his arm, not a best-seller but usually stiff reading, a biography of Ezra Pound, a book on Wittgenstein, a treatise on Western thought.

His name was Peter, just like my older brother's, and he later told me that he lived in the rehab for at least a week before he realized I was not a baseball player but a writer.

"You just look like a baseball player," Peter insisted. "You certainly don't look like any writer I ever met."

My own brother Peter had been to more detoxes and rehabs in twenty-five years than I could remember. We hadn't been close for years. Other than two younger brothers' weddings where I saw him, I can't remember when I ran into him in ten years.

Jimmy had stopped talking to me more than a decade earlier when he decided that my first novel was libelous and that he should have sued me.

But within a week out of the rehab, I ran into Peter, a taxicab driver in New York, who had been sober for close to a year. Jimmy had close to twenty years of sobriety as did my mother, too. The old man was still tooting on the sly, even after a stroke.

My other brothers and sisters were in different phases of clean and sober, too, all but a younger brother who was homeless and adrift in a bottle.

When I think about my family I can get awfully sad. But this is not that kind of story, I don't think. It was good to reunite with Peter after so many years, even in conversation, when he still defined his territories, baseball, bar-brawling, and now driving a cab.

The man I met for coffee, though, didn't have an ounce of ball player about him. He was thin to the point of emaciation, hollow-eyed, and bald, a man who looked as though he'd been through the ringer several thousand times and decided he was going to stay alive to spite a lot of people who either had contracts on him or just didn't like him one bit. He's the one who gets mistaken for the Robert Duvall of *Tender Mercies;* I'm the one who everyone thinks used to play baseball.

II

MINORS

From *What's a Nice Harvard Boy Like You Doing in the Bushes?*

Rick Wolff

Charleston, S.C.
May 16, 1973

THIS IS OUR SECOND trip here and I have found Charleston to be full of charm. Of course, there are some run-down places, but for the most part it's an intriguing city. For one thing, it's small and quaint, squeezed up against the ocean and full of cramped, cobblestone streets. Even more enticing are the palm trees that line the streets—just like being in Florida again.

The city is replete with Revolutionary and Civil War monuments and plaques, and in many ways Charleston reminds me very strongly of Boston. Except for the palm trees, of course.

To my greater delight, as Tis, Fern and I went sightseeing, we discovered an old museum right around the corner from our motel, a beautiful old white building done in antebellum style, as are most of the homes here.

We eagerly went inside and gazed for a couple of hours at the most wonderful collection of junk I have ever seen, everything from Civil War uniforms to Brazilian shrunken heads. It was quite a show.

At night we played the Charleston Pirates on their home field, which is known as College Park (it belongs to The Citadel, which is located in Charleston). My excitement continued to build, for this is a true stadium, enclosed by large cinder-block walls and bleachers able to hold thousands of people. Wow, I thought the first time I saw it, this is the big leagues.

Unfortunately, the field didn't measure up to the exterior surroundings. The dirt part of the infield was unique, at least to me, for I had never fielded a ground ball on seashells before. Generously speckled with bits and pieces of white chips, the infield looked like a reclaimed Atlantis.

To get used to this strange surface before the game, I decided to commit baseball's version of hara-kiri and asked one of the pitchers to hit me a few ground balls. After fending a dozen or so bad hops off my chest, neck, legs and other crucial parts of my body, I came to the astute conclusion that the field was, in its own way, something special.

The secret of playing here is purely mental. Just imagine you're enjoying a day at the beach and the rest comes easy. You can fool yourself into fielding grounders at Charleston just by playing your own shell game.

We won the game, 3-2, but I was hitless in four at-bats and made an error. Errors, I decided, hurt a lot more than hitless nights.

On this particular boot, I charged what appeared to be a normal, routine grounder. Just as I reached for it, it seemed to skip off the shells, glance off my glove, bounce off my chest, and then I swear, hide from me as my panic-stricken fingers groped to dig it out of the low-tide debris around my feet.

I think the official scorer was waiting for this big moment. He was faster pressing the "E" button than I was finding the ball. There came the red glow on the scoreboard as the error sign sadistically mocked my effort.

No flash on and off, either. It lit up and stayed on for what seemed an eternity so that the whole world would know that I had been charged with an error.

Baseball is the only sport, probably the only profession in the world, where one's errors are announced, exhibited, displayed, printed and publicized so that everybody can laugh at you or curse you out.

En Route from Charleston to Anderson
May 17

It was after midnight when we boarded our bus for the four-and-a-half-hour trip back to Anderson. It was not a pleasant thing to look forward to, but we had won two games, which made the trip less annoying.

I kept thinking about Harvard baseball bus rides to such remote places as Hanover, New Hampshire, and Princeton, New Jersey, when the guys just brought along their school books and read, a veritable library on wheels. The long, boring hours seemed like an eternity. A pitcher might be reading Pico della Mirandola's treatise "On The Dignity Of Man," while the shortstop was totally absorbed in his biochemistry of nonvertebrate animals. Educated, but boring.

As we left Charleston, we stopped at a red light, right next to a playground. It was midnight, but there were kids playing basketball. They were pretty good and most of the guys on the bus watched them as we waited for the light to change.

Suddenly and unexpectedly, Brian Sheekey, the resident bon vivant of the team, broke the silence with an amazingly good imitation of Marv Albert, the New York Knickerbockers' radio announcer. Doing the play-by-play of the playground game, Sheekey, in the distinct Albert nasal tone, had us completely enthralled.

"Frazier over to Monroe . . . back to Frazier . . . Clyde with a jumper from fifteen feet . . . YESSSSS . . . Knicks lead by 89-75, and now a word from Schaefer Beer . . ."

Instant insanity erupted. Since many of the guys on the team are from the New York area, Sheek's impersonation was an instant smash. The Sheek just ate up the attention and proceeded to entertain for the next two hours. His skits ran from imitations of Albert, George Carlin, and Marlon Brando to a real novelty—a perfect impersonation of New York Mets announcer Bob Murphy, something that I'm certain had never been attempted before, anywhere. Sheekey was just great.

Then, when the Sheek ran out of steam, Steve Tissot took over. Tis, a veteran pitcher and self-appointed team philosopher, brought out his guitar and went through a wide range of songs. Everybody joined in, the extinct Singing Senators being reincarnated in the form of the Tuneful Tigers.

When this got a little boring, Steve Litras, our third baseman and a Groucho Marx freak, grabbed a pair of glasses, messed his hair, put a black comb over his upper lip, struck a cigar in his mouth and walked up and down the aisle in typical Grouchoesque fashion.

For the grand finale, as the bus entered into the town of Anderson after four in the morning, Tissot struck up the popular tune, "Yellow Submarine" and Sheekey was the band leader. They started marching up and down the aisle and everybody was singing and clapping along with them. We kept it up until everybody had filed out of the bus in the cold, dark, quiet Anderson Stadium parking lot.

Greenwood, N.C.
May 18

A visit to Greenwood means an opportunity to see the legendary knuckleballer Hoyt Wilhelm, who manages the Greenwood team. Hoyt is something of an enigma, especially to those of us who grew up following his career. And who didn't? He had such a long career.

Wilhelm doesn't have much to say and he usually pitches batting practice to his players. He seems to enjoy baffling his own players with his unbelievable knuckleball in batting practice just as much as he enjoyed baffling big-league hitters when he was an active player.

I decided to go behind the batting cage and look at Wilhelm work, just to get an idea of what it was like to hit against him. It didn't take me long to realize how difficult he must have been and why he was so successful. The impression I got from watching him was that the ball was stationary and the scenery behind it was moving.

Anderson, S.C.
June 24

The size and nature of the crowds that attend our home games vary with each game. Yet, as the season progresses, it is increasingly evident that some of the fans are loyal, true-blue Anderson rooters who come to every game no matter the weather, the opposition or our position in the standings. They're a mixed bunch, farmers with their families, teen-aged girls, widowed housewives, old men who reminisce of days gone by and few local characters who play loud roles in the stands as hecklers, noisemakers, umpire baiters or all-knowing strategists.

It's not unusual to hear someone cheer for a favorite player and to see that player acknowledge his backer with a tip of the cap. Attachments are formed, fan for player, player for fan.

One day, I was playing pepper in front of the stands. At one point, the ball went over the railing right in front of an elderly black gentleman. I went to retrieve the ball (in the minors the fans give the balls back) and the man eagerly picked up the baseball and with an awkward motion that exuded age and arthritis, tossed it back to me.

A little later, the ball went back in his direction again and I went to retrieve it. This time I made some comment to the old man about my obvious lack of skill as a pepper player, and he just leaned forward on his wooden cane and laughed a deep cackle. As he smiled, he exposed the only couple of teeth left in his head and I realized that he must have been very old indeed. His dark, black skin covered his bony frame tightly and his hands were gnarled like the branches of an oak tree. His face was friendly and covered with a peach-like white fuzz of whiskers.

Before I could get back to the game, the old man started talking baseball, about whom he had seen play here in years past, about his days as a player, who his favorite player was and so on. He just rambled on, enjoying himself and pulling out memories as fast as he could. Finally, I excused myself and he urged me to play well and win.

Later, I did some investigating about him. I found out that he had been to every home game for over fifteen years. I heard he had also been a pretty fair pitcher back in his youth, playing in the "colored leagues" and was still revered around the area as a "local Satchel Paige."

Last night we played Gastonia and the old man was there in his customary seat. Around the third inning, there was a stir in the stands, but since I was out in the field and concentrating on the game, I couldn't really make out what was going on. But as the third out was recorded, we came hustling off the field and I could see the old man crouching over, his hand on his left side. There was a painful look on his face, the most agonizing look I have ever seen. His cane had fallen to the ground and he was gasping for breath. Around him some of the fans, mostly black, were in a panic. One woman was crying uncontrollably and a few younger men were running up the stadium steps, no doubt going for help.

It was an awful moment in my life. I felt helpless and unbelievably guilty as the ambulance squad came by and took the old man away. The game continued, but I couldn't do a thing to help the old man—I could only stand there and watch. I felt cold all over. I had to concentrate on winning a minor-league baseball game, which suddenly seemed dreadfully unimportant, even sacrilegious.

Today a public address announcement said the old man had been to every home game for so many years and that he had died last night. I didn't feel like playing, but the game went on.

Anderson, S.C.
July 1

Fern Poirier "died" today.

Everybody just sort of stopped what he was doing and hung his head in a moment of silence when the news was heard. Fern, one of our outfielders, had just been released.

In baseball, when a player is released or traded, his teammates say he "died."

For a while, nobody said anything. Very quietly, Fern walked over to his open wooden locker, took off his bag and began to pack his things. In a few minutes, he had finished—all that remained in his locker was the Anderson uniform—and Fern started making the rounds, saying his goodbyes to his teammates. Then he picked up his baseball bag and stoically walked out of the clubhouse door—and out of our lives.

Tis came over and asked, "Why Fern? He was just beginning to get going, starting to hit the ball well."

Jeff Natchez, our center fielder, sat on the clubhouse bench and shook his head. "Gee, he was such a nice guy. How come they released him?"

There was no answer. One minute Fern is a professional baseball player, laughing and joking and as loose as a ballplayer should be, and the next minute Len Okrie asks him to step into his office and, suddenly, Fern's dream of becoming a major leaguer has ended.

Getting released, like dying, is inevitable. Still, it's tough to endure. How do you go home in the middle of the season and tell your friends you just weren't good enough? It's hard to admit to your friends. It's even harder to admit it to yourself.

Waterloo, Iowa
May 20, 1974

Forgive me for saying it, but now I know how Napoleon felt. I just met my Waterloo.

Because of poor weather, we hadn't played in four days. And because Oke has been alternating me with Lloyd Sprockett, I hadn't played in eight days when I got the call today. It had rained all day and there was no batting practice and so I went to the plate cold.

In my first at-bat, I struck out, although I got three pretty good rips. My second at-bat I was ready. I got my eye back and worked the count to 3-2. I got right on top of the plate to guard it and the pitch came in low and away. I know it was low and away because I had to lean over quite a bit to see it.

"Streee-rike threeeee!" the umpire squealed.

Naturally, I had a few choice comments to make to him.

In my third at-bat, I was super-determined to hit the ball somewhere.

Again I worked the count to 3-2 and crowded the plate. This time I watched the pitch come in high and tight. I held my ground, then pulled my head out of the way at the last split second.

"Steee-rike threeeee!" shouted the umpire, sounding like a broken record.

Now I had just gotten the hat trick, three K's in one game, and I let the ump have it, but good. After listening to my barrage, he threatened me.

"One more word out of you and you're gone," he warned.

I mused over this option, then replied: "The way I'm going tonight, that wouldn't be a bad idea."

The ump smiled and countered: "Just for that remark, you're in for the remainder of the game."

Now for my fourth at-bat. We were trailing, 1-0, in the eighth when I came to bat with runners on first and second. I worked the count to 3-1, then laced an outside fastball down the right-field line. It curved foul by inches.

The count was 3-2 again. The fans were on me now and as I stepped back into the batter's box, I gazed at the ump. He was looking straight at me and I swear I saw a grin on his face.

Now I was set. This was going to be the pitch that would make or break my night. The pitcher wound up and threw his fastball. I swung and here's how it was reported in the newspaper:

> The Royals' big save was by second baseman Dan Hansen when he back-handed a line drive off the bat of Rick Wolff with two Pilots on base and two out in the eighth.

Joe Torre says that the hardest thing in baseball is "to learn that you're going to fail seven out of ten times." I think he's right, but knowing that doesn't take the sting out of failing. No matter how philosophical you get, it still hurts not to succeed.

Quite frankly, I haven't been playing well. I'm trying just as hard as before, but somehow things aren't dropping in.

The other day, Kevin Slattery and I were talking to some sixth-graders at an elementary school. They were amazed when we told them we got paid about $20 a game.

"Don't you ever play for fun?" a cute little girl asked.

Now, how do you answer a question like that?

From *Short Season*

Jerry Klinkowitz

Ball Two

COSTY PEDRAZA'S FIRST PITCH has been low and outside, almost past the catcher, forcing him to lunge head-first toward the base line and start this first inning with a snootful of dirt. He swings back on his heels and pumps his mitt upward, urging Costy to keep the slider from breaking too soon, then snaps the ball back to him on the mound.

Billy Harmon, who's playing second this game, wanders over to the bag between pitches and motions to Eddie at short. Eddie's English isn't much, but still better than Costy's, and so he's the guy who translates minor-league plays and instructions from the manager. Eddie's from Panama, though, and since Costy is only eight weeks off the plane from the Dominican their Spanish can get mixed up, meaning utterly different things.

One wet afternoon when Eddie suggested taking their raincoats to the park Costy thought he was talking about rubber diapers. Another time Eddie saw Costy talking with a pretty young woman near the dugout and walked over to compliment her hairdo. But Eddie's *pelo* was not at all what the word meant to Costy, who almost decked him right there. So Eddie's wound up thinking that this new kid is a little bit bananas, and vice versa.

But the little bit of English Billy and Eddie share—evolved as roommates through spring training and the first weeks of A-ball— keeps the middle infield free of ambiguities and fistfights. Billy has caught the pitcher's signal to them, a shrug of the left shoulder, which means he'll wait until the catcher calls for a fastball, so any grounder will surely go to Eddie's side of the bag. "Your ball, man," Billy says with his glove shielding his lips. "You bet," Eddie answers, his favorite American phrase, which handles just about anything.

As Costy paws the mound and the infield gets back into position, the benchwarmers pick their topic for the day. The madly erratic clubhouse shower that scalded one of them and nearly froze another has them thinking about water, and after a bit of grumbling Buddy Knox, the reserve infielder whose beer gut is growing with each day's lack of play, starts the second-string outfield on their pet obsession: discovering the headwaters of the Mississippi.

The Mighty Mississip' is a big item in their lives this year. Two of the clubs they play in Iowa are river towns, and for road games in Wisconsin and Illinois they cross it every trip. Lynn Parson, whose California hipness finds everything about the Midwest cutesy quaint, has been telling the bench how he and Rafael Quinones traced it to its source during three days of rainouts at Eau Claire last summer.

Out in the bull pen the long-reliever, two middle men, and the reserve catcher are—like the pitching coach who's joined them—just slouching and staring as if their game hasn't begun. The players sit quietly and Mack isn't thinking about anything at all. Costy paws while all the action's in the dugout.

"It started that first day we'd planned on the Eau Galle," Lynn recalls. "Yeah, you said the reservoir was full of walleyes," Buddy adds, and for a moment there's some thought about Wisconsin game fish. Their rivals in Madison, after all, are called the Muskies, and the fans have a fish cheer and everything. But now Lynn reminds them that the Eau Galle looked mean that day. "Storms?" the new batboy asks. "Nope, bunch of boys in campers acting like the place was locals only," Lynn scoffs. "So Rafael and I took our little All-Americas tour to the river and just headed on up. When we found Lake Wabedo Raffy phoned to be sure the game's called off and we fished all night."

"Fish stories!" Billy spits across the dugout as he says it and notes that Pedraza is shaking off a lot of signs. Some game, if this is only his second pitch. Mack spots the delay from the bull pen and leans out from the bench to see if the manager wants his help. But Carl is motionless on the dugout step, just resting on his knee and staring like the others toward the field.

Lynn fills the gap as Costy fidgets and Carl stares. "Hey, these good folks at Wabedo felt bad we didn't get a walleye strike, so next day they sent us further north." "Still raining?" Buddy asks and Lynn says sure, they decided to chance it and see how the Mississippi looked north of

Reginald. "I hear you can step right across it, there," Carl turns around to say, surprising everyone that he's been listening, but Lynn protests to all of them: "No way, kids, all the way through Sainer it's still a good twenty-feet wide and faster than a demon." Carl turns back, remembering those long-distance calls from a half-day's drive away. "We rained out again, Skip?" What could he have told Kansas City if they'd called — a left-fielder and star shortstop were two days A.W.O.L., looking for a place they could straddle the Mississippi River?

The catcher goes back to one finger — fastball — and this time Costy nods okay. What's this, he can't read numbers? The catcher's flashed it to him twice before, but now he gets the message — this shrewd Dominican is confusing the batter, making him think all sorts of exotic pitches and locations, when in fact it's going to be the straight one down Main, okay!

Costy fingers the ball and leans back in his stretch. Billy glances over to check that Eddie's in position, but Eddie's not with it at all — he's mooning over toward the dugout where Carl's perched on the top step, trying to ignore the jockies behind him. Billy wants to yell a "Hey, man!" but Costy's spooked enough from that first bad pitch. What on earth is Eddie up to? There's his little *niña* — the cute young shagger who's been flirting with him ever since his fence-hopper in batting practice nipped her ankle. She's in the first-row box over the dugout, where kids don't belong anyway and certainly not when they're shagging. "Hey man, *trouble,*" Billy wants to yell, but he doesn't have the words and what a can of worms, what a crazy Latin mess to get into. Maybe one of the older Spanish players — Quinones if he comes back down from Chattanooga — can straighten Eddie out. Mason City, Iowa, sure isn't Panama, or anyplace else but Iowa for that matter.

"Quinones, my man Raf-a-el!" Lynn is musing. "Wanted me to play winter ball in Colombia, said we'd get to Venezuela, meet his wife and kids." "Yeah, but what about the river?" Buddy prompts, now obsessed himself. "How far up did you guys get, did you ever see it get, like, real small?" He wants an answer — every third day this story gets started and then Lynn is called in to pinch hit or reserve, or following some other action just gets bored with it and changes subjects.

Lynn doesn't answer, as he's joined Carl in puzzling over Pedraza's actions on the mound. Costy's dropped his arm and has stepped off the rubber, staring toward Jim Smith the catcher as if he's in a daze. Smitty has called to Carl and is shrugging his shoulders, asking if he should check with Costy on the mound. "Sanmarda!" Carl calls to his shortstop, "Sanmarda, *vete*"—one of the few Spanish words he knows, as he gestures Eddie over toward the pitcher. "Settle him down, hey?" "You bet!" Eddie thinks to himself as he trots in toward Costy.

"Mi amigo, mi compadre," Costy is thinking happily as Eddie joins him on the mound, with Billy and the other infielders looking on suspiciously from their positions. But then Eddie greets him with the words Costy would use to summon a waiter or correct a servant, and his grin changes to a pucker, ready to spit. "What's the problem?" Costy says to break the tension, meaning it friendly enough but Eddie takes it to mean his own problem.

"I got no problems, man, it's you that's not pitching."

"I am too pitching, why don't you play shortstop like these Yankees pay you to?"

"I can't catch what they don't hit what you don't throw, baby!" Eddie says, again meaning it friendly, doing his best to put the funny words his teammates use into Spanish slang. But he's answered with a thick spray of tobacco juice across his uniform top.

"¿Niño? ¿Niño?" Costy is screaming. Eddie's looking down at his shirt, wondering what he's said, and is knocked clean off his feet by Costy's swift shove.

Costy is now bellowing insults and kicking at poor Eddie, who's struggling in the dust to find his feet. He's halfway up, finding unsure balance on the mound's steep slope, when Pedraza knees him in the chin and sends him head-over-heels toward the plate.

By this time Carl is out there, pinning Costy's arms from behind, while Jim blocks off Eddie, who's standing again but somewhat tipsy from the two quick blows. Both benches have emptied, but no one else is fighting—just the American players turning toward their Latin colleagues to ask what on earth is going on. "Shortstop called him a kid," the Angels' batter is telling the ump. "Down in the Dominican you'd say that to your own child, but for any other kid, not related, you know, it means a brat, a dirty kid in the streets, you know." "No, I didn't know that," the umpire says, not really listening, as he wonders how to discipline this mess.

He walks toward Carl, who's released Costy on the mound. Not having the least idea what to say, he simply takes a schoolmarmish, traffic-cop attitude and prepares to stare the manager down. "Don't look at me," Carl protests, "I don't understand these Latinos any better than you do." The ump is still silent. "Now don't go tossing anybody," Carl warns, anticipating an argument, "my boys didn't touch the other team, this is all my business, not yours." "Are they staying in?" the ump asks. Carl looks around to see that Eddie is still a bit woozy and bleeding from the mouth. "Shortstop's coming out," he decides, "pitcher stays in." The ump looks skeptical. "Hey, we played a doubleheader last night, I don't *have* anybody else!" Carl pleads, and the ump lets him off. But as he turns back to the plate he gives Carl a stern warning: "When I crew your game, *do not* play those bozos together, got me?"

As he passes the mound, Carl has three words for his pitcher. "Pedraza—hundred dollars!" He points as if to underscore, then stalks back to the bench. Costy looks about helplessly and settles on first baseman Andy Thompson, Spanish-speaking from home and college. Andy answers his mute question in clear, grammar-book language: "He's fined you one hundred dollars, Costy. Now behave!"

The players finally clear, but not until Lynn and the Angels' third baseman have finished up their chat. "Hear your showers are out, man," the infielder has said, and Lynn is giving him the whole run-down on how old Mack came running out naked through the clubhouse, scalded and steaming like a lobster. "Old Mack?" the Angel twists his head, "That's awesome! Bet he'll get it fixed, those old guys don't put up with none of this shabby A-ball stuff."

Lynn starts in on the great shower-leak story as the two teams brush past each other toward their dugouts. "We looked for it all last year, figured there had to be an absolute source, something real small-like, you know," he's telling the Angel as Buddy and the bench jockeys pass by.

"So where'd you find it?" the third baseman asks, as Buddy and the others stop to hear Lynn's answer.

"In the hot-water tap for the sink, you never would believe it!" Lynn explains as he slaps his rival with his glove and trots back to the bench.

Buddy is transfixed by wonder and disbelief. "Hey Skip," he calls as he approaches Carl, "Parson finally told us where's the source!"

"The source?" Carl asks, not following and not caring.

"Of the Mississippi, of the river!" Buddy exclaims. "It's in some kitchen sink, some leaky faucet!"

Carl just stares, writing off this senseless line to the general lunacy that has prevailed since Costy's first pitch. He's thrown a few tosses to get loose again, and Escobar's in at short. The ump pulls down his mask and calls for play, squatting behind the plate. Smitty signals a fastball and it comes in high, a mile out of the strike zone.

Five Bad Hands and the Wild Mouse Folds

The Mason City Royals are bussing it across the state, and an hour out of Bettendorf catcher Jim Smith announces that he's finished up his league chart. "Bettendorf!" yells Johnny Mueller before Jim can even begin, "Smells like catfish in the showers!" "Dubuque!" Joey choruses in, "Cat yuck in the rugs!" One by one they check off the Midcontinent League cities, small burgs of forty thousand folks or so where sometimes there isn't even a Holiday Inn, not that their GM could afford it. The Royals go into each city four times a year, and Jeff has booked them seasonal rates in motels that would otherwise stand empty. And for good reason. "Madison: big June bugs mashed up in the sheets! Quad Cities: smells like dead stuff in the walls!" Eddie perks up, senses his turn. "Caedar Rapeeds!" he trills in his high Panamanian accent, "¡La cucaracha!" Jim shouts for order, claiming they've got it all wrong. He runs down his own list of sundry pests and vermin, noting approval and shrugging off complaints ("The zitty waitress is in Peoria, moron"). But everyone agrees he's saved the best for last. "Eau Claire!" he sings out, and the whole bus answers in a single voice, "The wild mouse!"

Their four-game sweep in Bettendorf primes them for the Northern Division, and the luxury of an off-day's travel gets them into Eau Claire early enough for some serious poker.

> You gotta lend me five
> Just to keep me alive.

Donny the left fielder is making up a new ditty for each hand, fitting the beat of slapping cards, jingling chips, and popping can tops. For a minor-league baseball club the Royals make a good rhythm section when they're playing for blood; it sounds like a bass line behind a nasty whining Mick Jagger song.

> I'd pay you back quick
> But my brother got sick,

and Andy is dealing out another hand. "Garbage," he calls, not his hand but the name of this particular poker round, each dealer calling his pick. Two queens, two deuces. Should he play on a double pair when everybody's drawing three, tossing three, drawing two more?

> How about a ten
> till I see you again?

But he's a long way from borrowing. Nobody's had much good stuff that night, so the pots and losses have been small. The game was better on the bus up from Bettendorf, part of the crazy energy from the ballpark riot two nights before. "Game called on account of madness" the paper read, the Royals won on a forfeit called by the ump, and next night the stands were full hoping for a repeat. Lots of action, but all legal—a dozen home runs between the two teams, tied a league record, score like a football game, 14-13, one of the writers said he'd head it "Dodgers miss point after." Plus all sorts of good baseball. Carl's sucker pick-off worked three times; he was wrong, the runners never learn. Four wins in Bettendorf on top of the game from Wisky Rapids puts them way, way out front, and now when they finish in Eau Claire they'll be looking at a lazy four game/four day series in Dubuque odds say they'll sweep. Oh, oh, Eau Claire. Donny knows a girl up here who'll cook for him all week, so that's six dollars meal money for the poker pot each night. Right now she's across the courtyard watching TV with the players' wives.

Mitch is calling, the crazy bastard. He's the only Eau Claire player they'll let in the game, and only because he's shot his credit with his teammates. Calling the last five hands and the best he's had is a pair of aces. The poor goof. Matt, who took counseling courses when he pitched college ball, says the guy is lonely and that he's only playing cards as a substitute for making friends, which he can't seem to do. So he plays poker like a hyperactive eight-year-old. Maybe he doesn't understand the game.

> Just lend me twenty
> and I'll show you guys plenty.

For sure, he doesn't understand that Donny is singing about him.

The guys turn in at two, and within an hour the motel is quiet. But sometime later Angel hears his roommate get up and head for the john, and in a moment it sounds like a war going on in there. He pushes the door open just in time to see Jim's bat poised over the commode.

The bat slams down with a vengeance, shattering the fixtures and sending shards of porcelain and ceramic tile to the corners of the room. "Take *that*," Jim growls, and swings to position himself for the next blow. But his target is nowhere to be seen. "Close the door, close the lousy DOOR," he yells at Angel, who is calling in Spanish for Ed to come on down and see the fun. It's 4:00 A.M., lights out was two hours ago, but everyone is waking up as word spreads through the Northland Motel—Jim Smith is clubbing out the wild mouse!

Jim is standing on the toilet, his thirty-six-ounce Louisville Slugger bearing his own stamped signature broken off in his hands. "Angel, Angel, you got a bat up here?" he calls, and Angel laughs back, "No, man, I don't sleep with my bat." "Get me something, come on, get me something," Jim screams again, but now Johnny and Buddy are at the door with the mosquito spray Buddy had brought for the murky Bettendorf dugout. "This stuff is industrial strength," he tells the room, "just turn off that fan, close the door, and we'll gas the thing through the ventilator." "It's in the can?" Johnny asks, and Jim shouts back, "Yeah man, it's in the shower and I almost had it but these bats go to pieces, you know."

Buddy's up on the dresser, shaking and spraying his insect repellent through the bathroom vent. Angel starts to cough and sneeze. "Hey, man, you're killing me, turn on the air conditioner." "Forget it, you want to pull it all out?" Buddy protests.

"Listen," Johnny says, "you need a ton of that stuff to even stone it, this is the wild mouse." Every night in Eau Claire this season the mouse has hassled them—chewing gloves, glutting itself on chip dip from the poker table, and one-by-one keeping them all awake. Of course they'd like to flatten it, with baseball bats, bug spray, or the TV.

"That's it," Johnny announces. "It's gonna want out of that bathroom real bad," he reasons, "so turn out all the lights and get me up here on the dresser with something big." "Smitty's behind," Buddy suggests, but Johnny already has the twenty-three inch vintage black-and-white TV in his arms. "Bombs over Tokyo" he yells as Angel slips open the door, the mouse scoots out, and the television is dropped from an altitude of seven feet. It hasn't been unplugged.

A sickening roar and phosphorous shower fill the room, condensers sputtering and the main power tubes flashing red and yellow and spitting out sparks. Everyone's yelling and cheering like mad. "Don't touch it, don't touch it," Johnny yells to Angel, "you'll electrocute yourself." He jumps down from the dresser and over to the wall, where he unplugs the guttering set.

"Oh boy, oh boy," Jim is repeating. Nobody's hurt but the room's a mess, from the smoldering TV to the sooted-up walls. They kick away the TV's shell and there's the charred corpse of a tiny mouse.

"Try mouth to mouth, I think it's still breathing," Johnny says, but nobody's laughing. The team has this entire wing so nobody's heard the bedlam, but tomorrow morning, oh tomorrow morning. "Is Carl's light on?" Jim asks and Angel looks across the court to the coaches' room and it's dark. "I think they're still out," Angel says, but no one knows how to cover this.

"Let's say we were robbed," Buddy offers lamely. No one responds. A few sparks from the TV and Buddy jumps. "Easy, man," Johnny cautions, "it holds two thousand volts, don't touch it."

"I'm calling Jeff," Jim says, and reaches for the phone. Eight for an outside line, 515 for Mason City, then their GM's home number. "You killed a lousy mouse?" Jeff screeches in his tinny Bronx accent, "a lousy *mouse?*" "Yeah, well you see there's some damage up here, not a lot, but if Carl thinks he has to represent it to you and Mr. Howard. . . ." Jeff agrees to put a call into Carl at the desk, he'll get it any minute now that the after-hours bars are closed, and try to take the guys off the hook. The six players in the room will pay all damages from next month's salary. The TV is the worst, maybe the bathroom, but they'll cover it. "And listen, man," Jim pleads, "from now on can you book us in some other place up here?"

"At their pleasure," Jeff assures them. "At their pleasure, I'm sure."

Eddie and the *Niña*

Jolene is a Class-A shagger. For two hours before each game she sits on the concrete retaining wall beyond the left-field fence and chases batting-practice balls that make it out. Six or seven do every late afternoon, sometimes a dozen or more, and today has been especially good—fifteen practically new Midcontinent League balls fill her pockets and batting helmet by six o'clock. Most of them are scuffed just three times: the first that took them out of last night's game, second by the wallop out of the park today, and third for the grass, gravel, or concrete where they hit just now.

The Mason City Royals' GM will pay her a quarter for each ball when she reports her total at the month's end. But tonight she carries a higher mark of distinction, for her hero, Eddie Sanmarda, has sent a screaming liner to the top of the left-field wall, just a foot away from the foul pole, and with a momentum-gaining bounce it's taken a beeline for Jolene's ankle and stung her good. For a while she mugs it up and walks with an exaggerated limp, but fifteen minutes before game time it's swelled up and hurts real bad.

A fan takes her to the dugout. "Mr. Peterson," he says to the manager who's worrying over his lineup card, "one of your shaggers caught a line drive on her ankle, maybe the trainer could give her some ice." Carl lifts her over and, dream of dreams, she's in the Royals' dugout. Chet the trainer pulls down her sock, feels that there's no break, and applies an ice pack. He listens to her story then calls Ed over to see his work. Eddie speaks little English but he knows his sockamayocking rampage has hurt this little *niña*, so he grabs a clean game ball and presents it to her as his first trophy of atonement. Then he chases back to concessions for a hot dog and big orange drink, his spikes clattering on the steel walkway. Bill White, the stadium announcer, has introduced the managers and umps, the first three hitters, and is waiting on Eddie as he stumbles back through the boxes, so Ed runs out to his position from the stands. Bill is two-thirds down the lineup and the whole infield is out there before anyone notices Ed standing at second, gloveless, dripping mustard and orange pop on the bag.

That night Mason City wins 6-2, a good game with no errors and three home runs. Ed hits the first but pulls up lame rounding first base. Carl has to help him around third to home and in minutes his leg is packed in ice. Jolene's still there in all her glory so she bums two quarters from the trainer and fetches Ed a Coke.

If Ed Sanmarda makes the major leagues he'll be the first starting shortstop who can feed an entire team for less than five dollars, another minor-league skill gone to waste in the bigs. By mid-June in his first year with Mason City he has fed his teammates, all twenty-two of them, on eight successive Sundays. Meal money is passed out Monday mornings and it never lasts a week.

Spanish-American cooking? Yes, in a way. But nothing Eddie or his family ate in Panama. His down-and-out enchiladas are purely a concoction of American convenience food, a mélange of cheap ingredients chosen after his first half-hour in an Iowa food store.

Three packages of supersoft tortillas at 69¢ each, full count twenty-four, which answers for every man on the team. A can of mild taco sauce for these soft-mouthed gringos, only 19¢. A round of Colby cheese, the biggest investment at $2.44. That leaves 30¢ of his five (hidden in his hatband Monday) for some closed-out jalapeño peppers he's found at the Swiss Colony Gourmet Shop, unquestionably the best food buy in Mason City and perhaps the whole United States. These are for himself, Joey, and Manuel; the Yankee boys tried them once and howled for water, like throwing gasoline on their fires until Eddie told them just to suck on sugar for a while. "Panama Pizzas," Donny Moore called them, refusing to roll the tortillas like Eddie showed. One of these babies, a foot long and three inches high when tightly rolled and broiled, keeps their bellies filled from Sunday night to Monday morning, when the meal money comes and it's back to Mac's and Burger King.

Given his relatively few words of English Eddie finds it amazing he can have so many Anglo friends. When the Royals' scout told him he'd start in Mason City his parents were concerned—How would he get along, with whom could he even speak? The scout, a veteran of the Mexican leagues and the majors, assured them there would be other Latin players—Herman Escobar from Cuba by way of Miami, Angel Naboa from northern Mexico, Monterrey, plus there was Andy Thompson from Ybor City in Tampa, half-Spanish, who was majoring in Romance languages at South Florida—but that even without these Spanish-speaking kids Eddie would find it easy to get along.

Baseball has its own language of movement, the scout explained and Eddie soon found out. On the field the game's natural rhythm of threes—three strikes, three outs, three bases, nine innings, nine players— gave his actions a familiar mold. Playing deep for the first two outs, in on the grass when he expected a bunt, pegging the ball to first and running off the field with his teammates—all this made Ed and the guys partners in a dance that flowed between the base lines. In the dugout they became a captive audience to the other team's spectacle with its own echo of the same old song.

Warm-ups before the game, the cadence afterward of bagging bats and balls, loading the bus, fifteen minutes back to the motel, and then a couple hours' cards or TV before bed. The five months from April through August across eight Midwestern towns flowed easy, like a river, its currents obvious from the first time around.

Assigned to share a room with Billy Harmon, whose Spanish was as weak as his own English, Eddie found no trouble—their body language carried directly from the field, and as roommates they had more to say to each other than Angel and Herman, or any of the English-speaking pairs. "¿Quieres algunos chips y Pepsi?" Eddie would call from the kitchenette and Billy would nod and answer, saying "Sure, bring some cheese if we got some." One night around a darkened motel pool they talked for hours, their voices floating through the dusk like music from another world. Eddie spoke of his parents back home, Billy about the ball he'd played in high school, and though neither knew for sure what the other was saying each felt good about their talk. When Ed and Herman played the infield they laughed and chattered, rattling the batters with their private jokes. But with Eddie at short and Billy at second they played with the quiet of brothers.

Eddie had been signed in August off a sandlot team organized by the United Methodist mission in Panama City. He was nineteen years old and had never played much ball before that summer, favoring jai alai up to then. But the Methodists had been pulling kids off the courts, and Reverend Styles, their coach, was so struck by Eddie's natural talent that he wrote every major-league club about his find.

Scouts from Kansas City, Chicago, and Toronto answered his letters, and during the All-Star break a man from the Royals flew down. This was the day Eddie hit two home runs and played the infield like a dervish—to show him off, Reverend Styles shifted him around every two innings from third to short to second and to first. The scout took his report back to Kansas City on the next plane and three weeks later called with an offer. As a crack infielder who could hit, Ed would be their number-one pick from the nondraftable Latin Americans. Report to Sarasota in March for rookie camp and then, depending on the older utility infielders, he'd have a spot with Double A Chattanooga or A-ball's Mason City. In his part of Panama City, $630 a month American was a fortune, so Ed gladly signed. The Methodists were right: jai alai would waste him and he was too small for soccer.

In Sarasota he was rudely disappointed. The American players showed off tricks he'd never dreamed of and the coaches ignored his lusterless play. But in the second week when the veteran players came in for workouts the Royals' starting shortstop broke an ankle on a practice slide and everyone moved up a notch—the reserve infielder to short, Neddy Ralston from Triple A Tacoma to the Kansas City bench, Mason City's shortstop to Chattanooga—and Eddie had the A-ball job by default.

Carl now gave more attention and liked what he saw. He spent more time with Eddie, showing him how to watch the ball's rotation: bottom over top a fastball, top over bottom a curve, sideways with a white dot in the middle a slider, which was thrown three-quarter arm as well. Mack threw ball after ball with Carl catching and calling each of them for Eddie, who was soon sending every one to the wall. Woody

Brown, the Chattanooga manager, now watched, too, so Carl cut the practice sessions before he lost his man.

On April 2 camp was broken and the parent team headed up to K.C. for the opener. The farm kids were given the chance to ride along on the charter and Eddie said yes to see his first pro game. He spent three days in Kansas City sick on Yankee food—the players ordered thick rare steaks so he did too and nearly vomited; a steak in Panama means well-cooked, cut-up beef in rice and bananas. He found a taco stand near the bus station, and, even though the putrid little things were made with hamburger, he bought his own jalapeño sauce at a nearby Quik-Trip and made them edible.

He rode a bus from Kansas City up to Chicago, twelve hours, just to spend a day walking among the tall buildings on Michigan Avenue. In the Art Institute he prayed before the El Greco he'd seen in his mother's Catholic missal. At the Y they spoke Spanish, more Spanish than English, and the Honduran clerk told him it was better to pay the ninety bucks and fly to Mason City, bus connections were that bad. On the airline bus he sat with a Mexicana stewardess who took him to the Ozark ticket counter and then all the way to gate F-11, through this airport bigger and busier than any he'd ever seen. Forty minutes in the air a passenger pointed out the Mississippi, way over its banks at flood stage, and Eddie couldn't believe it wasn't a long, wide lake.

At the Mason City airport, so small and desolate, he was lost. Seeing no buses and afraid of cabs, he started walking down the highway toward town. A sheriff's deputy picked him up, saw his baseball gear, and drove him to the Quality Inn, where the ballplayers stayed. Thankfully Carl was in the lobby to book his room. Tomorrow he'd have his apartment with Billy, the blond and baby-faced second baseman who'd been his friend in camp.

April 13 was the home opener, then a second game with Wisconsin Rapids before heading up to Eau Claire. Right off Ed was hitting and hitting well, surprising himself in this cold weather when sometimes fewer than fifty fans came out for the night games. Other players were complaining that their hands stung and their joints ached, wanting the managers to shift the weekend games to afternoons, but Ed was in his glory. The night lights made the ball's seams stand out like scars on his uncle's cheeks, and Carl had taught him to watch so well that he routinely sent the fastballs screaming through the hole and lifted a few hanging curves out beyond the wall.

By May 1 he had twenty hits and fifteen R.B.I.s, an amazing clutch percentage. By June 1 he was up to fifty-five and forty, and in one amazing week—June 6–12, against Madison, Quad Cities, and Cedar Rapids—drove in another fifteen runs, virtually the only Mason City player producing scores. Carl would surely have faced losing him to Chattanooga by now, but Kansas City's All-Star shortstop was coming back and the organization had an extra infielder plugging up the tubes.

Lynn Parson, the hip black outfielder from Berkeley, California, started telling Eddie about "making his hundred." Poor in English and worse in slang, Eddie groped for the meaning, so Joey came over to explain. One hundred R.B.I.s is an achievement even in 162 major-league games; in A-ball's short season of 140 it is a rare accomplishment indeed. "You gotta make your hundred," Lynn crooned and Eddie got the idea. "Ninety-nine," the black player sang, "and a half won't do."

School's been out since June 9 and Jolene's been here for batting practice each afternoon. By coming in for the games she risks her job, because the GM wants the shaggers to stay out and chase fouls or home runs. But her ankle still hurts, she tells him, and she can't strain it running in the dark when the teenage beer-drinkers out on the bank give her competition. The GM's New York savvy has been flashing "lawsuit" ever since that line drive nipped her, so he doesn't complain. "Are you shagging BP tomorrow night?" he asks and Jolene answers with an impish grin, heading down to play some catch with Ed.

Hitting .340 with all those R.B.I.s exempts Eddie from the team's ribbing, so he's started being more forward with the kid. Johnny Mueller the superstar sits on the outside bench taking love notes from the little girls who scamper back and forth down the grandstand runway. Billy's perched on the wall, laughing at Johnny and wishing for some adulation of his own. But Jolene is Queen of the Silver Dollar, reigning monarch of the Mason City Park Commission Stadium, where she stands along the baseline tossing balls back and forth with Ed.

"Eddie," she yells so everyone can hear, "here's my slider," and with her glove she waves that brush-cross motion the pitcher makes in warm-ups to indicate a fast-breaking ball. "No, no, *niña*, no no!" Eddie shouts back—kids shouldn't try to throw breaking stuff till their arms are developed; she could hurt herself for life. But Jolene's slider floats in soft as a butterfly, hardly any spin, and Eddie hopes they come at him like this during the game. "Your slider," he tries in English as he flips the ball back, "she is a beeg balloon!" The bench laughs. "Okay, nut face," Jolene snarls, and sends a smoking fastball at his groin.

For three nights' running Jolene comes in for catch, and after Friday's game she's perched on the dugout roof as the team troops in after a 1-0 win over Cedar Rapids. Eddie's been hitless, a seventeen-game streak broken, but the sight of his little *niña* cheers him. "Wanna cone?" Jolene asks, and Eddie, puzzled, looks to Andy Thompson who says "*Helado*, man, *helado.* 'Cept it ain't *helado.*"

There's a Dairy Dreem just three blocks from the ballpark, and Eddie, who rarely carries money, reaches into the deep lining of his fine broad hat for Sunday's five.

"And what does your daddy want?" the lady asks as she hands the girl her Chocolate Whip special, and Jolene doubles over in a barely held laugh, snickering up at Eddie with that twisted impy smile that's been haunting all his dreams.

Triumphant Return

Rick Wolff

> Time is of the essence. The
> crowd and players
> Are the same age always,
>   but the man in the crowd
> Is older every season. . . .
>   Rolfe Humphries
>   *Polo Grounds*

FIFTEEN YEARS AGO I played my last season of professional baseball for the Clinton (Iowa) Pilots. It was a Detroit farm team at the time, but Clinton has since become part of the San Francisco organization. It has been renamed the Giants, but it is still in the Class A Midwest League. I've undergone some changes too. Now I'm 38, and I'm an editor who leads the domesticated life of a New York suburbanite — wife, two children, station wagon. But this June I got a chance to go back to the Midwest League to play in a few games as a minor leaguer again and to report on just how life in the cornfields of baseball has changed over the years since I admitted that sliders are awfully tough to hit and that at 24, I was getting too old to play a kids' game.

Within 24 hours after I left Manhattan and found myself trying to squeeze into a pair of double-knit game pants in South Bend, Ind. — home of the Class A South Bend White Sox of the Midwest League — something happened. Something that I cannot account for, something that should never have happened, something that could only happen on a ball field in the middle of America.

WEDNESDAY EVENING   Stanley Coveleski Stadium is located in downtown South Bend. You go down Main, make a right on Western, and you can't miss it. In a town with only a couple of multistory buildings, the stadium light standards are a major feature of the skyline. The ballpark is right across the street from Union Station and the rail yard, right next to the old Studebaker plant.

Rick Patterson, the field manager of the White Sox, greeted me, gave me the once-over and told me straight out with his Southern baseball twang, "Don't worry, Rick. We're going to treat you just like any other ballplayer here. That's what you want, isn't it?"

"You bet."

"Then go with Scott [Johnson, the trainer] and get suited up. And stick around for tonight's game. Who knows? We may need you."

"Well, skipper, to tell you the truth," I found myself saying, "I thought that maybe I'd just work out a bit tonight and then shower and go back to the hotel. It's been a long travel day, you know." I winced as soon as I said the words.

"Yeah, sure," Patterson said. "Whatever you want."

I went along with Johnson to find a uniform big enough to fit my expanded waistline and a cap small enough to protect the scant hair left on my head. Along the way, I got a real good look at "the Cove." First off, understand that the Midwest League ballparks I played in had wooden stands, usually with a peeling coat of green paint and always with as many splinters as your derriere could handle. The clubhouses were cramped quarters equipped with nails on which to hang your clothes, and the showers—which were always clogged—never had a thought of hot water.

But the Cove, just a year old, was minor-league heaven. Each player had a personal stall in the big clubhouse. The trainer's room was equally big and complete with all the latest gizmos of medical technology. And there was a weight and training room full of equipment. Then there was the manager's office. Did I mention that the entire place was carpeted? Now, out these doors you can take the elevator to the general manager's office. Elevator? In Class A? I asked one of my new teammates if all the ballparks in the Midwest League were like the Cove. He smirked and said, "Are you kidding?"

A few minutes later, the deed had been done. I looked in the full-length mirror in the clubhouse, and the mild-mannered editor from New York had been transformed into an official member of the South Bend White Sox. Yeah, the double-knit pants were a bit tight, and the low-cut stirrups weren't exactly my style. But there was no mistaking it—I looked like a ballplayer. After 15 years, I was back on the roster.

The pregame workout went fine. At the start of the evening's game with the Burlington (Iowa) Braves, I sat back on the dugout bench (aluminum) and watched the Sox take a 7-0 lead behind 21-year-old lefthander Freddy Dabney. In fact, Dabney was coasting along with a no-hitter into the sixth inning when he accidentally clipped a Braves batter, who then promptly charged the mound.

Within seconds I found myself in the midst of a nasty brawl that left one Burlington player flat on his back with a bad cut on his nose and another with his knee crunched. Dabney had suffered a broken finger on his nonpitching hand, and to add to the indignity, he was one of several players given the heave-ho for having had a major role in the fight. So much for Dabney's no-hitter.

Back on the bench I felt a stirring of pride to have been one of the first of the White Sox to join in the fray. Not that I threw any punches, but I was on the field, holding back bodies, trying to reestablish a sense of order. I mean, it's been a long time since we had a bench-clearer at one of our editorial meetings. I was chuckling to myself when Patterson yelled down at me in the bottom of the eighth, "Wolff, grab a bat—you're up next!"

The last thing I wanted to do tonight was pinch-hit. Especially in a game where feelings were red-hot. After all, it was now getting chilly; my arms and legs ached a bit. Then there was the matter of not having seen a minor-league fastball, curveball or slider up close and personal in more than a decade. And I had *never* seen a split-fingered fastball from the batter's box.

But the skipper had issued an order. So I grabbed a helmet and a bat. A wooden bat, a genuine Louisville Slugger. I tried to remember how to swab it with the pine-tar rag.

By the eighth inning, the game was well in hand, and nobody in the stands seemed to pay much attention to the "new kid" coming to bat. And quite frankly, there wasn't much to report. The 22-year-old Burlington righthander fed me a steady diet of blurry fastballs and hard sliders that seemed to break off at right angles. All I dreamed of doing was making contact, and that's all I did. With a 2-2 count, I lunged at a slider and tapped a weak roller out to short. I lumbered down to first, where I was an easy out, and then found myself heading out to the field for the ninth.

The first two visiting batters fanned, and the final man up hit a routine, powder-puff grounder to me. I picked it up cleanly, whisked it over to first and then, to my surprise, found myself engulfed by my teammates. From their perspective, it was something just short of miraculous for this fossil to have hit a dribbler to short and fielded a grounder. As we went up the runway to the clubhouse, I pulled one of the Sox coaches, Kirk Champion, off to the side and asked about the team's reaction to my play.

"Look, Rick, it's like this. The consensus is that you're definitely going to hurt us as a team," Champion said with a straight face. "The real question is, How badly will you hurt yourself?"

THURSDAY EVENING At game time, the temperature was 49 degrees with a sharp breeze out of the north. I took infield practice, checked the lineup card, and found my name penciled in for the ninth slot. I actually felt pretty good; I even had the first play of the night come my way at second, which I again handled.

Burlington was starting a lefty, and as my teammates returned from the plate, I quizzed each one on what the pitcher was throwing. "Aw, he's just throwing pus," third baseman Greg Roth angrily said. "Nothing but pus." That reassuring thought began to point up evidence that perhaps minor-league ball hadn't changed all that much. All batters, no matter what the era, always claim that the opposing pitcher is throwing nothing more than pus—even if the pus does happen to cross the plate at 90 mph plus.

I came to bat to lead off the bottom of the third. By now, the crowd of more than 5,000 (the Chicken was in town for the evening) began to take note of the old-timer. I fouled off a couple of pitches down the right-field line and then—with an 0-2 count—laced a clean, solid, line-drive hit into right center. Nobody was more surprised than I was. What I remember more than anything else was that glorious feeling of hitting a pitch right on the money with a wooden bat, that true feeling of a bat conquering a pitch.

In the fifth inning it happened again—another shot to right. In the sixth, I hit a one-hopper to short, but on my fourth time up, in the eighth inning, I lofted the ball to right for a sacrifice fly and my first RBI in the Midwest League in 15 years. In the field, I was making the plays, picking up grounders, catching pop-ups, taking care of business. I was charged with one error. That occurred when a pickoff throw from the pitcher literally went through my glove; the ball broke one of the strings between the fingers. Remember—I had been using that glove before most of my teammates had been born.

Late in the game, I began to notice a change in my teammates: Wayne Busby, our hyperkinetic shortstop from Mississippi, said, "Hey, old-timer, you better keep your cap on, 'cause people are going to start thinking there are two Golden Domes here in South Bend." And from one of the pitchers, "Tell us, Rick, you must have known him, what kind of player *was* Babe Ruth?" I had become the target of some old-fashioned needling — the ultimate acceptance in baseball. Even the Latin American kids got involved. I caught Clemente Alavarez, our talented catcher, pointing at me and saying to infielder Leo Tejada, *"Mucho loco, si?"*

It was a glorious, wondrous evening, and I was even awarded the game ball by Patterson, who laughed and shook his head in disbelief. And, of course, the White Sox had won again, 4-1. I showered and looked around for a celebratory beer.

"Sorry, old man, but no beer in the clubhouse," I was told. "Organizational policy."

No beer? After a win? Things have changed a bit. Sometimes, I guess, it's for the better.

FRIDAY EVENING A crowd of 3,000 curious fans came out, all eager to see whether the oldest player in South Bend Sox history could somehow keep the magic going. I hadn't slept much the previous evening; even an ample dose of Extra-Strength Tylenol couldn't keep my throbbing legs from demanding that I come to my senses and return to the safe confines of suburbia.

But game time came at dusk and Patterson even moved me up to eighth in the order. When I walked on four straight pitches on my first at-bat, I could hear the manager of the Burlington club, Jim Saul, screaming at his befuddled young pitcher, "C'mon, just throw strikes to this old geezer. He can't touch you! He can't even see you!"

I next came to bat in the fourth inning with a teammate on second and first base open. The Braves pitched to me instead of intentionally walking me, which made me furious. I hit a scorcher. The first baseman was just able to snare it in the air, and then he fired to second to double up the runner. O.K., it was an out, but it was yet another solid shot right on the sweet part of the bat. In the seventh, the Braves started a reverse shift with everybody shaded heavily toward right on me. Again feeling my oats, I pulled a liner down the third-base line for a base hit.

Finally, in the eighth, I came to bat with men on second and third. "Geez, you've gotten your hits, your RBI, your walks," squeaked Busby.

"You might as well go for it all and try to smack one over the Pepsi sign." Nice thought, but even fantasy has its limits. Yet on the first pitch, I swung, made contact, and saw the ball headed for extra-base land in right center field. Out of the corner of my eye, I saw the ball bounce on one hop against the wall, and I cruised into second with a stand-up double and two more RBIs. It was at this point that I realized the fans were on their feet, giving me an ovation and cheering my name. Even the Burlington shortstop came over to me and asked, "No offense, mister, but how the hell are you doing this?"

Patterson sent in a pinch runner, and I came off the field with both arms in a triumphant Kirk Gibson–style salute. Amid a sea of high fives and happy congratulations from my teammates, Patterson started laughing and gave me a big bear hug of approval on the dugout steps. "Old man," he chortled, "you just did what every old ballplayer has dreamed of doing. To come back one more time and do it again. By golly, you did it!"

And that was that. Over the three days, the Sox had won three, and I had finished 4 for 7, with three RBIs, one BB, one SF, one E and a league-leading .571 BA. The next morning, under sober gray skies, I headed back to New York and to my seat on the 7:59 train. The South Bend White Sox climbed on a bus and headed for a three-game series in Kenosha, Wis.

But for a brief moment, I had been able to go back and experience minor-league ball again: The unique smell of fresh pine tar. The grainy grip of a wooden bat. The sound of spikes clacking on a cement runway. That final pregame rush of adrenaline as you stand at attention during the national anthem. The playful but biting wit of teammates. And, of course, the pure joy of hitting a pitch solidly for a base hit.

Jim Bouton, another ballplayer who knows something about comebacks, once wrote that "you spend a good piece of your life gripping a baseball and in the end it turns out that it was the other way around all the time."

FOOTNOTE South Bend White Sox: In case you need some extra offense for the pennant drive in September, you still have my phone number.

III

SCOUTS

From *Dollar Sign on the Muscle*

Kevin Kerrane

Hugh ALEXANDER WAS pretty damn tight with management. In 1981 he was working for an organization that credited its own overhauled scouting staff and farm system for the team's evolution into a consistent National League power, and within that organization he had the status of "special-assignment scout." This meant that he routinely evaluated professional rather than amateur players, either as future opponents or as possible acquisitions through trade. It also meant that he had one of the best jobs in scouting.

Special-assignment scouts are among the few baseball scouts making more than $30,000 a year, and they receive major-league accommodations as well as occasional public recognition (sports-writers usually call them superscouts). In contrast to the evaluation of amateur players, special-assignment work involves less intuition and projection and more detailed analysis and strategic thinking. Some of these scouts, like Jim Russo of the Orioles, are often cited by their colleagues as the sharpest observers in the business.

One phase of special-assignment scouting is typified by the Philadelphia Phillies' 1980 World Series "book" on the Kansas City Royals, a sixty-page analysis prepared by Hugh Alexander and two other senior scouts, Jim Baumer and Moose Johnson. The report outlined the patterns and preferences of each Kansas City pitcher, graded the range and arm of each Kansas City fielder, and suggested defensive alignments and pitching strategy against each Kansas City hitter. The notes on how to pitch to George Brett were understandably vague ("Outstanding high fastball hitter; don't let him beat you"). The scouts

had no hope of isolating a weakness that had eluded American League
pitchers all season but were simply trying to limit the damage Brett
could do, which meant "keeping the rabbits off the bases." The rabbits
were Willie Wilson, U. L. Washington, and Frank White—all blindingly
fast, capable of distracting pitchers and flustering fielders by stealing a
base or taking an extra one with apparent ease, setting the stage for the
big hits by Brett. On White, for example, the report was quite specific:
"Likes to pull when ahead of count; may go opposite field when
behind. First-ball, fastball, high-ball hitter—pitch down. Can change
speeds on him; has trouble with breaking balls. Will bunt for base hits
to 1st or 3b side." The analysis of every hitter was followed by a
detailed chart for positioning each fielder. Through the six games of
that World Series the three rabbits hit 12 for 73 (.164) with only 5
walks and 3 stolen bases; they struck out 23 times. And George Brett
came to bat with a total of 14 runners on base.

    During the regular season Alexander stayed about five days ahead
of the Phillies, providing advance reports on the team they were
scheduled to play next. "If I'm in the same town with the team when
they start a series, I go into the clubhouse before the game and talk to
the team myself. I go over all the other team's players—who's hot,
who's hurt, who's playing even though he's hurt, who can take the
extra base, who can throw from the outfield. How we're gonna position our outfielders is a big thing. And I talk to the pitchers—I might
say, 'Bull Durham is a wild-swingin' guy, won't draw too many walks'
—but I *never* tell 'em how to pitch to a hitter. Who the hell am I to tell
Steve Carlton how to pitch? I just say, 'Hey, I've watched this club play
four games this week, and this is what I saw other pitchers get their hitters out with.' Because if I was Steve Carlton, and some old guy told me
'You have to throw this hitter exactly this way,' I'd say, 'Go fuck yourself.' He's gonna pitch his own game anyway, and I admire him for that."

    Alexander also sized up each opposing player as a potential Phillie
and he consulted with Paul Owens on every trade. It was Owens, his
one-time scouting rival, who lured him away from the Dodgers in 1971
and made him a kind of baseball *consigliere*. The rapport between
these men was a shared philosophy of old-fashioned scouting that
really amounted to a philosophy of life. When Owens characterized
the Philadelphia system at the start of the 1981 season, he defined it in
terms of Hugh Alexander's style of rugged individualism: "We want
guys who aren't afraid to dent a fender, take a chance, put their names
out. Aggressive scouts—they're the ones who find you aggressive players."

Owens's prime example of aggressive scouting was the signing of pitcher Marty Bystrom. In 1976 Bystrom, just out of high school, was ignored in the June draft. That fall, at Miami-Dade Community College South on a baseball scholarship, he pitched four straight shutouts. Then the scouts came sniffing around, because Bystrom, as an undrafted junior-college student, was eligible to sign a pro contract at any time. A Philadelphia scout, the late Catfish Smith, asked Miami-Dade coach Charlie Greene for a special workout for Bystrom so that two other scouts, Hugh Alexander and Gust Poulos, could see him.

"At this workout," according to Greene, "Alexander assured me that he wanted a chance to see Marty to make recommendations for the January draft, and that he would never sign one of our players until the season was over." Two days later Bystrom's father phoned Greene with the news that Hugh Alexander was at the house trying to sign Marty. Greene rushed over, joined the talks, and—when he heard the bonus figure of $35,000—finally encouraged the Bystroms to accept it. Gust Poulos, who had opposed the signing because it would mean breaking his promise to Greene, was subsequently fired by the Phillies.

Charlie Greene told this story as a tale of treachery. The Phillies (including Marty Bystrom) interpreted it as an example of the kind of initiative still possible in modern scouting. A scout's job is to get the good player, not to find ways not to. And if your first teacher was Cy Slapnicka, and if you've just written up a pitcher in a report like this—

> Tall, lean, long arms and young, good body. Good delivery, high ¾, except he hooks his arm some behind his back, but not bad, and his control with this delivery is real good. Workouts with pitchers are deceiving, I realize. However, this boy showed an outstanding fastball at times, with good life and velocity, fair curveball but good sweeping-type slider. Threw some straight changes. Good hard worker in workout.

—the rest comes naturally.

"I told Poulos, 'Our chances of getting Bystrom in the draft are *remote*. I have a job to do.' And I don't care about that coach—how horseshit he says I am or whatever—because he had a gentlemen's agreement among scouts that they wouldn't sign his players, that they'd wait and draft 'em. That agreement was an easy way out for the scouts: they didn't have to make the big decision or try to outbid one another, and they said, 'Let's don't break this bond we have with the school. Let's all take our chances, and we'll all do pretty well.' I'm not criticizing scouts, because I love scouts, but they took the easy way out.

"Today a scout's toughest competitors might be college coaches instead of other scouts. At the four-year schools, when they offer a scholarship, they usually don't tell the boy that it's not guaranteed, that it can be taken away for *athletic* reasons. It's not a four-year deal; it's one-one-one-one. But they're not gonna say that. The college coaches go around the edges a little bit.

"Course, if *I* was a college coach, I'd probably do the same thing. . . . It's like the survival of the fittest. Right?"

Hugh and I are sitting behind a backstop at the Carpenter Complex in Clearwater, Florida. From around us, on the four fields extending like cloverleaves from the central clubhouse, come the sounds of spring training, a soft waterfall of thwocks and thuds in the morning sun. In front of us Keith Moreland is taking batting practice.

"A pure hitter," Hugh says. "Look how he keeps the front shoulder closed and takes the whole body into the pitch . . . " (Moreland cracks a line drive to left) "with a nice short stride."

"Do you use things like that to project? Could you tell from his mechanics that a high-school hitter was a good one, even if he went o-for-four when you saw him?"

"Maybe. But on a one-game look I might be more confident to say that he was a *bad* one—you know, if he was an overstrider or had a big hitch in his swing."

"Branch Rickey said that overstriding can't be corrected, that a scout should just forget about a prospect who's a chronic overstrider."

"Rickey was right, he sure was. But he meant more than just taking too big a step. Look."

Hugh stands up and assumes a right-handed batting-stance. In slow-motion he mimes a bad swing. What I notice right away is less the big stride than the upper body already opening out—the left shoulder turning to the left and up, the right shoulder dropping, and the swing becoming snarled as the right elbow swivels down. "Tell me what I'm doing wrong," he says.

"You look like a golfer about to hit a slice. You're all opened up before the bat even crosses the plate."

"Yeah, and see how my arms are *not* extended. They should be, but I've jammed myself."

"And that's all because of your stride?"

Hugh shrugs, as if to say that cause and effect can't be so easily disentangled. "The big stride is usually a tip-off that a guy's whole *system* of hitting a ball is wrong. That's why it's not a matter of simple correction. It means his lower body's not coordinated with his upper half. It goes together with a slow bat, because the big stride takes more time, and it goes together with committing himself too soon, so he opens his body or gives up his hands when he should keep 'em back."

He slowly repeats the same mistakes, and then takes the swing farther through. "Here's another tip-off. When the bat crosses the plate, the top hand should stay on top. But if I do *this*" (Hugh's lowered right shoulder and elbow now lead his right hand below the plane of the imaginary bat), "I'll never be a good hitter as long as my ass points down. Now look at this."

Hugh takes his stance again, but something is different. It might be that he glares out at the imaginary pitcher—or that he really seems to visualize a ball and sets to attack it the way a hungry player named Hugh Alexander did in 1937 when he hit his way to the major leagues. The slow-motion stride is short, led by the front shoulder. The body stays closed as the arms extend fully, and . . . "Look at my hands! See?"

The right hand is above the plane of the imaginary bat and the imaginary left hand. "Look," he says again at the moment of impact, and I can feel a real ball jumping off a real bat and shooting toward the left center-field gap for sure extra bases.

Clearing the Decks

Peter Pascarelli

October 8, 1984

SAN DIEGO—Some teams make trades only as a last resort, tiptoeing upon such ventures as if walking on a mine field and rarely daring to gamble on a move.

Other teams are a little more willing to venture into trade talks but prefer a hush-hush style, revealing nothing to inquisitors and concealing their intentions as if they were state secrets.

Then there are the Philadelphia Phillies. No clandestine methods are included in their arsenal, no masked intentions or secrets. No one has to wonder if the Phillies are interested in joining the trade market.

Instead, they unleash their front-office pointmen like so many sharks in a feeding frenzy. Phils officials make no effort to hide whom they're talking to and what they're looking for, talking loudly about their intentions with an almost hyperactive openness and flair.

This winter's main goal, at least the stated one, will be to find pitching help. Many factors contributed to Philadelphia's 1984 collapse, but one of the most important was the poor second-half performance by the Phils' bull pen. By trading Willie Hernandez to Detroit in perhaps the worst trade of the previous year, the Phillies lost a dependable performer who bloomed into superstardom with the Tigers. Without Hernandez around, relief ace Al Holland ended up having to carry more of the load. And he tailed off down the stretch, ending the year with a mind-numbing streak of 11 blown leads and ties over the final six weeks.

So relief pitching is the Phils' primary need as perceived at season's end.

Reprinted with permission of Macmillan Publishing Company from *A Baseball Winter*, edited by Terry Pluto and Jeffrey Neuman. Copyright © 1986 Macmillan Publishing Company.

It is also clear what the Phils have to offer in exchange for pitching. Their scouts and coaches seemed in general agreement that catcher Bo Diaz, who was injured during most of the 1984 season; shortstop Ivan DeJesus, who had an awful season offensively and defensively; and assorted other spare parts are expendable.

With that game plan, the Phils descended upon the World Series. The Series is annually attended by club executives from all major-league teams, so it becomes the first opportunity for clubs to start feeling out each other about their off-season plans.

Giles, in the season's final-weekend think tank, gave the go-ahead for a quick sweep of the other clubs by his various trade negotiators. The hope was that the Phils could make a quick trading score and accelerate their rebuilding schedule.

So Giles okayed having top scouts Alexander, Ray Shore, and Moose Johnson attend the Series along with himself and his three top front-office aides, Owens, Siegle, and Baumer. They begin their quest tonight, the eve of the Series opener, at a lavish party thrown at lush Balboa Park by the San Diego Padres. Phils representatives attack unsuspecting officials of other clubs over fresh seafood and cocktails.

In sharp contrast to the feverish Phillies are the Mets. Their needs are no less well defined, and what they have to offer is every bit as clear, but they try to avoid holding their trade talks over a public address system. If at all possible, they keep a low profile, not revealing their intentions unless absolutely necessary. They feel no need for a quick kill here; they are content to plant a few seeds, and in at least one case, fertilize a seed long since planted.

It was October 2, 1983, at Shea Stadium in New York that Frank Cashen had first dared to covet Gary Carter. On that day, the Mets were to apply the finishing touch to their second successive last-place finish. Even so, they swept a double-header from the underachieving Montreal Expos, depriving them of second place.

Cashen sat with John McHale, and recognized the torment in McHale's demeanor. Another season of promise and disappointment. McHale was discomforted enough to indicate the Expos might consider personnel changes. Cashen, seizing the moment, said, "If you're ever going to dismantle, I'd be interested in Gary Carter."

At the time of this first mention of Carter, the Expos would no sooner have dealt their all-star catcher than the Mets would have dealt Darryl Strawberry. Carter was the cornerstone of the Expos' organization, and cornerstones come with unwritten no-trade clauses. Carter was to the Expos what Tom Seaver and Pete Rose had been in their respective first tours with the Mets and Reds: the player most closely associated with the team. A club doesn't casually deal its signature player.

This is not to say a club will never trade its "franchise" either; the Mets traded Seaver in 1977, and the Reds allowed Rose to leave after the 1978 season. Cashen himself had pried Keith Hernandez away from the Cardinals in 1983.

Aware that "untouchables" are an endangered species, Cashen occasionally reiterated his interest in Carter to McHale. He did so at Shea Stadium on September 21. McHale only pointed out Carter's no-trade provision. Cashen found no reason to be encouraged other than the knowledge that his own organization was better equipped to supply the Expos' demands than it had been a year earlier. If McHale only would say, "So make me an offer."

Developments would soon lead McHale to speak those words. Murray Cook had been named Expos general manager and had had the opportunity to evaluate the players, whose unlimited potential and limited success had annually perplexed and frustrated their fans across Canada.

Cook, who earlier in the summer had escaped the Yankees asylum, found deficiencies in the Expos' regular lineup, and concluded that overall improvement could be achieved most readily by trading one of their stars. He made recommendations to his new employer, Charles Bronfman, and immediate superior, McHale. "Carter is the one who would bring the greatest return," he said. Cook was never instructed to "dump" Carter and the gigantic financial obligation of his contract. But the seven-year, $13.1 million contract has become a burden for a franchise with decreasing attendance. Cook was told, "Do what you have to do."

October 9

SAN DIEGO—After the first game of the Series, Jim Baumer is ensconced in the corner of a postgame hospitality suite talking with Milwaukee scout Dee Fondy while John Felske stands nearby. "We've been here two days and I think we've talked to every club in baseball," says Felske with a touch of wonder in his voice. "When Bill Giles and his people want to make a trade, they are unbelievable."

Meanwhile, Hugh Alexander is buttonholing his various cronies and confidants, the most notable being a kindred spirit named Jack McKeon, who as general manager of the Padres has earned the nickname "Trader Jack" for his brash willingness to make deal after deal in building San Diego into champions.

"I can't help Hughie with finding a pitcher or a shortstop or a power hitter, the three things he says he's looking for," says McKeon. "But Hughie and me always check with each other. Maybe we can work one of our three-way deals where I throw in something to get another club involved, get Hughie what he needs, and help myself, too. But I think Hughie's a little too anxious to do something right now. Teams don't like to jump this early."

Nevertheless, Alexander and his band press on. They talk most seriously to people from Atlanta, Montreal, the New York Mets, Milwaukee, and Cincinnati. Tomorrow afternoon, Giles will convene his whole group at a poolside meeting for an update.

October 10

SAN DIEGO—Brandishing a yellow legal pad that lists all the various equations the Phillies are trying to complete, Giles runs down the options after 48 hours of negotiating. Lo and behold, it seems that Alexander has begun to wedge out a possible deal with Atlanta. The Braves are interested in Diaz and might be willing to relinquish one of two relief pitchers—Donnie Moore or Jeff Dedmon.

"I think we can do something, I really do," declares Alexander. "You know Uncle Hugh; if there's a chance, I'm going to keep on those suckers until I wear them down."

October 11

DETROIT—The scene shifts to Detroit for games three, four, and five of the Series. Joe McIlvaine, the Mets' recently promoted director of player personnel, chats with Red Sox general manager Lou Gorman, the former Mets vice-president, while Frank Cashen presses—gently—for Gary Carter. "What are you going to do with Jim Rice if you can't re-sign him?" McIlvaine asks. Gorman offers no definitive answer. And the Mets exploration ends there.

The Phillies continue their open attempt to make a deal. While other club officials socialize and talk shop only in the most general way, Giles, Shore, Alexander, and Johnson bore in on active negotiations.

But their attempts begin to loom futile as the week wears on. Their talks with Atlanta hit a snag when the Braves become concerned about the condition of Diaz's knee, which was operated upon twice during the season. The Phillies offer to share their medical reports, in an effort to assure the Braves that Diaz is not damaged goods.

October 13

DETROIT—The Phillies are resigned to the fact that aside from possibly laying the groundwork for future talks, their effort for a quick score is a failure.

It is just too early for other clubs to make final trade decisions. And club executives from other clubs admit that they are a little put off by the Phils' aggressiveness. Given Philadelphia's recent track record, many clubs plan to make the Phillies wait and hopefully force the club to dig into its pool of young prospects.

By late evening, the Phillies' contingent is making flight reservations home. And Alexander, Shore, and Johnson, several cocktails into the evening, are beginning to wind down.

They have talked to so many teams for so many hours that they are beginning to lose their equilibrium. A jokester then suggests to Alexander that if he is so desperate to make a trade, he should try to work out a deal with Shore. "Give Snacks (Shore's nickname) Shane Rawley and Jeff Stone, and he might give you Juan Samuel," suggests the observer. "Now that might not be so bad a deal," Alexander replies. A dazed Johnson stands next to the conversation, nodding his head.

Then a light bulb goes off above his head. "Hey, Snacks and Hughie can't make a trade, they work for the same club," declares Johnson.

Thus educated, the final Phils survivors straggle home to trade another day.

Free Agency for World Leaders

Gerald Rosen

IT WAS AN IDEA whose time had come, but it took a prolonged strike to achieve it: free agency for world leaders.

At first it was a difficult concept for many to accept. Irrational loyalties and ancient ties to nations and to various ideas, religions, and principles seemed to stand in the way, in spite of the fact that virtually everybody could see that in the case of a professional athlete, for a person to be tied to one club for his entire career, without the possibility of selling his services in the free market to the highest bidder, was akin to chattle slavery.

But how quickly the world public came around once the excitement surrounding the possibility of a first-class bidding war began to surface. And now, after the first poststrike winter meetings have concluded, the results are in, and believe me fans, they are more dramatic and far reaching than anyone could have anticipated just a few short months ago.

Mikhail Gorbachev to the United States ($2,500,000)

Virtually everybody's candidate for manager of the year in '87, Gorbachev took a has-been team, a perennial second place finisher, and turned them into a certain contender for top honors. The U.S. is hungry for youth, dynamism, vision, and purpose, and Gorbachev clearly fits the bill. His pretty wife didn't hurt, and besides, to many in the U.S., he seems to be the only person available who understands economics. The U.S. is betting he'll be able to get the great powerhouse rolling again and they could be right.

Ronald Reagan to Russia ($1,500,000)

A lot of money for a seasoned veteran but Russia is just entering the TV age and they're clearly betting that the Old Master still has some of that media magic left. Besides, his "free enterprise" and "get the government in Moscow off our backs" talk could be just the thing for a bureaucratic Russian economy that seems to be permanently suffering from a premature hardening of the arteries. (Word has it that the Russkies threw in $200,000 to bring along Senator Joe Biden of Delaware to write the old master's speeches.)

Moammar Khadafy to Italy ($700,000)

The Italians are definitely taking a chance here, giving up so much cash to the leader of a small nation, but the word is they are basing this offer on the rumors that Khadafy likes to dress in women's clothing. If this is true, the Italians are betting big bucks that he'll be hit in the spring fashion shows in Milan, and with the shorter skirts this year, his great legs could be worth a fortune.

Margaret Thatcher to Argentina ($650,000)

"If you can't beat them, join them" appears to be the Argentinians' philosophy. Heavily impressed by the way the Iron Lady kicked their pampasses in the Falklands War, the Argentines seem to be making their move now to get Mrs. Thatcher on their side the next time around. Rumor has it that Mrs. Thatcher is already taking elocution lessons so she will sound upper class in Spanish.

Prince Rainier to Iran ($1,450,000)

A lot of money for a club that barely has expansion team status in the big leagues, but after years of harsh measures, hysteria, crusades, and regimentation under the fanatical Ayatolla, the Iranians appear to be sick of the high-pitched life-style, and who better to lead them out of this era than the easy-going Prince, who has mastered the art of living graciously and doing virtually nothing. The Iranians obviously were attracted by the fact that he's handsome, easy-going, he skis, yachts, and scuba dives, and, in a country where all the women are hidden or veiled, the fact that the Prince has two lovely daughters who don't wear much clothing was not lost on the mullahs.

Queen Elizabeth to the U.S. ($14,000,000)

A real shocker! But it makes sense when you realize that many Americans have wanted a royal family for 200 years, ever since what started out as a simple tax rebellion got out of hand and wound up losing them the entire royal connection before it was over. There were some doubts at first about paying the Queen more than Dave Winfield, but the fact that Prince Charles and Princess Di might join her over here evoked visions of the return of Camelot and effectively silenced the dissenters.

Emperor Hirohito to England ($1,600,000)

Another stunner! Impressed by his dedicated leadership of his people in World War II, this poor island nation went deep into its pockets to come up with the big bucks. A sentimental choice at heart, it was nonetheless popular with British fans, who love symbols of stability and tradition. Rumor has it the British clinched the deal when they assured the Emperor that Buckingham Palace came under the London Rent Control Ordinance.

Former Haitian President "Baby Doc" Duvalier to France ($600,000)

The French, accused by virtually all the world press of being irrational in this bid, replied: "We know this makes no sense, but it's our country and we'll run it any way we like."

Ferdinand and Imelda Marcos ($500,000)

To the U.S., to host the Jim and Tammy Show on national TV. The U.S. reportedly just barely outbid Italy, which offered the former dictator $400,000 just to bring his wife to live in their country and buy her shoes there.

Idi Amin

Still unclaimed at press time, but his agent, Ira Sutman of Beverly Hills, claims the former butcher of Uganda "has lots of irons in the fire" and "is looking absolutely marvelous."

IV

PLAYERS

From *Foul Ball!*

Alison Gordon

THE GHOSTS ALL COME OUT on opening day, lurking happily in the outfield corners, floating through the dugouts, raising small eddies of red-clay dust around second base, settling into the bleachers with the flesh-and-blood paying customers.

They are the ghosts of baseball and gather wherever the game is played, not just in historic venues like Comiskey Park and Yankee Stadium. They even come to modern horrors like Exhibition Stadium on the shores of Lake Ontario. They don't even have to go through customs.

Some of the ghosts are dressed in baggy flannel uniforms with their stirrup straps barely showing an inch of white over their polished black shoetops. Others wear dark jackets, high collars and ties, and straw boaters on their heads. The women have fox-furs draped across their shoulders and hats with a jaunty tilt. They sit incongruously among their rude modern counterparts who use language once reserved for the locker rooms under the stands, but in all their hearts is the same joy.

Baseball is as eternal as green grass and blue sky, and has been passed down through the generations, both on the diamond and in the stands. There are Ty Cobb and Babe Ruth, shagging flies in the outfield. Jackie Robinson, Honus Wagner, and Lou Gehrig take infield practice with Willie Upshaw, Alfredo Griffin, and Damaso Garcia. Cy Young leans against the bull-pen fence while Dave Stieb warms up before the game. And every fan in the stands carries a memory of a father or a grandfather who took him to his first game, and the line goes back for more than a century.

From *Foul Balls* by Alison Gordon. Used by permission of the Canadian Publishers, McClelland and Stewart, Toronto.

Despite the changes in the game: despite skintight uniforms in shocking colors and night games and the designated hitter, despite silly seven-foot-tall furry animals cavorting on the dugout roofs and plastic playing fields, the game is still the same as the day it was decided to put the bases that magical ninety feet apart and the mound sixty feet, six inches from home plate.

I once stood outside Fenway Park in Boston, a place where the ghosts never go away, and watched a vigorous man of middle years helping, with infinite care, a frail and elderly gentleman through the milling crowds to the entry gate. Through the tears that came unexpectedly to my eyes I saw the old man strong and important forty years before, holding the hand of a confused and excited five-year-old, showing him the way.

Baseball's best moments don't always happen on the field.

The dugout is a special place, at once utilitarian and almost sacred, a place of physical and spiritual renewal where players can hide from accusing eyes and spend a few moments with men who are surely their friends while outside the spectators howl and opposing players glare their game-time hatred.

It is a cosy cave, whether it is set down from the playing field by steep steps like the ones in Detroit and Baltimore or a field-level modern adaptation like the one in Toronto, a dug-in.

Before a game, before batting practice has even begun, there's the feeling of a private club here. Players hang from the dugout roof, stretching, or lounge on the narrow benches, chewing tobacco and spitting it on the floor, already stained and disgusting from generations of juice, splintered and pitted from generations of sharp spikes.

The dugout isn't pretty, but it's home. Here is where the tales are told, over and over again. Usually the stories are old ones, with even rookies digging back into their early minor-league days for conversation, when they talk at all. Usually, following unwritten rules, rookies listen to coaches and veterans talking about players and ballparks only they know.

"You remember Fred Smumphl?" one coach asks.

"Yeah, I played with him in Rochester," another answers. "Now he could hit. He could *flat* hit."

Nods all around. A player leans on his bat and spits.

"Not only that, he could throw," he chimes in. "He could *flat* throw. I remember one time in winter ball I saw him throw out Jose

Alapwunnra — remember him? — and Fred must have been forty at the time."

"Yup." Pause, spit. "Jose could run, too."

"I played against him in Mexico." Agreement from down the bench. "He could *flat* run."

Like the oral tradition of any group, the stories are comforting, a reminder of the sanctity of the game. A reminder that in this world a man is measured by a simple yardstick. Education doesn't matter; nor does family background. In fact, high breeding and college degrees are suspect. What matters are hands and wrists and legs and heart, and the guys in the dugout know all about those.

They are workmen surrounded by their tools before their shift begins. Their bats are in the rack at the end of the dugout, compartmentalized by uniform number so that each player can find his own quickly and choose from several: the batting practice bat, taped on the barrel; the gamer, with several good hits left in it; and the backups. Each has the player's number written in felt pen on the butt of the handle either by the bat boy or the player himself, depending on his superstition. Some players have secret signs or hexes for luck, a particular style of numeral that has worked in the past, elaborate as the graffiti on a New York subway car.

The helmets are on top of the rack, numbered on the back, some battered, some brand new. Players take them from team to team when they are traded, painting their new team colors on top of the old.

Big, square canvas bags with zippered tops hold balls, ready for batting practice and infield drills. These are used balls, scuffed and grass-stained: new balls are used only in games and for pitching workouts. There are towels folded and laid on the ledge behind the benches.

The water fountain holds a place of honor in most dugouts, inevitably bearing the scars of countless kicks and bat attacks by players who have failed at the plate. Somehow the water cooler is always to blame; but it keeps bubbling cheerfully, supplying cold, if somewhat brackish, water for thirsty throats.

The players are in charge of their own gloves, and these lie on the steps and benches. Players have practice gloves, too, either new ones they are working into shape to use in a game or, for some infielders, smaller models for practice to improve their fielding. Like the batter who swings a weight in the on-deck circle so that his bat will feel light and free at the plate, the fielder uses the small glove so that his bigger gamer will catch more balls.

Many players and most coaches arrive early on game days, leaving the hotel at 2:00 for a 7:30 game on the road, because the unstructured rituals are as important to them as the formal warm-ups to come. They play cards in the clubhouse, gossip in the dugout, or sun themselves in the empty stands.

The team bus arrives with the stragglers shortly after 5:00, and by 5:30 almost everybody is on the field. It's the home team's turn for batting practice first, so the visitors stretch and warm up, often chatting with a friend from the opposing team while doing it, or stand behind the batting cage and heckle.

This is the private time, the time when the diamond belongs to them. Soon the gates will open and they will be on show, but for now the only people in the park are the ones who belong there: players, the press, ground crew, vendors and ushers getting their final briefing in the stands. An umpire is always on duty, standing by the dugout in street clothes, supposedly enforcing the rule against fraternization between opposing team members. There is a sweet calm.

In the bull pen, the pitchers work out with their coach, especially the starters who aren't scheduled to pitch for a couple of days. Dave Stieb or Jim Clancy goes out with Al Widmar to work on a new pitch or perfect an old one. The tutelage will last as long as their careers.

While the home team takes batting practice, the visitors warm up, playing catch, slow toss at first at relatively close range, then harder and harder, farther and farther. Some play pepper, a simple fielding game that can get very intense. A player with a bat taps the ball toward a line of three or four fielders, one after the other. The fielder catches the ball and tosses it back to the batter to hit. A fielder who misses must move to the bottom of the line and if the batter misses, the first fielder gets to bat, usually over vociferous protest.

It's almost worth the price of the ticket to come out early and watch the Milwaukee Brewers play their variation on pepper, called flip. It is a viciously played game in which the ball is flipped from glove to glove among jostling players who do their best to make the next guy miss it. A game does not go by without several players sent sprawling by body checks more at home in a hockey rink. Most major-league teams have banned flip for fear of injuries, but it is as much a part of the Brewers' macho image as Pete Vuckovich's scowl.

Lloyd Moseby is always a joy to watch in pregame play. He may be a hero now to Little League dreamers, but he has lively fantasies of his own and before the working day begins, he is Walter Mitty in spikes.

Playing catch, usually with Willie Upshaw, Moseby becomes a pitcher, throwing sliders, curveballs, and changeups, commenting on each as it hits Upshaw's glove. He's like every twelve-year-old who has ever done a play-by-play of his fielding games against the front steps.

"A hard slider—strike three!" he shouts, raising his arms over his head in triumph. "Moseby notches his twentieth save! How about that?"

In batting practice, Moseby hits one into the left-field stands, an opposite-field home run, and dances out of the cage screaming, "I don't believe it! The Blue Jays win the pennant! The Blue Jays win the pennant!"

Not content with chasing fly balls in his normal center-field turf, Moseby asks the coaches to hit ground balls to him at third base. He makes great diving stops and rifles the ball to first, laughing when he misses. He then comes into the dugout to confide, quite seriously, that he could be the greatest third baseman ever to play the game. There is always that kind of joy in the best of the players, though few of them have Moseby's exuberance.

These moments before the game are as much a part of the pleasure of baseball as the game itself and typify the special nature of the sport as well as anything else. Let football players spend their pregame period throwing up and getting mean. Baseball players spend theirs getting loose. The relaxed intensity necessary to play the game well is the reason for the tradition of zaniness that has built up in baseball.

The fans who come out early, who are there when the gates open an hour and a half before game time, share in this. They can watch big, ugly Cliff Johnson pick up tiny Garth Iorg (in baseball, anyone under 5'11" is referred to as a "little man") and race him around in a fireman's carry. They can hear the insults being shouted from dugout to dugout, cheerful jibes about the players' ability, looks, drinking capacity, or, these days, salary. The players mimic each other mercilessly. One player jumps out of his dugout with a bat and replays the way another bailed out on an inside pitch the night before, and members of both teams point at the embarrassed culprit and laugh uproariously.

As game time approaches, everyone gets a bit more serious. The starting pitcher retreats to the clubhouse where, like a matador, he dons his psychological suit of lights. Some pitchers refuse to go on the field before a start, but even the most even-keeled need a short quiet period alone. The other players settle into familiar routines, the same drills they have done from the lowest minors right on up before every game, day or night, with no exception, even during the World Series. These are the drills that help the players switch off their minds and fine-tune their reflexes for the game ahead.

Batting practice is taken in groups of four or five, the starters separately from the extra men. Each player first bunts twice, once down the first-base line, once toward third. They begin with six or seven swings, depending on the time available, taking turns, and work down until they are popping in and out of the cage, taking one swing each while the next group watches the clock and complains they are taking too much time. (Baseball players all have selective arithmetical amnesia. When they're in the cage, they can't figure out how many swings make five. When they're outside waiting, their math improves.)

The batting coach usually leans against the back of the cage watching. Occasionally he comments between swings or takes a player aside between turns with some advice.

The rest of the players are busy in the field, shagging flies in the outfield (although pitchers' shagging looks suspiciously like standing around with arms folded talking to the next guy) or fielding infield ground balls, hit by coaches standing beside the batting cage on either side.

After both teams have had batting practice and the protective screens and cages have been rolled away, it's time for the final drills: outfielders catch fly balls and base hits and practice throwing to third and home; then the infielders practice fielding and throwing to different bases and to home; the pitchers stand in foul territory, first playing pepper, then relaying balls from the outfield back to the coaches; the catchers practice fielding bunts.

As the drills end, the players leave the field one by one, fielding one last ground ball as each leaves until only the catcher remains. One final popup and he's free to go and the ground crew race out with their rakes and barrows full of lime to fluff up the infield one last time.

The umpires stroll onto the field at last, with their hulking authority, and wait for the lineup cards to be delivered to them at the plate by a representative of each team. Then they all solemnly discuss the ground rules they have gone over dozens of times before.

The rituals whet the fans' appetites, and they greet the home team with great cheers when they run on the field and doff their caps for the anthems. Whenever the Blue Jays or Expos play, both American and Canadian anthems are played. Larry Millson of the *Globe and Mail* once estimated that if each anthem averages a minute and a half, players for Canadian teams spend a full eight hours listening to anthems in the course of a 162-game season—a working day's worth of phony patriotism.

A dream game is always played in the sunshine, memory omitting the lights or the cold of reality. It is watched from the boxes down the first-base line in Fenway Park in Boston or Royals Stadium in Kansas City, with a hot dog from Detroit in one hand and a beer from Milwaukee in another, surrounded by Baltimore fans waiting for the operatic vendor from Al Lang Field in St. Petersburg to pass by, singing "East Side, West Side" in a ringing baritone. Dreams are like that, you remember the best.

The game proceeds at just the right pace: the one detractors call boring. It is gentle and relaxed, full of spaces for reflection or conversation, quiet moments in which to relish a play just made or a confrontation about to occur. What's the rush? The longer the game, the more there is to enjoy.

It's hard to understand people who hate baseball, but easy to pity them. Never to have felt the surge of joy watching a ball sail over the fence or a fielder making a running, leaping catch is to have missed a great pleasure indeed. For that matter, to have missed the anger and despair when the ball sailing over the fence beats your favorite team in an important game is equally sad, because the caring feels so good. To find baseball boring is to have missed drama and nuance, the laughter and the tears that come from joy or sorrow. It's a shame.

The unfortunate thing about baseball for the novice fan is that the more you know about it the more attractive it becomes, and there aren't enough teachers to go around.

It's not hard to find the excitement in a high-scoring game the home team wins, but the pleasure of a pitchers' duel is more elusive. To find the joy in a low-scoring game, you have to understand that the central confrontation of the game is being won by the pitcher, this time, but the battle is rejoined with each pitch.

That's what is at the core of the sport. Standing on a hill precisely ten inches high is a man who uses every bit of muscle and talent and brain he has to throw a ball harder or with more spin of one kind or another than anyone in the stands ever could. He has a lone enemy and eight accomplices on the field with him. His catcher is crouched behind the plate doing some (or, occasionally, all) of his thinking for him, suggesting which pitches to throw. Seven other men, four in the infield and three in the outfield, are ready to make the pitcher look good. His enemy stands next to the plate with a stick in his hand, all by himself. It's as simple as that. The guy with the stick is trying to hit the ball thrown by the man on the hill, preferably out of range of the gloved accomplices.

The complications come in when we peek inside each man's head, the real battleground of baseball. The pitcher and catcher remember what they have learned from the scouts and from their own experience with the hitter. Does he have trouble with curveballs? Will he go for the slider low and outside? Does he swing at the first pitch or watch it? In short, is there an easy way to get this guy out? The fielders are remembering, too. Does the hitter pull the ball? Should the outfielders shade him to left or right? What's the pitcher going to throw?

The hitter, for his part, is reviewing what he knows about the pitcher and catcher, while trying to watch the fielders in case they open a hole he can hit through. All of the celebration goes on in the time it takes the pitcher to get the sign from the catcher, wind up, and throw the ball, to the accompaniment of a hellacious hullabaloo from the paying customers in the stands.

Add a base runner or two and the equation becomes even more complex. The pitcher and catcher are worrying that the runner will try to steal and are trying to prevent it. The catcher will often call for a fastball with men on base to give himself a fighting chance.

That will please the hitter, because fastballs are easier to hit, but he has to worry about the base runner, too. He gets signs from the third-base coach to tell him whether he should swing or not, hit behind the runner into right field, or simply swing away. And, oh yes, he has to hit a round ball with a round bat, reckoned by some to be the most difficult endeavor in all of sport.

The experienced fans understand all of this, and even have some thinking of their own to do. Anyone can see the hitter's batting average on the scoreboard and guess at his chances, but the ardent fans know more. They might remember the last time the two players squared off, when the pitcher gave up a home run, or know that the hitter is in a three-game slump. They might even know that the pitcher's wife just had a baby and he's tired.

The numbers define the game, but so do human factors. These athletes, unencumbered (with the exception of catchers) by the padding, helmets, and masks of hockey and football, have faces, and their isolation on the field gives them no place to hide. This is one reason that newspapers and magazines profile these players more than they do those in football or hockey, and why readers are eager to learn more about them.

Their personalities also show clearly in the way they play. No one watching Pete Rose in action can have any doubt about the type of man he is. Compare the way Eddie Murray arrogantly approaches the plate with the excuse-me diffidence of Todd Cruz and see if you can figure out which is the slugger. This body language even shows what kind of a day a player is having. The difference between a relief pitcher struggling for control and the same one in command of his game is like watching two different men.

Sometimes the confrontation is classic, usually when it is the team's best pitcher against the other team's best hitter when the game is on the line. There's intimidation on both sides. The batter digs his spikes into the dirt and glares, saying with his eyes, "Throw the damn ball."

The pitcher responds. He throws it right at the batter's throat. "Out of my way, mother. Get back where you belong."

The batter picks himself up out of the dirt and laughs. The fans howl for the pitcher's head. The show goes on.

In Yankee Stadium on October 10, 1980, the confrontation was between George Brett, the Royal third baseman who had hit .390 in the regular season, and Goose Gossage, the Yankee reliever who had a 2.27 earned run average and twenty saves. The league's best reliever was up against the league's best hitter in the third game of the league championship series, but it was even more than that. It was also the fourth time the two teams had met in the playoffs, and the Yankees had won the three previous times. The Royals had never made it to the World Series but they had a 2-0 lead in games this time. They were hungry.

The score was 2-1 Yankees in the seventh inning and there were two men on when Brett came to bat, speedy Willie Wilson and U. L. Washington. Brett hadn't had a hit in seven at bats.

There were 56,000 fans in the stands, and every one of them was screaming: "GOOooOoose, GOOooOoose" echoed off the pillared facades of the historic park. They were banshees, drowning out the few voices shouting in the visiting dugout: "It's going to happen! It's going to happen!"

It was a moment so exciting, so purely dramatic, that years later it still gives me chills. In memory the two are frozen for an instant before Gossage threw his first pitch. Then whap, it was over in the blink of an eye — the delivery, the swing, and then the ball flying harder and faster than physics should allow into the third deck of the right-field grandstand. There was no doubt about it. Brett was the Royals and Gossage the Yankees, and the series was won and lost on that single pitch.

In April of 1982 I remembered that night again after another confrontation almost as classic, though not as crucial. Reggie Jackson was making his first trip back to New York in an Angel uniform after going to California as a free agent when the Yankees didn't try to sign him. Jackson was bitter, as were the New York fans who had adored him through five years and three World Series. They felt, Jackson and his fans, that Yankee owner George Steinbrenner had let them all down.

The day before Jackson's return, Steinbrenner tried to upstage the event by firing manager Bob Lemon for the second time in five years and rehiring the man Lemon had replaced the season before, Gene Michael.

Jackson had been slumping, with a .173 batting average so far that season, and his nine hits had all been singles. He was at the ballpark early, taking extra batting practice and holding a press conference. ("Hi, guys, I'm Reggie," he began.)

When the lineups were announced, 35,000 fans gave Jackson a standing ovation. They cheered his first at bat, a weak popup. His second time up, he singled, and the fans chanted "Reg-gie, Reg-gie!" as they had so many times before.

Finally, when he hit the first pitch Ron Guidry threw his third time at bat off the facing of the third tier in right field, they stood and chanted "Steinbrenner sucks," over and over. It was as if they had rehearsed it for weeks, so clearly were the unlovely words enunciated by men and women, boys and girls, young and old, in perfect unison. And even the Yankees couldn't quite hold back their smiles as they stood on the field and listened.

On the way downtown after the game I encountered a gleeful cabbie, a middle-aged man who had lived in New York and hated the Yankees all his life. His radio was tuned to the Yankee network.

"Reggie stuck it in Steinbrenner's ear, didn't he?" the cabbie gloated. "I was on the Brooklyn Bridge when he hit it."

As the ride continued through the less appetizing parts of Harlem the man talked about other great moments in baseball history, including Brett's home run two seasons previously. "That was a great one, too," he chortled. "I was gassing up the cab over in the Bronx when he hit it."

It finally dawned on me that this very dedicated fan saw very few games. He was too busy trying to support a family to take nights or afternoons off, but he listened to every game on his radio and fixed them in his own peculiar geography.

The Giants were the cabbie's team before they went west, and his all-time hero was Willie Mays. "When he retired, they gave him a day," he said, evoking the majesty of the occasion. "I'll never forget it. When he made his speech I just pulled the cab over to the side of 85th Street and cried. It was like he was my father."

Baseball has more than moments like those two home runs, those sweet moments of revenge. What makes baseball special is almost daily surprise. Watching tiny Alfredo Griffin hit a home run is as delightful as watching elephantine Cliff Johnson steal a base because each is so unexpected that fans laugh and clap each other on the back. Did you *see* that? Players in the dugout hide their smiles behind their hands, and Griffin crosses the plate or Johnson dusts his uniform off at second trying to look cool, as if it happened every day.

If it wasn't for surprise only a handful of the twenty-six teams in the major leagues could survive. The others wouldn't draw flies to watch them lose, overmatched, game after game. But baseball is the underdog's sport, and on any given day virtually anything can happen, and that's what keeps fans showing up to see even the least successful teams. Because any team can win any game; because a Gold Glove can make an error and a bum can make a great play; because the worst team in baseball can score twenty runs some days baseball is still alive. A trip to the ballpark is full of anticipation: what's going to happen today?

In the early Blue Jay years, all fans could hope for was astounding surprises. They got their share, but the underdog battle I remember best was fought out of town, in Yankee Stadium. It was a game few others will recall so vividly. Tommy John and Billy Martin might, even though it had no real bearing on a championship. Phil Huffman will never forget it.

The Blue Jays started a four-game series in New York on June 19, 1979. Now these were truly dreadful players having a terrible year, and it was a midweek series, but there were 36,000 crazed fans on hand that Tuesday night. Not for the Blue Jays, no, but to welcome back Billy Martin as manager.

At the beginning of the week, Steinbrenner, perhaps realizing that advance ticket sales were pathetic for the series, perhaps wanting to guarantee Martin a few quick wins, had announced that Bad Billy would replace Bob Lemon, the man who had replaced him the season before. The move was cynically motivated, but the fans lined up around the block to be there.

To further ensure success, Martin moved John (10-2 at the time) up a game in the starting rotation to pitch the first night against the hapless Jays. All they had to face the ace was Huffman, a fuzzy-cheeked rookie with a 3-7 record who would turn twenty-one the next day. Huffman, although he tried to hide it with a moustache that refused to grow, had the fair freckled face, mischievous grin, and baby-blue eyes of a Norman Rockwell painting.

Banners hung from every tier of the stadium to welcome Martin back, and when he came jogging out of the dugout with the lineup card before the game the din was frightening, especially to Huffman, out in the bull pen warming up. "When they all started yelling for Billy, I got the chills," he recalled afterwards. "I got the butterflies real bad. I was so pumped up I couldn't even hear the names of the batters when they were announced."

It was probably just as well. If he had realized who he was facing he probably wouldn't have got them out, but he lasted six innings, holding the Yankees to three runs while the Blue Jays had every blooper they hit drop in. They ended up winning the game 5-4. David slew Goliath, and the cynics lost their shirts.

The heroes of that night were men who will never be called to Cooperstown. Not one of them lasted in the majors past the end of the next season. Huffman lost eighteen games that year and was sent to the minors, never to return. Tom Buskey, the journeyman reliever who saved the game, now works for the state employment office in Pennsylvania and coaches a junior college team. J. J. Cannon, who made the catch of the game to rob Graig Nettles of a home run, now coaches in the low Blue Jay minors.

It's nice to think that those men, Cannon and Buskey and Huffman, have that game to remember, and you know they remember it still. That was the night when they were truly big league. The Cinderella night when they beat the Yankees, broke all those New York hearts, and felt like they could play forever. Their lives have turned back into pumpkins and field mice, but they still carry the glass slipper around in their minds.

I remember Cannon's catch in particular. He was a late-inning defensive replacement for the genial, lead-footed Otto Velez in right field, and when Nettles hit the ball, Cannon was the only one in the park who didn't believe it was gone and that the Yankees had won the game. He raced back into the right-field corner, timing his leap to the flight of the ball, as he later explained it, and snatched it off the padding at the top of the fence, ten feet high.

It was a perfect moment, a perfect catch, and he hangs up there frozen in my memory for all time, the cheering fans frozen behind him at the very moment they realize they've been robbed, their jaws slackening out of the smiles of triumph.

I remember Huffman, too. There are more reporters in Yankee Stadium than anywhere else in the league, especially on a night like this one, vultures coming out to circle Martin again. They all wanted to talk to the kid pitcher who had spoiled Billy's fun. Huffman was all calm bravado and offhand—nothing to it, just another day in a big-league pitcher's life, ho hum—convincing unless you had suffered with him through the seven losses and seen the doubt and despair in his eyes. He was a kid in over his head, and he knew it, but he was enjoying the bluff. I waited until the New Yorkers had left before I talked to him.

"What about the first pitch in the third inning?" I asked, about a ball thrown so wildly it sailed over the catcher's head and hit the screen, totally out of control.

Huffman looked around to make sure we were alone and then began to giggle. He laughed and laughed and didn't stop until he had used all the happiness up. Then he went out with the big guys and had a birthday celebration he will never forget.

These moments are the soul of baseball: the ball perfectly hit, perfectly caught, or perfectly thrown; the strikeout that ends a game, the pitcher's hand punching the air, the catcher running toward the mound. We can unwrap the moments later, when it's quiet, and enjoy them all over again. Each fan has a private collection, and his moments are more precious than another fan's whole game.

I certainly cherish Huffman's game more than another one played almost two years later, even though the second game already has its own niche in the Hall of Fame, and in Len Barker's heart. It was a pretty boring night in Cleveland on Friday night, May 15, 1981. Two lackluster teams, in contention for nothing more interesting than last place, were meeting because the schedule told them to, and nobody much cared. Paid attendance was announced as 7,290 but some of those who had paid for tickets obviously had stayed at home. Those who showed up looked like no more than a handful in the huge park. The Blue Jays and Indians drew big crowds only on bat day.

It was a chilly evening and neither team was doing anything very exciting. The Indians scored a couple of unearned runs in the first inning, but Luis Leal kept it close with a good pitching job. Barker, for his part, hadn't allowed a Blue Jay to reach base by hit, walk, or error; but this caused little excitement in the press box.

Partial no-hitters are more common than one might think. Baseball writers see them all the time. The first couple of times it's exciting, but after that it's just an excuse to set up a pool. After three no-hit innings, a dollar will buy you one of ten numbered slips of paper. The number you get, from one to nine, indicates what position you hold in the batting order, and the zero gives you the no-hitter to cheer for. The guy who pulled that slip that night groaned.

Even five perfect innings aren't really unusual. Players say they don't start noticing until after the sixth, after the second time through the batting order. That's why Barker's perfect innings that night, one after another, didn't cause much of a stir at first.

This wasn't Nolan Ryan out there, for Pete's sake. This was Len Barker and the Indians, and someone was bound to get on base sooner or later. Even the Blue Jays, no matter how they were slumping (they had been shut out in two previous games), would get on base with a hit, a walk, or an error before the game was over.

In the press box we simply waited for the play that would open the game up and noticed admiringly that the game, however dull, was moving along nicely. There was a chance to get our stories in before deadline.

Only as the game began winding down did the excitement begin. As the seventh inning passed, then the eighth, a strange, superstitious silence filled the stadium. The clapping and cheering were slightly subdued, the balance seemed so precarious. All eyes were on Barker as he left the mound after an inning, and then came back for the next. This large, rather ordinary pitcher became a different man.

In the press box we had been making jokes about the legitimacy of such a feat against the Blue Jays and whether it should carry an asterisk in the record books, but we stopped kibitzing and began to watch each pitch carefully, trying to fix it in our minds. This wasn't just another boring game — this was history!

We called our editors, spoiling their hopes for an easy night: "Uh, I know you don't want to hear this on deadline, but we might have a perfect game here."

During the top of the ninth inning, with the Indians up to bat, Terry Pluto, the beat writer from the *Cleveland Plain Dealer*, rushed breathlessly into the press box. It was every writer's nightmare come true. Len Barker was pitching a perfect game, and Pluto had taken the day off.

He watched with the rest of us as Barker walked to the mound in the bottom of the ninth, picked up the ball, and immediately bobbled and dropped it. His nerves were showing. The scoreboard in center field flashed the answer to the night's trivia question: "The Toronto Blue Jays and Seattle Mariners." The question had asked which two teams had never been involved in a no-hitter in the major leagues. It looked mightily like the jinx was on, but Barker, calmer than anybody in the place, faced his last three men and got them.

Ernie Whitt, the last batter, hit a fly ball into center field. Rick Manning ran in and caught it, then kept on running with it clutched in his hand, fought through the mob on the mound, and gave it to Barker. Whitt dragged his bat back to the Blue Jay dugout, where the rest of the team just stood and watched, completely stunned. They stayed on the field for a long time, waiting with the rest of the crowd for Barker to come back out on the field and acknowledge the cheers.

Whitt insisted to me later, even off the record, that he had been trying as hard as he ever did to get a hit in that last at bat. He wanted to ensure that Barker had earned it. He said that when he had come in to pinch-hit he had even considered pulling a Babe Ruth, pointing into center field to show where he was going to hit it out. All in all, it wasn't the way he wanted to get into the history books.

There had not been a perfect game pitched since 1968, when Catfish Hunter did it to the Minnesota Twins for the Oakland A's. One after another, Barker had set down twenty-seven Blue Jays. No hits, no walks, no errors. Two foul outs, five fly ball outs, nine groundouts, eleven strikeouts. It was perfect, and it was, for the most part, a yawn. Funny.

When it was over, Barker's hands were shaking with after-the-fact jitters as he passed champagne around to his teammates. (Every ballclub must have a secret supply of bubbly hidden away for such occasions.) He said he felt like he was "in an airplane 45,000 feet off the ground."

Someone mentioned Addie Joss, the last Indian to pitch a perfect game (in 1908, against the White Sox), but Barker had never heard of him. "But whoever he was," he said, "I'm sure he pitched a hell of a game!"

It was almost an anticlimax, but the sense of history was strong. We were there. We saw it happen. And don't you know that in years to come the people who claim to have been there that night could fill the stadium to the rafters.

There was something especially nice about seeing it pitched in that cavernous old barn of a ballpark, a fitting place for history to be made. I watched half a thousand games from the press box in my five years on the beat, but never even came close again.

I could identify with Pluto the next season when Jim Clancy took a perfect game into the ninth inning against the Twins while I was taking a few days off to get married. I was listening to the game on the radio at home, trying to decide whether to rush down to the stadium to see the end of it. Clancy was one of my favorite players, and I hated the thought of him throwing it without me. The first batter in the inning took the quandary away with a bloop single, and Clancy became just another pitcher who almost made it.

Perfect games are rare. The special combination of skill and luck necessary has rolled around in the major leagues only eight times this century. Luckily for us all, a game doesn't need to be perfect to be splendid.

Time Loves a Haircut

Bill Cardoso

"ALL RIGHT, BUDDY, sit down and I'll see what I can do," said the old outfielder, now thirty-nine and twenty pounds heavier at 201 than he was when he left the game in 1981, playing for Vera Cruz in the Mexican League.

Bernie Carbo, the Cincinnati Reds' No. 1 draft choice in 1965, chosen ahead of Johnny Bench. Bernie Carbo, clutch hitter, home run hitter. Bernie Carbo, who kept the many visages of Buddha in his locker. Bernie Carbo, who, it is said, never knew what day it was, let alone where he was.

Well, we're in Wyandotte, Michigan, downriver from Detroit. Bernie's neck of the woods these days. We are in a brown two-story building where Bernie Carbo's We Are Family Hair Stylists shares space with Nunzio's Construction Services Inc. The salon had been a real estate office until Bernie moved in with his clippers and his "family," Sonia and Dorothy, colleagues in the world of lock and tress.

"That tail, yeah," Bernie was saying of the single lock of hair starting to trail down the nape of my neck. "Extension, you call 'em? I like that. Ride 'em, cowboy. You see mine? I got a tail. I had mine new when I went to Saudi Arabia in, what? Three years ago. I went to Saudi Arabia to do a baseball clinic. I couldn't believe it. All these kids were running around, big gold necklaces and Mercedes-Benzes and everything like that. And they all had tails. Every one of them had a tail. And that's when I came back and said, those tails are pretty neat. And I started growing a tail.

"So, I've had it for a few years. And then I bleached it. Put some bleach in it. Back then I had my hair a little bit longer. Then I went shorter. I like it shorter, like yours. I'm gonna blow it a little bit." The blow-dryer purred.

"It looks all right. You're getting the works. I'm gonna give you what we used to call—remember the ducktail? The duck ass? Heh-heh. The DA? The *lively* DA! DA with a tail! The tail is really not off-center. But it's the way your hair grows. Oh, that tail looks good. You look like a movie star. Hah hah hah." Bernie was clipping away.

"Yeah, man, you know what? My first full year, in 1970. Sparky Anderson was my manager? I said, I'm going to get me a perm. I'll be the first white ballplayer to have an Afro. In 1970, in San Diego. Paid forty-five dollars. That was a lot of money then." Indeed.

"Went back to the ballpark. Sparky took one look at me and said, 'You ain't playing today. You ain't playing tomorrow. You ain't playing until you get that hair cut!'"

Now Sonia, who had been Bernie's instructor at Virginia Farrell's hair school before she joined the family, spoke. "Hey, look, Bernie, Bill ain't got no stockings on!"

I'm stuck in the Hamptons, Sonia. Socks ain't legal there.

"Hey, you know what?" said Bernie. "You laugh about the no stockings. Sonia laughs. Listen to this. When I was in St. Louis, this lawyer came in to read a letter from Mr. Busch. Mr. Busch was going to give us a pep talk: 'Hey, you guys, you gotta go out there and win. You know, you don't win a championship playing like this.' And the lawyer that was reading it didn't have any socks on. I walked up to him and said, 'Hey, you don't got any socks on. Do you mind if I read that letter?' He says, 'Yeah, you can read it.' And the next day I got released. I got released for asking him about his no socks."

My word! How's my extension?

"Good. Don't touch it! I'll tell you what, though. Your hair is not the easiest to cut. Swirls all over the place. It's cra-zy! Strong hair. Your hair sticks out on the sides there. The tail is—see how that is right now? That's in the middle of your hair. But watch how your hair grows. See? Look at that. That's something, isn't it? It grows right into a circle."

I'll have to *mousse* it?

"Not *mousse* it! I'll *grease* that son of a gun. We'll grease it. Get it all nice and greased. But look how nice the neck is. I'll comb it to grow toward the middle, into that DA. And worn a little close to the neck like this. And let that tail grow down like this. And when it gets long enough, we can braid it. Let that tail start growing out.

"See, mine's a little bit longer than that. Mine was long, but Sonia cut it. When yours gets a little bit longer, braid it. Do you trim your mustache? Do you like it off your lip?"

I like it bandito-style. Zapata.

"Oh, wild and crazy, eh?"

Yup.

"I'll just trim it a little bit here. Relax. Close your lips." Bernie snipped away. "Looking good! Yeah, when I went to that fantasy camp the Red Sox have in Winter Haven I took my clippers with me. It was the worst thing I did the whole damn week. I was giving the whole fantasy camp haircuts. Shaving their beards. Bill Lee had a beard. And his wife wanted me to shave it off. Bill's over in Rome now, doing a clinic. So, I shaved it off. The whole thing. Gave him a haircut."

Clip clip. "I thought the '75 Boston Red Sox was the best team I ever played on. That's including the Big Red Machine in '70. We played the World Series in '75 without Jimmy Rice. He had a broken wrist. Who's to say, if he played, I probably wouldn't have hit my two pinch-hit home runs. Do you want this above the ears, or do you like it on the ears?"

A little over the top of the ears.

"Just a little bit over the top? That's the style, to show your ears a little bit. You like it to cover the ears a little?"

No. The new style, Bernie. I want to be with it, now that I'm finally in the eighties.

"I tell you, Bill, the extension doesn't look that bad. Yeah, I did the Red Sox fantasy camp with Dom DiMaggio. I did the Cincinnati Reds, too. There ain't too many I can't do. I played on enough teams. I'll tell you that.

"The most fun team, though, was the Boston Red Sox. See, I don't actually say I was a Cincinnati Reds man. Although I'd like to see Rose and those guys win. But I'm a Boston Red Sock. The only reason was Mr. Yawkey. He's the one who made my day. He was in the clubhouse one day. I walked in and said, 'What'd we do? Hire another old man?' He had a pair of brown pants on. Old shoes. A work shirt. And he comes my way and says, 'Bernardo! How're you doing? I'm Mr. Yawkey.'

"And I went, 'Mr. Yawkey!' Wasn't he great? He really cared for his players, I'll tell you that. Too bad he had to go and pass away. Well, I'm almost done. You look like a movie star! All right now, I'll just clean you up a little bit. Well, what do you think? The tail's looking *good!* I wish it was longer. Then I could braid.

"Too bad the old man didn't live, eh? I'd probably still be playing for the Boston Red Sox if he was still living. You know what happened? In '75 I hit those two pinch-hit home runs. And that was the year my contract was up. And I had to sign, right? So, I got a 20 percent cut in pay after that World Series. That damn Haywood Sullivan and Buddy LeRoux took over the club in '77, and they gave me a 20 percent cut. And then they traded me to Milwau—who'd they trade me to, Cleveland? They traded me to Cleveland, didn't they? No, that was in 1977. No, they traded me to Milwaukee. I went to Milwaukee. That's when my wife was nine months pregnant and stuff like that. Took a 20 percent cut in pay. Couldn't believe they treated me like that. Mr. Yawkey probably would've given me a nice contract. Just like he did prior to that.

"But I think your tail really turned out nice. I don't know if these tails are gonna be in style that long, or what. What do you think? Three years? Three years. You know who started the tail? The Japanese. The Japanese!

"Yeah. Bill, you need to let this grow just a little bit longer. There you go, looking like a movie star! I told my father I was gonna be a haircutter when I grew up, and he said, 'No you're not. You're gonna be a ballplayer.' See, one side of the family had too many boys and no girls, and the other side—my father's—was all girls. So, I'd get together with the girls and try to straighten my hair, or I'd do their hair."

And then one day, his career at an end, it all came true. Bernie was tending bar at the Bump Shop in Lincoln Park, in the downriver area of Detroit, when a customer, Allison McKay, talked him into going to hair school with her.

"You know, Bill, the most fun I used to have, even when I was having trouble playing ball and stuff, you know what I'd do? I'd stop at the side of a ballpark, where there were kids playing, you know, throwing the ball all over the field and everything. And I'd stop and watch them because of all the fun they were having. And I just tried to realize, hey, I had a lot of fun when I played when I was a kid, too. If I could just get that frame of mind. You know what I mean?"

Absolutely.

"But how do you like the haircut, Bill?"

Why, it's beautiful, Bernardo.

Understanding Alvarado

Max Apple

Castro THOUGHT IT WAS no accident that Achilles "Archie" Alvarado held the world record for being hit in the head by a pitched ball.

"Because he was a hero even then," Fidel said, "because he stood like a hero with his neck proudly over the plate."

When people asked Mrs. Alvarado what she thought of her husband's career, she said, "Chisox OK, the rest of the league stinks. Archie, he liked to play everyday, bench him and his knees ached, his fingers swelled, his tongue forgot English. He would say, 'Estelle, let's split, let's scram, *vámonos a* Cuba. What we owe to Chisox?'

"I'd calm him down. 'Arch,' I'd say, 'Arch, Chisox have been plenty good to us. Paid five gees more than Tribe, first-class hotels, white roomies on the road, good press.'

" 'Estelle,' he would say, 'I can't take it no more. They got me down to clubbing in the pinch and only against southpaws. They cut Chico Carasquel and Sammy Esposito and Jungle Jim Rivera. What we owe to Chisox?'

"When it got like that, I would say, 'Talk to Zloto,' and Zloto would say, 'Man, you Latinos sure are hotheads. I once got nine hits in a row for the Birds, was Rookie of the Year for the Bosox. I have the largest hands in either league and what do you think I do? I sit on the bench and spit-shine my street shoes. Look there, you can see your greasy black mug in 'em.' Zloto always knew how to handle Alvarado."

Zloto came to Havana, showed Fidel his hands, talked about the '50s. Fidel said, "They took our good men and put them in Yankee uniforms, in Bosox, Chisox, Dodgers, Birds. They took our manhood,

Zloto. They took our Achilles and called him 'Archie.' Hector Gonzalez they called 'Ramrod,' Jesús Ortiz they made a 'Jayo.' They treated Cuban manhood like a bowl of chicos and ricos. Yes, we have no bananas but we got vine-ripened Latinos who play good ball all year, stick their heads over the plate and wait for the Revolution. Fidel Castro gave it to them. It was three and two on me in Camagüey around November 1960. There were less than two dozen of us. Batista had all roads blocked and there was hardly enough ammunition left to kill some rabbits. He could have starved us out but he got greedy, he wanted the quick inning. When I saw that he was coming in with his best stuff with his dark one out over the middle, I said to Che and to Francisco Muniz, 'Habana for Christmas,' and I lined his facist pitch up his capitalist ass."

"I'm not impressed," Zloto said. "When I heard about the Bay of Pigs I said to myself, 'Let's wipe those oinks right off the face of the earth.' You took Cuba, our best farm property, and went Commie with it. You took our best arms, Castro, our speed- and our curveball artists. You dried up our Cuban diamonds."

"Zloto, Zloto," Fidel said. "Look at this picture of your buddy, 'Archie' Alvarado. Don't you like him better as 'Achilles'? Look at his uniform, look at his AK 47 rifle."

"I liked him better when he was number twenty-three and used a thirty-six-inch Hillerich and Bradsby Louisville Slugger to pound out line drives in Comiskey Park."

"There's no more Comiskey Park," Fidel said. "No more Grace, no more Chuck Comiskey to come down after a tough extra-inning loss and buy a drink for the whole clubhouse. No more free Bulova watches. The Chisox are run by an insurance company now. You punch a time clock before batting practice and they charge for overtime in the whirlpool bath."

"That's goddamn pinko propaganda," Zloto said.

"You've been outta the game, big Victor," Fidel said. "You've been sitting too long out in Arizona being a dental assistant. You haven't been on the old diamonds, now astro-turfed, closed to the sun and air-conditioned. You have not seen the bleachers go to two-fifty. While you've been in Arizona the world changed, Zloto. Look at our Achilles, four fractured skulls, thirteen years in the big time. Played all over the outfield, played first and played third. A lifetime mark of two ninety-nine and RBIs in the thousands. He never got an Achilles day from Chisox, Bosox, Tribe, or Birds. When he came home Fidel made him a

day, made him a Reservist colonel. I did this because Achilles Alvarado
is not chickenshit. You, Zloto, know this better than anyone.

"Achilles said to me the first time we met, 'Fidel, the big time is
over for Archie Alvarado, but send me to the cane fields, give me a
machete and I'll prove that Alvarado has enough arm left to do
something for Cuba.' A hero, this Achilles 'Archie' Alvarado, but they
sent him back to us a broken-down, used-up pinch hitter with no eye,
no arm, and no speed.

"'Achilles, Archie,' I said, 'the Revolution was not made for Chisox,
Bosox, Bengals, and Birds. We didn't take Habana for chicos and ricos.
Cuba Libre doesn't give a flying fuck for RBIs. The clutch hit is every
minute here, baby brother. Cuba loves you for your Cuban heart. I'll
make you a colonel, a starter in the only game that counts. Your
batting average will be counted in lives saved, in people educated, fed,
and protected from capitalist exploitation.'"

"Cut the shit, Fidel," Zloto said. "I'm here because Archie will be
eligible for his pension in September. He'll pull in a thousand a month
for the rest of his days. That'll buy a lot of bananas down here, won't
it?

"You may think that you understand Alvarado, Fidel, but I knew
the man for eight years, roomed with him on the Chisox and the
Bosox. I've seen him high, seen him in slumps you wouldn't believe.
I've seen him in the dugout after being picked off first in a crucial
situation. You wouldn't know what that's like, Castro. I'm talking
about a man who has just met a fastball and stroked it over the infield.
He has made the wide turn at first and watched the resin of his
footprint settle around the bag. He has thrown off the batting helmet
and pulled the soft, long-billed cap from his hip pocket. The coach has
slapped his ass and twenty, thirty, maybe forty thousand Chisox fans
start stomping their feet while the organ plays 'Charge,' and then he is
picked off in a flash, caught scratching his crotch a foot from the bag.
And it's all over. You hear eighty thousand feet stop stomping. The
first baseman snickers behind his glove; even the ump smiles. I've seen
Alvarado at times like that cry like a baby. He'd throw a towel over his
head and say, 'Zloto, I'm a no-good dummy. Good hit and no head. We
coulda won it all here in the top of the ninth. That Yankee pitcher is
good for shit. My dumb-ass move ruined the Chisox chances.' He
would sit in front of his locker taking it real hard until the GM or even
Chuck Comiskey himself would come down and say, 'Archie, it's just
one game that you blew with a dumb move. We're still in it, still in the

thick of the race. You'll help these Sox plenty during the rest of the year. Now take your shower and get your ass over to a Mexican restaurant.' The Alvarado that I knew, Castro, that Alvarado could come back the next afternoon, sometimes the next inning, and change the complexion of a game."

Fidel laughed and lit a cigar. "Zloto, you've been away too long. The Archie you knew, this man went out of style with saddle shoes and hula-hoops. Since the days you're talking about when Alvarado cried over a pick-off play, since then Che and Muniz are dead and two Kennedys assassinated. There have been wars in the Far East and Middle East and in Bangladesh. There have been campus shootings, a revolution of the Red Guard, an ouster of Khrushchev, a fascist massacre in Indonesia, two revolutions in Uruguay, fourteen additions to the U.N. There has been détente and Watergate and a Washington-Peking understanding and where have you been, Zloto? You've been in Tucson, Arizona, reading the newspaper on Sunday and cleaning teeth. Even dental techniques have changed. Look at your fluorides and your gum brushing method."

"All right, boys," Mrs. Alvarado said, "enough is enough. What are we going to prove anyway by reminiscing about the good old days? Zloto means well. He came here as a friend. Twelve grand a year for life is not small potatoes to Archie and me. In the Windy City or in Beantown we could live in a nice integrated neighborhood on that kind of money and pick up a little extra by giving autographs at Chevy dealerships. Fidel, you know that Archie always wanted to stay in the game. In one interview he told Bill Fuller of the *Sun-Times* that he wanted to manage the Chisox someday. They didn't want any black Cuban managers in the American League, not then. But, like you say, Fidel, a lot of water has gone under the bridge since those last days when Archie was catching slivers for the Bosox, Chisox, and Birds. These days, there might even be some kind of front-office job to round off that pension. Who knows, it might be more than he made twenty years ago when he led the league in RBIs."

Castro said, "Estelle, apart from all ideological arguments, you are just dreaming. Achilles was never a U.S. citizen. After a dozen years as one of Castro's colonels, do you really think Uncle Sam is going to say, 'Cm'on up here, Archie, take a front-office job and rake in the cash'? Do you really think America works that way, Estelle? I know Zloto thinks that, but you've been down here all this time, don't you understand capitalist exploitation by now?"

Estelle said, "Fidel, I'm not saying that we are going to give up the ideals of the Revolution and I'm not deluded by the easy capitalist life. I am thinking about only getting what's coming to us. Alvarado put in the time, he should get the pension."

"That's the whole reason I took a week off to come down here," Zloto said. "The commissioner called me up—he heard we were buddies— and said, 'Zloto, you might be in a position to do your old friend Alvarado some good, that is if you're willing to travel.' The commissioner absolutely guaranteed that Archie would get his pension if he came back up and established residence. The commissioner of baseball is not about to start mailing monthly checks through the Swiss embassy, and I don't blame him. The commissioner is not even saying you have to stay permanently in the U.S. He is just saying, 'Come up, get an apartment, make a few guest appearances, an interview or two, and then do whatever the hell you want.'"

Fidel said, "Yes, go up to America and tell them how mean Fidel is, how bad the sugar crop was, and how poor and hungry we Cubans are. Tell them what they want to hear and they'll pension you off. The Achilles I know would swallow poison before he'd kowtow to the memory of John Foster Dulles that way. They sent an Archie back home, but Cuba Libre reminded him he was really an Achilles."

"Fidel, let's not get sentimental," Mrs. Alvarado said. "Let's talk turkey. We want the twelve grand a year, right?"

"Right, but only because it is the fruit of Achilles' own labor."

"OK, in order to get the money we have to go back."

"I could take it up in the United Nations, I could put the pressure on. Kissinger is very shaky in Latin America. He knows we all know that he doesn't give a fuck about any country except Venezuela. I could do it through Waldheim, and nobody would have to know. Then we could threaten to go public if they hold out on what's coming to him."

Zloto said, "America doesn't hold out on anybody, Castro. Ask Joe Stalin's daughter, if you don't believe me. You guys are batting your heads against the wall by hating us. There's nothing to hate. We want a square deal for everyone. In this case, too. As for Kissinger, he might carry some weight with the Arabs, but the commissioner of baseball cannot be pressured. That damned fool Alvarado should have become a citizen while he was playing in the States. I didn't know he wasn't a citizen. It was just crazy not to become one. Every other Latin does."

"But our Achilles, he was always different," Castro said. "He always knew that the Chisox, Bosox, Birds, and Braves didn't own the real thing. The real Achilles Alvarado was in Camagüey with me, in Bolivia with Che, with Mao on the Long March."

"The real Achilles was just too lazy to do things right," Mrs. Alvarado said. "He didn't want to fill out complicated papers, so he stayed an alien. As long as he had a job, it didn't matter."

"Zloto," Fidel said, "you one-time Rookie of the Year, now a fat, tooth-cleaning capitalist, you want to settle this the way Achilles would settle this? I mean why should we bring in Kissinger and Waldheim and everyone else? I say if a man believes in the Revolution, what's a pension to him? You think I couldn't have been a Wall Street lawyer? And what about our Doctor Che? You don't think he would have made a big pension in the AMA? I say our Achilles has recovered his Cuban manhood. He won't want to go back. Estelle does not speak for him."

"Fidel is right," she said, "I do not speak for Archie Alvarado, I only write his English for him."

"If Estelle wants to go back and be exploited, let her go. Do you want those television announcers calling you Mrs. Archie again as if you had stepped from the squares of a comic strip? Does the wife of a colonel in the Cuban Army sound like a comic-strip girl to you, Zloto?"

"Fidel," Estelle said, "don't forget the issue is not so large. Only a trip to the Windy City or Beantown, maybe less than two weeks in all."

"You are forgetting," Fidel said, "what happened to Kid Gavilan when he went back to see an eye surgeon in New York. They put his picture in *Sepia* and in the *National Enquirer,* the news services showed him with his bulging eye being hugged by a smooth-faced Sugar Ray Robinson. They wanted it to seem like this: here are two retired Negro fighters. One is a tap dancer in Las Vegas, the other has for ten years been working in the cane fields of Castro's Cuba. Look at how healthy the American Negro is. His teeth are white as ever, his step lithe in Stetson shoes, while our Kid Gavilan, once of the bolo punch that decked all welterweights, our Kid stumbles through the clinics of New York in worker's boots and his eye bulges from the excesses of the Revolution. They degraded the Kid and the Revolution and they sent him home with a red, white, and blue eye patch. That's how they treated Kid Gavilan, and they'll do the same to Achilles Alvarado."

"Well, goddamn," Zloto said, "I've had enough talk. I want to see Alvarado; whether he wants to do it is up to him."

"That," Castro said, "is typical bourgeois thinking. You would alienate the man from his fellows, let him think that his decision is personal and lonely, that it represents only the whims of an Alvarado and does not speak for the larger aspirations of all Cubans, and all exploited peoples. The wants of an Alvarado are the wants of the people. He is not a Richard Nixon to hide out in Camp David surrounded by bodyguards while generals all over the world are ready to press the buttons of annihilation."

"No more bullshit, I want to see Alvarado."

Estelle said, "He is in Oriente Province on maneuvers with the army. He will be gone for . . . for how long, Fidel?"

"Achilles Alvarado's unit is scheduled for six months in Oriente. I could bring him back to see you, Zloto, but we don't operate that way. A man's duty to his country comes before all else."

"Then I'm going up to see him and deliver the commissioner's letter. I don't trust anybody else around here to do it for me."

"We'll all go," Fidel said. "In Cuba Libre, no man goes it alone."

II

On Maneuvers in Oriente Province

The Ninth Infantry Unit of the Cuban Army is on spring maneuvers. Oriente is lush and hilly. There are villages every few miles in which happy farmers drink dark beer brewed with local hops. The Ninth Army bivouacs all over the province and assembles each morning at six A.M. to the sound of the bugle. The soldiers eat a leisurely breakfast and plan the next day's march. By two P.M., they are set up somewhere and ready for an afternoon of recreation. Colonel Alvarado is the only member of the Ninth Infantry with major-league experience, but there are a few older men who have played professional baseball in the minor leagues. Because there is no adequate protective equipment, army regulations prohibit hardball, but the Ninth Infantry plays fast-pitch softball, which is almost as grueling.

When Fidel, Zloto, and Estelle drive up to the Ninth Army's makeshift diamond, it is the seventh inning of a four-four game between the Reds and Whites. A former pitcher from Iowa City in the Three I League is on the mound for the Reds. Colonel Alvarado, without faceguard or chest protector, is the umpire behind the plate. His head, as in the old days, seems extremely vulnerable as it bobs behind the waving bat just inches from the arc of a powerful swing. He counts on luck and fast reflexes to save him from foul tips that could crush his adam's apple.

When the jeep pulls up, Reds and Whites come to immediate attention, then raise their caps in an "Olé" for Fidel.

"These are liberated men, Zloto. The army does not own their lives. When their duties are completed they can do as they wish. We have no bedchecks, no passes, nobody is AWOL. If a man has a reason to leave, he tells his officer and he leaves. With us, it is an honor to be a soldier."

When Zloto spots Alvarado behind the plate, he runs toward him and hugs his old friend. He rubs Alvarado's woolly black head with his oversize hands. Estelle is next to embrace her husband, a short businesslike kiss, and then Fidel embraces the umpire as enthusiastically as Zloto did. An army photographer catches the look of the umpire surprised by embraces from an old friend, a wife, and a Prime Minister in the seventh inning of a close game.

"Men of the Revolution." Fidel has advanced to the pitcher's mound, the highest ground. The congregated Reds and Whites gather around the makeshift infield. "Men of the Revolution, we are gathered here to test the resolve of your umpire, Colonel Alvarado. The Revolution is tested in many ways. This time it is the usual thing, the capitalist lure of money. Yet it is no simple issue. It is money that rightfully belongs to Colonel Alvarado, but they would degrade him by forcing him to claim it. To come there, so that the capitalist press can say, 'Look what the Revolution has done to one of the stars of the fifties. Look at his stooped, arthritic back, his gnarled hands, from years in the cane fields.' They never cared about his inadequate English when they used him, but now they will laugh at his accent and his paltry vocabulary. When they ask him about Cuba, he will stumble and they will deride us all with the smiles of their golden teeth.

"The commissioner of baseball has sent us this behemoth, this Polish-American veteran of eleven campaigns in the American League, Victor Zloto, who some of you may remember as Rookie of the Year in 1945. This Zloto is not an evil man, he is only a capitalist tool. They use his friendship for the colonel as a bait. Zloto speaks for free enterprise. He has two cars, a boat, and his own home. His province is represented by their hero of the right, Barry Goldwater, who wanted to bomb Hanoi to pieces. Zloto wants the colonel to come back, to go through the necessary charade to claim his rightful pension and then return to us if he wishes. Mrs. Alvarado shares this view. I say no Cuban man should become a pawn for even one hour."

"What does the colonel say?" someone yells from the infield. "Does the colonel want to go back?"

The umpire is standing behind Castro. He is holding his wife's hand while Zloto's long arm encircles both of them. Castro turns to his colonel. "What do you say, Achilles Alvarado?"

Zloto says, "It's twelve grand a year, Archie, and all you have to do is show up just once. If you want to stay, you can. I know you don't like being a two-bit umpire and colonel down here. I know you don't give a shit about revolutions and things like that."

Castro says, "The colonel is thinking about his long career with the Chisox, Bosox, Tribe, and Birds. He is thinking about his four fractured skulls. He justifiably wants that pension. And I, his Prime Minister and his friend, I want him to have that pension, too. Believe me, soldiers, I want this long-suffering victim of exploitation to recover a small part of what they owe to him and to all victims of racism and oppression."

Colonel Alvarado grips tightly his wife's small hand. He looks down and kicks up clouds of dust with his army boots. He is silent. Zloto says, "It's not fair to do this, Castro. You damn well know it. You get him up here in front of the army and make a speech so it will look like he's a traitor if he puts in his pension claim. You staged all this because you are afraid that in a fair choice, Archie would listen to reason just like Estelle did. You can bet that I'm going to tell the commissioner how you put Archie on the spot out here. I'm going to tell him that Archie is a softball umpire. This is worse than Joe Louis being a wrestling referee."

"Think fast, Yankee," one of the ballplayers yells as he lobs a softball at Zloto's perspiring face. The big first baseman's hand closes over the ball as if it were a large mushroom. He tosses it to Castro. "I wish we could play it out, Fidel, just you and I, like a world series or a one-on-one basketball game. I wish all political stuff could work out like baseball with everybody where they belong at the end of the season and only one champion of the world."

"Of course, you would like that, Zloto, so long as you Yankee capitalists were the champions."

"The best team would win. If you have the material and the management, you win; it's that simple."

"Not as simple as you are, Zloto. But why should we stand here and argue political philosophy? We are interrupting a game, no? You have accused Fidel of not giving Alvarado a fair opportunity. I will do this with you, Zloto, if Achilles agrees, I will do this. Fidel will pitch to you. If you get a clean hit, you can take Alvarado back on the first plane. If not, Alvarado stays. It will be more than fair. This gives you a great advantage. A former big-leaguer against an out-of-shape Prime Minister. My best pitch should be cake for you. You can go back and tell the commissioner that you got a hit off Castro. Barry Goldwater will kiss your fingertips for that."

Zloto smiles, "You're on, Castro, if it's OK with Archie and Estelle." Colonel Alvarado still eyes the soft dirt, he shrugs his shoulders. Castro says, "Do you think this is a just experience for you, Achilles Alvarado? This is like a medieval tournament, with you as the prize. This smacks of capitalism. But this once, Fidel will do it, if you agree that your fate shall be so decided."

"What's all this about fate and justice," Estelle says. She takes the ball from Castro. "Archie had eleven brothers and sisters and hardly a good meal until he came up to the Chisox. He cracked his wrist in an all-star game and that cost him maybe four or five years in the big leagues because the bones didn't heal right. It's a mean, impersonal world with everything always up for grabs. Alvarado knows it, and he accepts it. He is a religious man." She throws the ball to her Prime Minister. "Get it over with."

The teams take their places with Castro replacing the Three I League pitcher. Zloto removes his jacket, shirt, and necktie. He is six-five and weighs over 250. His chest hairs are gray, but he swings three bats smoothly in a windmill motion as he loosens his muscles. Castro warms up with the catcher. The Prime Minister has a surprisingly good motion, more sidearm than underhand. The ball comes in and sinks to a right-handed batter like Zloto. Colonel Alvarado takes his place behind home plate, which is a large army canteen.

"Achilles Alvarado," says Castro, "you wish to be the umpire in this contest?"

"Why not?" Zloto says. "It's his pension, let him call the balls and strikes. If it's a walk or an error, we'll take it over. Otherwise, a hit I win, an out you win."

"Play ball!" the umpire says. Castro winds up twice, and his first pitch is so far outside that the catcher diving across the plate cannot even lay his glove on the ball. Fidel stamps his foot.

"Ball one," says the umpire.

The infield is alive with chatter: "The old dark one, Fidel," they are yelling. "Relax, pitcher, this ox is an easy out, he can't see your stuff, there's eight of us behind you, Fidel, let him hit."

Zloto grins at the Prime Minister. "Put it down the middle, Mr. Pink, I dare you."

Fidel winds and delivers. Zloto's big hands swing the bat so fast that the catcher doesn't have a chance to blink. He has connected and the ball soars a hundred feet over the head of the left fielder, who watches with astonishment the descending arc of the power-driven ball.

"Foul ball," says the umpire, eyeing the stretched clothesline which ended far short of where Zloto's fly ball dropped.

The power hitter grins again. "When I straighten one out, Castro, I'm gonna hit it clear out of Cuba. I never played in a little country before."

Castro removes his green army cap and runs his stubby fingers through his hair. He turns his back to the batter and looks toward his outfield. With a tired motion, he orders his center fielder to move toward left center, then he signals all three outfielders to move deeper. Estelle Alvarado stands in foul territory down the first-base line, almost in the spot of her complimentary box seat at the Chisox home games.

Zloto is measuring the outside corner of the canteen with a calm deliberate swing. He does not take his eyes off the pitcher. Castro winds and delivers another wild one, high and inside. Zloto leans away but the ball nicks his bat and dribbles into foul territory where Estelle picks it up and throws it back to Castro.

"One ball, two strikes," says the umpire.

"Lucky again, Castro," the batter calls out, "but it only takes one, that's all I need from you."

The Prime Minister and the aging Rookie of the Year eye one another across the 60 feet from mound to plate. Castro rubs the imagined gloss from the ball and pulls at his army socks. With the tip of a thin Cuban softball bat, Zloto knocks the dirt from the soles of his Florsheim shoes. The infielders have grown silent. Castro looks again at his outfield and behind it at the green and gentle hills of Oriente Province. He winds and delivers a low fastball.

"Strike three," says the umpire. Zloto keeps his bat cocked. Estelle Alvarado rushes to her husband. She is crying hysterically. Fidel runs in at top speed to embrace both Alvarados at home plate. Zloto drops the bat, "It was a fair call, Archie," he says to the umpire. "I got caught looking."

"Like Uncle Sam," Castro says, as the soldiers stream in yelling, "Fidel, Fidel, the strikeout artist." Castro waves his arms for silence.

"Not Fidel, men, but Achilles Alvarado, a hero of the Cuban people. A light for the Third World."

"Third World for Alvarado. Third strike for Zloto," an infielder shouts, as the Ninth Army raises Fidel, Achilles, and Estelle to their shoulders in a joyful march down the first-base line. The Prime Minister, the umpire, and the lady gleam in the sun like captured weapons.

Zloto has put on his shirt and tie. He looks now like a businessman, tired after a long day at a convention. Fidel is jubilant among his men. The umpire tips his cap to the army and calms his wife still tearful atop the bobbing shoulders of the Cuban Ninth.

"Alvarado," Estelle says, "you honest ump, you Latin patriot, you veteran of many a clutch situation. Are you happy, you fractured skull?"

"Actually," Alvarado whispers in her ear, "the pitch was a little inside. But what the hell, it's only a game."

From *High Inside*

Danielle Gagnon Torrez

IN MAY OF 1980, I visited Fenway Park for the last time. I rarely came early enough for batting practice anymore (usually two hours before a game), but today was different. I'd been to a lawyer's office and had come over to the park directly afterward. It would be my last chance to see Mike for a long while. I'd been meeting with a divorce lawyer for many weeks, and he'd devised a plan. Mike had joked in the past that if I ever divorced him, I'd have to find him in order to serve the papers. My lawyer advised that I keep everything secret. The papers would be handed to Mike while he was on the road. Since he'd be leaving for a road trip after tonight's game, the plan would be executed within a couple of days. I was still riddled with doubt, still upset about actually having to end my marriage once and for all. But I forced my fears below. I had to do this, had to go through with it.

I looked out at the bright ball field. All these fully grown men scampering around in odd white suits and visored caps. I thought of how they'd once been cute little boys. I remembered a day outside Yankee Stadium. Mike and I were in our Cadillac and carefully squeaking through one of those crazy mob scenes. Suddenly, Mike stopped the car.

"What's wrong?" I asked.

He didn't answer. I saw a skinny boy with dark hair staring intently, hopelessly, at each passing car. He was praying, I knew, for an autograph. He strained forward while his mother crossed her arms over his chest and held him close. The two of them looked lost and out of place, like Mike the night I'd met him. Then the kid saw Mike beckoning to him. His child's eyes and mouth opened wide with delight. He leaped toward us, not even glancing toward the oncoming cars. Mike grinned at him and opened his window, though just a crack. Other hands, other arms, were pushing at the car all the way around. Behind us, horns honked like mad. Mike ignored it all and took the crumpled program from the boy's hands. The child's fingers, with bitten nails, curled around the inside of the window, brown eyes watched intently as Mike signed a page and passed it back. The boy lit up wildly but then ducked his head shyly as Mike smiled back.

Mike said something to him in Spanish, then rolled up his window. He gave me a quick, embarrassed look, then sat up very straight and drove on without looking at me again. It was as though he were telling me: "All right, I did it. I stopped for a kid, but I don't want to talk about it. Just don't say anything."

I was so proud of him that day, very grateful he could perform such a kind act. But I wondered also how healthy it was for a young boy to grow up around so much adulation, both seeing it and perhaps wanting it one day for himself. Did I want Iannick, for example, following his daddy's footsteps? There was so much good about this game, but so much bad that came with it.

I looked at the rafters of Fenway Park. This place had seemed so crumbly when we'd first come here two years before. Tonight, however, I felt a funny, nostalgic warmth. It was like leaving an old friend. I would really miss this old park, and all the other parks, too. I knew, though, I'd never really be welcome here again. Like other wives who had "divorced baseball," I was about to disappear. I would no longer be a part of this team. I would no longer be Mike Torrez's wife.

I watched Mike doing his usual sprints from left to right field. Then he walked and chatted for a while with Dennis Eckersley. Then once again, sprinted. I watched him as I had watched him many times before. He was drenched with perspiration, the towel around his neck heavy and limp and not much help. Then he spotted me sitting with Susan, my housekeeper, and with Iannick, who was unimpressed and busy with a stuffed animal. From way across the field, Mike's great smile contrasted sharply with his dark, sunburnt face. Suddenly, he began trotting towards us, avoiding in the process a player, a line drive, and a TV camera.

He was spied by a ten-year-old boy who clutched a baseball. The boy ran toward the railing as a crowd gathered and pleaded with Mike for autographs. I made my way through them, and Mike pulled me against him, hard, and smacked me on the cheek. Then he picked up our son and disappeared into the dugout.

Back at my seat, I saw the ten-year-old boy again, now darting up my aisle. With big strides, he climbed two steps at a time, losing his balance as he reached me, then tripping and landing right in my lap. We both broke out laughing as I helped him to his feet.

"Mrs. Torrez," he said, "please sign my ball?" I looked down at his dirty ball, held so preciously and tightly by tiny fingers. There were a few scribbles on the ball near traces of scuffed grass stains. One scribble belonged to Mike. I examined the *T* in Torrez: so simple, yet so strong, the name climbing high, determined. It was so much like the man and his personality. Looking up, I saw Mike and Iannick reappearing, our son's small mouth smeared with orange soda. Mike was beaming with pride as he carried Iannick back to me, and for a moment, nothing else mattered. This is what I had wanted so long to see—father and son, happy, together.

I grabbed the boy's pen and hurriedly wrote out my name. Danielle Gagnon Torrez. I crossed my *T* with Mike's on purpose. I was touching him, this time, forever. I held onto the ball for a moment, just savoring. I could not simply let go of this last piece of my life all by myself.

The boy took the ball from my hand, while I managed to hold back the tears burning my eyes. Then, I gave the boy a weak, trembling smile. His face looked confused and full of question. But he looked down at his ball and began turning it around and around.

"Gee, thanks, Mrs. Torrez!" he cried.

I turned my eyes toward the field. At this point, it took all I had to bring a hand over my head to wave at my husband. Mike was sprinting over to deep left field now and waving back. He was saying goodbye, I knew, for just a couple of weeks.

But I was saying goodbye forever.

From *The Seventh Babe*

Jerome Charyn

"DRINK YOUR HONEY and hot milk, Mr. James."

Fuck off.

Garl wasn't impolite to the fat nurse. He sipped the beverage she had prepared for him. He was seventy-nine years old. His three baby brothers had put him in Holyoke House last year. Garl paid the bills. He had a small pension and something of a bank account. His brothers would phone him from time to time, ask him about the pain in his legs, but they wouldn't come to Holyoke. It was too far away. Shem was a lawyer. Laurence was a brain surgeon. Theodore was a stock and bond man who was retiring to the Florida Keys.

How could Garl have been close with his brothers? He played ball summer and winter to see them through college. Shem, Laurence, and Theodore established themselves, made long careers, and Garl was happy for his brothers. He spilled the honey and hot milk into a flower bowl after the fat nurse had gone.

There was Red Sox fever in Holyoke and all of Massachusetts. Boston sat on top of the American League, thirteen games ahead of its rivals. The orderlies at the nursing home remembered that Garl had once played center field for the Sox. So they considered him an expert on anything to do with the club.

"What about Yaz? Jesus, he'll be thirty-nine this month . . . And Jim Rice? Can you believe that man's power? . . . and who's a better catcher than Carlton Fisk? . . . the Boomer at first and Hobson in the corner . . . banging in a hundred and twelve runs . . ."

"His arm is weak," Garl said.

The orderlies looked at the old man. "You crazy? He's a goddamn hero . . . going with a hurt shoulder."

"Bushwah, he can't make the throw."

"Wise guy, who won the Man of the Year Award, Hobson or you?"

They had a conference among themselves. They didn't want to rile the old man. They heard how he fell off a flagpole fifty years ago. They were crafty with Garl, leading him away from the current Sox.

"Who's the best third baseman you ever saw?"

They figured he'd say Brooks Robinson, Billy Cox, or Graig Nettles, their enemy on the Yanks.

"Pharaoh Yarbull. No one could chew his glove."

The orderlies were mystified. "What team was he on?"

"The Cincinnati Colored Giants."

He was spiteful and shrewd, this old man, reaching into the nigger leagues to arrive at a third baseman that none of them could have known about.

"Was your Pharaoh a righty or a lefty at the plate?"

"He hit from the left side," Garl said.

"Then he had to change hands when he took the field."

"No, he was lefty all the way."

The orderlies knew their baseball. They weren't toys for any flag-pole man. A lefty third baseman? Only niggers would tolerate such a freak. "How did he go around the horn with that left hand? He'd have to be an acrobat."

"He could go around the horn, through the horn, anywhere you like."

Demented. They had to feed orange juice to an old fool. They began to doubt he'd ever been on the Sox.

"Who's your next choice, old man?"

"Babe Ragland."

"Was he a lefty too?" they tittered.

"All the way."

"With the Black Yankees, or what?"

"Ragland was with the Red Sox."

A fury began to grow inside the orderlies. In a different year they might have ripped off his clothes and allowed him to bake on the lawn. Why should they give a crap? Boston was destroying the American League. The old man could invent all the lefty third basemen he wanted. Would they forget a Babe Ragland if he'd held down third for the Sox? They scratched their heads and pulled fiercely on their chins.

"Hey, there was a guy . . . he came up from an orphanage, hit a lot of singles, and was thrown out of baseball by the commissioner himself."

"That's the Babe . . ."

This obscure mouse was better than Cox and Nettles and their own Butch? Demented. They'd have to keep the old man from climbing another flagpole. They wrapped the blood-pressure cuff around his arm, squeezed the bulb, took four individual readings, put a check on the old man's chart, laughed to themselves, *Babe Ragland, Babe Ragland,* and told Garl to stick to a diet of lettuce and orange juice.

He was glad when they removed their trays and bottles and cuffs. They didn't torture him at Holyoke House. But he despised the charts, the hot milk, and the sound of their blood-pressure bulb. His legs had caved in, and that's the reason his brothers conspired to get him into a nursing home, so Garl would stop falling in the street. He refused to sit in a wheelchair. He had a cane, and he would hobble about. But mostly he stuck to his room.

He'd been forty years a baseball coach and master of Greek at a college in the Hampshire hills. Garl had never married. Women stayed with him. He would hug their bodies at night. But nothing seemed to last. He was ashamed to admit that he'd forgotten them. It wasn't the fault of his dotage. Garl remembered every busher he had played with. And one redhead. Marylou. Her lips would peck at him in his sleep. Old man as he was, he would eat off her body. Look for freckles on her shoulder.

He was a hunter in a nursing home, killing off old taboos. Garl had fucked himself. He'd denied the redhead and starved whatever passion there was in him. He should have married Marylou, taken her off the roster at Fenway Park, severed her from Hollis McKee. Garl always had the good excuse. He was a gypsy ballplayer with a family to support. How could he anger Hollis?

He lost Marylou to the swamps. He'd enter his eighties with the mark of her lips on him: a tired center fielder married to a redhead in his sleep when he could have had a waking-time wife. He was a constant boarder, living in hotels, rooming houses, and a nursing home. His wandering had brought him here, to Holyoke House. Hot milk and honey.

There was a tumult downstairs. A convict was loose in the nursing home. It sounded unreasonable to Garl. What would a convict be doing at Holyoke?

"Hiya, skip."

He did see a man in a convict's suit. Was it for halloween? Impossible. It was August now. The man reminded Garl of his brother Shem. Shem wouldn't come to Massachusetts.

The convict began to keen at him. He was reciting garbled bits of Sophocles . . . a freshman could have done a better job. The convict mixed up Ajax and the wound in Philoctetes' leg.

Garl wouldn't correct him. He liked how this convict sang in Greek.

"Babe, you son of a bitch. You scared the hell out of everybody."

Ragland was wearing the pajamas of the Cincinnati Colored Giants. The orderlies had sneaked upstairs with huge frying pans. They were ready to pounce on the kid.

"Go away," Garl screamed at them. The orderlies disappeared.

"Shit, I was only trying to visit you, Garl."

"People aren't used to the old-fashioned uniforms, kid."

The kid had to be seventy, or seventy-two. His back wasn't curled over. He didn't have wattles on his neck. His fingers were hooked and powerful: the proper claws of any third baseman.

"Babe, what's up? You didn't come all the way from Alabama or Wyoming to visit an old brother you once knew on the Red Sox and the Harry Heilmanns . . ."

"Ah, we're having an exhibition with some boys from Amherst summer school . . . a night game, Garl. And it's in the field next door. I was hoping you might come down and watch."

Garl jumped out of bed. He put on shirt and pants and grabbed hold of his cane. He hobbled behind Rags.

"I could carry you, Garl. It wouldn't be difficult."

"I can walk."

Garl met the orderlies on the stairs. "Come on with us," he said. "We're going to a night game."

Three orderlies, Rags, and Garl passed the nurses' office and ducked away from Holyoke House. It was a party of five scratchy men. The Babe led his party to a field across the road. The Amherst summer-school pickup team was waiting for the boss of the Colored Giants. These scrappling, big-necked boys were anxious to beat the ass off a band of country niggers. But the Cincinnatis had gone half white. Garl stared at them and recognized the kid's dilemma: these Giants were the rejects of a hundred tryout camps. "Sockamayocks," Garl said.

The kid agreed. "You take what you can get, skip."

Where were those landscape artists, the men who could sculpt a

baseball diamond on any field? The kid had four lumpy bases, crooked
foul lines, a batting cage with holes and wounds in the metal fabric,
and a pitcher's station that looked like dirt off a chickencoop.

Garl noticed an ancient fire truck in deep center field, a rat's nest
of cables, and lighting poles that gave the impression of giant tooth-
picks in the ground. The fire truck had bronchitis. It coughed a lot.
What about the Cincinnatis' mahogany Buicks? There were only three
of them left, and the mahogany was bitten off. The Buicks seemed
naked to Garl.

A redhead came out of the first Buick. Garl had to go to his cane,
or he would have flopped into the grass. *Marylou.* He prayed some
local god would toss a curtain over him, so he wouldn't have to see that
red hair. He put an elbow in front of his face. The beautiful witch was
no longer satisfied to peck him in his sleep. She followed Garl out of
the nursing home. Who could say what unholy thing she'd do to him
in the field?

"Since when are you so shy, Garland James? You used to look at
my mother."

Ah, it was only the girl. Marylou was dead.

"Sorry, Miz Iva, I didn't realize you were traveling with the team."

"You know Raggsy. He can't survive without a roommate."

Both of them laughed.

Shouldn't the girl have had some gray specks in her hair? She had
to be seventy, or sixty-nine? Did you kick old age in the pants when
you traveled with the Giants?

And who was on the hill for them, warming up his right arm? Yam
Murray's hundred-year-old shadow? Garl's legs were twisted and all,
but pathetic kneecaps couldn't interfere with his eagle eye: he spotted
the emery board in the pitcher's glove.

Garl hobbled over to Rags. "Don't confuse a sick old man. Who's
working for you on the hill? If it's not Yam Murray, it has to be his son."

"Wrong," Rags said. "It's the grandson."

"What's his name?"

"Yam Murray."

"Jumping Jesus," Garl said. "Whole generations of Yams . . . he kicks
like his grandpa. And I like the way he goes into the stretch. Rags, are
you holding him a prisoner? . . . why isn't he in the majors right now?"

"Shoulder trouble," the kid said. "He screwed around with knuckle-
balls and got himself hurt. The Dodgers had to let him go. That's all
right. He can pitch for me."

The kid couldn't blab too long. He had to play his spot. He lumbered off to third. The Amherst boys chuckled as he went into his crouch. They hadn't figured the boss would be part of the Giant infield. They could blow him down with the wind from their bats. They shouted to him, "Pop, do you have disability insurance?"

The kid told them to play ball.

"Then bring up the lights . . . it's black around home plate."

"Sorry," the kid said, and he signaled to the sockamayock in center field. The center fielder ran behind the fire truck. Garl heard a hiss. The poles shook in the ground. A light with a soft blue haze burned all over the diamond. This blue didn't hide the base paths; it was as if a mellow fog had rolled onto the field at noontime.

The summer-school team was satisfied.

Yam kicked from the mound and threw his emery ball into the cuffs of the first batter. He chopped at the pitch and banged a hard grounder into the hole. It would have gone through the shortstop, but the old man at third angled his body and it became a fucking knife that could stab a ground ball, recover itself, and hit the first baseman with a strike.

"He learned that from the Pharaoh," Garl said with a scowl. The Amherst boys shrugged. It had to be the night for graybeards. How else could you explain the catch? The orderlies touched Garl on his shirt. "Who is that old geezer?"

"Babe Ragland."

Two more innings of play and Garl had converted them.

"He's the best," the orderlies whispered. " . . . tell Nettles to move over, or Ragland will make the All-Star team."

The kid hopped, twisted, tossed strikes from between his legs. Amherst barely had the courage to go on with the game.

Garl could swear his kneecaps were on the mend. He was dancing near the third-base line. He listened to a crazy knock from the fire truck. The knock turned into a song. Women were serenading him from inside the truck. *Go with the Giants, go with the Giants.* Garl assumed his blood pressure was running high.

The sockamayocks beat Amherst summer school, 11-1. The center fielder switched off the lights. The truck was calm again.

The sockamayocks moved about the field like busy ants. They unearthed the lighting poles and carried them to the truck, dismantled the batting cage, picked up the pillow-bases and stored them in a Buick.

While Garl rocked on his feet, the orderlies were growing tense. They'd have to include Babe Ragland in their "immortals" list, put him ahead of Billy Cox, but what about the fat nurse? She would scream at them if she discovered that Mr. James had fled Holyoke House to watch college boys, scamps, niggers, and old men play on a warty field.

"Garland baby, we'd better shuffle back to the house."

Garl stared at the orderlies. "I have to say goodbye to the kid."

That medicine from the fire truck, the generator-song, had begun to wear off. Garl felt a burning in his leg. The flagpole injury was flaring up. Was it bravura or stupidity to fall off a pole in center field? Whenever the umps tossed him out of a game, Garl would sit near the piss trough at the neck of the tunnel and relay his signals to the bench. He was the captain of piss and manager of the Red Sox. Did he drop from that pole out of spite, after his brothers' education had been finished?

What could he declare about his own folly? That he loved Greek and the foolishness of cramming Sophocles into the skulls of boys? That he wanted his center field without the rigmarole and politics of a major-league club? He hadn't fallen off any pole. He'd jumped. To cripple himself and shout "fuck you" to Hollis.

"Skip, what's the matter?"

The Babe was standing in dusty pajamas.

"Rags, you should have left me on Quintana Roo . . . I'd have had a ripe old age among those bandits, eating shrubs and roots. I'm not partial to nursing homes . . . honey is bad for your teeth."

"Why don't you come with us?"

"I wasn't trained to be a batboy, Mr. Ragland . . . "

"I could give you center field."

"How?" Garl muttered. "With a dead knee . . . and a stick in my glove hand?"

"I'd rather have Garland James on one leg than any sockamayock . . . if the knee acts up, you can always manage the Giants. I have enough to do at third."

Crazy team. Crazy fire truck. Would they like him in Colorado when he turned eighty-six? He got into the Buick with Iva and Rags. Four sockamayocks sat in the back. Iva drove.

The orderlies were dumbfounded as the caravan took off. The Giants had kidnapped *their* old man. They chased the Buicks and the fire truck down the road. It went on for half a mile, until the wind was out of them. It was a fool's errand. They couldn't outrun a caravan. They'd have to return emptyhanded to Holyoke House.

They argued, pushed each other on the road. A furor was upon them to think up a story. How do you tell a nurse that you lost one old man? *Vanished.* That's the word. The old man had vanished on a walk in the fields. They could afford to whistle. Who cared about a nurse? They had their story now.

V

PROFESSORS

From *The Warsaw Sparks*

Gary Gildner

DARIUSZ WAS THIRTY-TWO. He had a flat-footed walk that reminded me of Charlie Chaplin in a hurry, but his round face was a small boy's delighted to his cheeks at being invited to tag along with the big guys. He was a member of the board of PZBall and a man who searched Warsaw for stars.

The first time I met Dariusz, he came knocking one January day on my classroom door at Warsaw University, where I was teaching a course in American literature. I was, in fact, deep into a discussion of who Ted Williams was, and what he represented to the main character of Russell Banks's novel, *Continental Drift*. I had brought to class my Detroit Tigers cap as a visual aid, and was wearing it when I answered the knock. Dariusz apologized profusely for interrupting, but he had heard at the American Embassy that I was a baseball player—and could we talk? Quickly? He had with him, to translate, a young man named Grzegorz, who was wearing, in addition to his winter coat, an old Rawlings mitt that had seen much use (and could have used, I noted, a good dose of neat's-foot oil). Caught by their visual aid, I invited them in. They said no, no, they only wanted to know if I would help the Warsaw baseball team. I said, "How? When?" They said we could discuss this tomorrow. The following afternoon they came to my apartment. Standing in the doorway, Grzegorz said, "Dariusz apologizes, but can you go with us?"

"Right now?" I said.

"Yes, if that is not inconvenient," said Grzegorz. "We are having practice tonight."

Minutes later we were pushed together on a rush-hour autobus,

Reprinted from *The Warsaw Sparks* by Gary Gildner by permission of the University of Iowa Press. Copyright 1990 by the University of Iowa Press.

making our way across town to Gwardia gymnasium, where I would meet the Skra players at their first practice of the season. It was the middle of January, the day already dark, I could see sleet falling in the headlights of cars going past. Suddenly Dariusz began searching around in his shoulder bag, and came out with a Topps bubblegum card of Dwight Gooden. Showing it to me, he said, "Much quickness. Very great, I think, yes? We *need* this." Grzegorz said, "What Dariusz is hoping you will do for the team is make us presentable. Last year was a disaster." I'd do what I could, I said. "What position do you play?" Grzegorz asked. I had to smile. I explained to him that I'd played high school and American Legion ball and had once been scouted by the Tigers after pitching a Legion no-hitter. But that was the high point of a short career. I developed arm trouble my last year in high school and became strictly a fan who played catch now and then. The Detroit cap in my duffel bag, I told Grzegorz, only meant that I was still crazy about the game and rooted for the Tigers.

The autobus pulled up at the Gwardia stop. As we walked in the snow to the gym, Grzegorz spoke Polish to Dariusz, and Dariusz, beaming, said to me, "You will pitch once more!" I said to Grzegorz, "Tell Dariusz I'll be very happy, and honored, to supply some coaching. But I'm forty-nine years old and I don't think I should attempt a comeback."

Grzegorz said, "A comeback?"

I said, "I'm too old to pitch."

Dariusz said, "A revelation! I am seeing much happiness. It's OK! It's OK!"

Now in Rybnik, eating breakfast with Tony and Alejandro, Dariusz looked worried. He counted the players twice. He asked Tony how he'd slept. Tony, in a sweater and warm-up jacket, said, *"Dobrze"* ("Fine"). He was a quiet, reserved, good-looking man with a mustache. Besides being our best and oldest player, he was also, at five-feet-two, our shortest . . . and the one who seemed most affected by the weather. We were most likely to see Tony at practice if the sun was shining. If it was the least bit chilly when he showed up, he wore, unless he was fielding, white cotton gloves. Dariusz then asked Alejandro how he felt, and Alejandro, already fidgeting to get going, said, *"Dobrze! Dobrze!"* Long-limbed, wiry, curly-haired Alejandro was the Sparks' talker, having played enough baseball in Cuba to know the tradition and value of chatter. When I heard him in the outfield crooning his Spanish-Polish interludes of encouragement and praise, his sputters of razz, I wished I had him in the infield, or behind the plate, to fire up his quieter teammates at close range. Out where he was, much of his song was lost on the wind. He too wanted to be closer to the action, if not everywhere at once. Often he'd suggest to me, after Froggy muffed a play at first base or a ball went through Norbert's legs at shortstop or Jake threw wild down to second, that he, Alejandro, could play first base, shortstop, catcher. "Pitch too maybe! OK?" At the beginning of practice when we warmed up our arms, he'd want me to observe his specialty, his submarine ball, which he delivered from an almost hairpin position, releasing the ball near his shoe tops. Never mind that a herky-jerky, all arms-and-legs motion (that is, a desire to fox the batter; that is, *style*) was his principal aim—which was also the case with his next specialty, the knuckler, and his next, the sinker. Never mind, he'd indicate, smiling grandly: he, Alejandro, Cuban tinker and confidence man, could pitch, *sí*, and catch (*"Fuego, amigo! Fuego!"* he'd yell from a catcher's crouch, thumping his mitt), and play anywhere else that I needed him. So far, that was center field, where he could catch any ball that was catchable, and then achieve—with speed and accuracy—home plate with his throw.

Tony and Alejandro were allowed to play on the team because PZBall had a rule that each club could take on three foreigners. The only other foreigner playing Polish baseball, as far as I knew, was a Cuban named Juan Echevarría. He was founder, coach, and first baseman of Robotniczny Klub Sportowy Stal Kutno. *Stal* means "steel" and Kutno is a town of 50,000 that makes steel; it's located 127 kilometers west of Warsaw. Echevarría, a contract worker in Poland who married a Kutno woman and decided to stay there, formed Stal Kutno in 1984. When anyone asked him about the history of Polish baseball, Dariusz would give plenty of verbal ink to Echevarría, mainly because Juan was the one who introduced him to the game. In the larger picture, Polish baseball's genealogy, Dariusz told me, went back to the old Polish game of *palant*, which went back to 1474. *Palant* had a bat (about half the size of a baseball bat), a leather ball (softer than a baseball, about twenty percent smaller), and a single base (a wooden post in the ground, placed a certain distance from where the batter stood). The batter played against a gathering of fielders. Like a tennis player serving, the batter hit the ball, then had to run to the post and back. He was "out" if a fielder either caught the ball in the air or, having fielded a grounder, hit the batter with the ball before he could get back to the starting point. According to Dariusz, *palant* was last played in Poland in 1967. "Death," he told me, "came natural in Silesia." Silesia is the coal-mining region in southern Poland where Rybnik is located; Rybnik is the town where the Polish Palant Union buried itself and then rose up as a softball team—thanks to the Czechs who taught it the rules. Klub Sportowy Silesia Rybnik became Poland's first softball team, Górnik Boguszowice became its second, and they played each other until 1982, at which time the Czechs taught them baseball. The Polish workers liked this game *bardzo, bardzo* ("very, very much"). Three more Silesian teams were quickly formed: another one in Rybnik (Kolejarz), one in Jastrzębie, and one in Rój-Zory. All five of these baseball teams were within twenty kilometers of each other. Then an outsider came in—Cyprzanów. Cyprzanów is a village of about 400 located ninety kilometers west, and a beautiful little turn south, of Rybnik. It is almost in Czechoslovakia, among rolling hills so storybook-like it seems right and proper that Cyprzanów is not even shown on the *Samochodowa Mapa Polski* (the official Polish road map). There is a church on a hill, and a red brick road winds through the village. The road leads to a creek. You cross over a bridge and come to a sheep meadow. That's where Ludowy Zespól Sportowy Cyprzanów (Folk Sports Union of Cyprzanów) plays baseball, among strict white chalk lines and clusters of sheep droppings that no one pays much attention to. Juan Echevarría's Kutno team was formed the same year as Cyprzanów's, and the next year, 1985, PZBall—with seven teams— began league play.

Most baseball diamonds in Poland were laid out on soccer fields, which usually resulted in a deep left field, an even deeper straight-away center field, and a short right field. Since almost all the players threw and batted right-handed and tended to hit the ball to left and center, that layout worked fairly well. (The occasional ball hit to deep right, and into the stands that were often there, was a ground-rule double.) What did not work well, however—and thank God it was dying out as the Poles came to understand baseball better—was their fussy practice of laying down canvas carpet on the pitcher's mound, at home plate, and along the base paths, to save the grass. When the field at Skra was being prepared for our first game that season, I told the Klub manager we were going to play baseball, not conduct a wedding, and I took the carpet away. The Górnik diamond did not have carpet; in fact, the base paths were dirt (or dirt and cinders—these guys were tough indeed) and the pitcher threw from a true mound. Right field was short—about 175 feet, ending in a thick stand of oak trees—but otherwise here was a real ball field. It was also very soggy from all the rain. Third base, in the worst shape, was a small pond. Tony found a shovel and, wearing his white cotton gloves, dug a hole about twelve feet away from the base—in foul territory—and then scooped out a canal leading from the pond to the hole. It was a wonderful piece of engineering: the water flowed.

The Junior Sparks did not flow. Neither did the Górnik Juniors, for that matter. They played a five-inning game (the limit for Juniors unless one team was ahead by ten runs after three innings; then a "knock down" was declared and the team behind spared further humiliation). They played a game in which two groups of adolescents slipped and rolled over in the wet grass a goodly number of times, made an occasional catch, an occasional put-out at first base, hit the ball maybe six times, walked a lot because they were small or afraid to swing the bat, struck out a lot because they were eager to swing at anything (especially when the pitch came in hat-high), and in short demonstrated that they had spent the important part of their youth bouncing soccer balls off their foreheads and feet instead of throwing and catching and hitting baseballs. The Junior Sparks were all seventeen and eighteen years old (eighteen was the cut-off for Juniors; there were no age restrictions for Seniors) and, except for one player, had never held a baseball until six months ago. (The exception was our center fielder, Paweł Tymiński, who had lived briefly in New York City.) I didn't know about the Górnik Juniors' experience, but they did not seem to possess any more skill or savvy than we did. That surprised me, in view of the fact that Boguszowice had been playing the game five years longer than Warsaw. It also surprised me that our Juniors were physically much bigger than theirs—I had expected to see size and muscle on *all* the players in Silesia. Our catcher, Mariusz ("Whale") Tumulski, a good eater who made his mother and grandmother happy over the years, was not an outrageously big kid for a Pole (six feet, 190 pounds), but he looked almost freakish next to those local boys. In any case, it was a sloppy game that Górnik won by a score of 14-12. The young Sparks were not overly disappointed. They knew they were learning a difficult sport and found consolation in the handful of decent plays they'd made. They also knew that the next game was the one that counted.

The Sunday following our loss to Jastrzębie, we hosted another Silesian team, Rój-Zory, whose name means "hive." "Like with bees," Pete told me. It was April 24, cold and overcast, and by the second inning of the Seniors game snowflakes were flying around. I counted six fans in the stands when it was over—Mariusz' girlfriend, Mark's girlfriend, Froggy's father and sister, Pizza Hut's father, and Vicki. We gave up three runs in the first inning—errors and walks—but then we started catching the ball and hitting it everywhere. In the bottom of the third, when we took a 15-3 lead, a Junior player—Paweł Tymiński—came running over to me and said, "Coach, Dariusz has a message for you. He thinks we can win by a knock down."

I looked up at Dariusz manning his microphone in the press box, cigarette smoke swirling around his head, and heard him explaining to the tiny audience that there was no Polish word for "homer." (Mariusz had just hit one.) I said to Paweł, "Maybe we can. But go tell Dariusz I'd rather not win by a knock down. We need the playing time. Tell Dariusz I'm thinking of making a lot of substitutions."

A tall, thin, altar boy–looking kid, Paweł hustled up the stadium steps to the press box. In a couple of minutes he was back, breathing hard. "Coach," he said, "I'm sorry to interrupt, but Dariusz wants me to say a knock down is no problem."

"Go tell Dariusz I'm going to start calling him George Steinbrenner," I said.

"I don't understand," Paweł said.

"Tell him *spokojnie.*"

"He says it is cold today."

"Tell him I know."

Paweł took off. Rój-Zory came up to bat and Mark, on the mound, walked the first two hitters. Then Dariusz was standing beside me, trying to look very casual. I yelled out to Mark to throw strikes.

Dariusz said, "Very cold this day."

The batter lined out to Froggy, who stepped on first for a double play.

"Did you see that, Dariusz? Hell, we should pray for snow all summer," I said.

"I see, yes, but—" Dariusz lit a cigarette. "Gary, what you think about knock down? Theoretic only. *Only* theoretic. What you think?"

"I don't like that rule," I said. "It's Little League."

Mark struck out the next batter and when the Sparks came in I told Adam, Pete, and July to warm up. Dariusz looked alarmed. He said, "They will pitch?"

"Maybe," I said.

"But why?"

"We're twelve runs ahead. They could use the practice."

"But Gary, Gary, Adam is maybe big nervous today. Maybe Pete, maybe July—all no good."

"How will they get better, Dariusz?"

"I know, I know, but—"

Adam, Pete, and July had plenty of time to get warm because we sent ten men to the plate that inning, scoring five more runs. Everyone was having fun, whooping it up. Mark borrowed a scarf from his girlfriend and wore it when he went up to hit. He smacked a double. Then everyone else borrowed scarves—from Froggy's sister, Vicki, Mariusz' girlfriend, from each other. Chuck Powers offered his parka to Tony, who already had on—beside the white gloves—two jackets and a hooded sweatshirt. We were all having fun in the swirling snowflakes except Dariusz, who was smoking and rolling up his Scoremaster as if he might try to smoke that too. "Must win. Must. Very important."

In the top of the fifth—we led, 20-3—I put Adam on the mound. I figured to let him get the first out, July the second, Pete the third. Rój-Zory had to score eight runs that inning to keep the game going.

Adam's first pitch bounced off home plate. His second pitch sailed over Jake's head—and the umpire's—into the stands. His third pitch almost hit the batter. I called time and went out to the mound. I put my arm around Adam's steaming shoulders. I could feel his heart pounding to escape. Jake joined us. "Jake, tell Adam to ease up on his fastball and just play catch with you, like in practice. Tell him nice and easy into your glove."

When play resumed, Adam threw a strike. He looked amazed that he could do such a thing. He threw another easy one—for strike two—and then raised his pitching arm in a salute, grinning as if the world might be an OK place after all. These were the first strikes he'd ever thrown in a game. Against Jastrzębie he threw eight consecutive balls to the only two batters he faced. If this big, strong, former javelin champion could pick up some confidence on the mound, we'd have a hell of a pitcher. He delivered again and the batter blooped a single just over Froggy's head. I told Jake to tell Adam that was OK, the pitch was in the strike zone. But I could see it was not OK with Dariusz, who paced back and forth behind our bench like a man in prison.

The next batter bounced a very slow roller to Tony that Tony wisely held onto—no chance to get anybody. "Adam's doing fine," I said to Jake. "Tell him to throw just a little harder." Adam walked the next batter—on a 3 and 2 count—and Dariusz, seeing the bases loaded, seemed to have stopped breathing. His face was plum-blue. Rój-Zory's next batter hit a big-hopper straight back to Adam; he caught the ball and threw it cleanly to first. He got his out. He was bursting. When I brought in July, Adam raced from the mound like a kid who had something good to tell his mother, and all the guys on the bench held up their palms for him to slap.

July gave up a walk to load the bases again, but fanned the next batter. When I called time to bring in Pete, I saw that Dariusz was now sitting on the bench with his face in his hands. We had a 20-4 lead and he couldn't bear to watch. Pete, who had the best control among all our pitchers, delivered two quick strikes and Dariusz was peeking through his fingers. The next pitch slipped out of Pete's hand and skittered past Jake. The runner on third scored. I didn't look at Dariusz; he might have been bleeding; for sure he was thinking that if Rój-Zory put on a rally, we had no more pitchers. But the batter popped up to Tony, and the umpire stood on home plate and declared a knock down. Dariusz rose from the bench like one who had come from a long and terrible journey. "History, history," I heard him rasp.

It was the Sparks' first victory ever, breaking a fifteen-game losing streak that began the previous year. Dariusz brought over a man whom he introduced to Chuck and me as "chief of Skra." In all the excitement I never caught his name, if it was given, and never saw him again. He was short, bushy about the eyebrows like Brezhnev, and all bundled up. A bulldog-looking gent. Dariusz hung on the man's grunts as if they were poetry.

In the happy shower room later, I said to him, "Did the chief want a knock down?"

"Chief of Skra? No."

"Why was it so important?"

"Knock down not important."

"Dariusz, you were very eager to win by a knock down. Do not give me bullshit." Then I yelled to Pete, who was enjoying a warm shower, "Hey, shoot that hose over here." I held Dariusz so he couldn't escape the spray.

"Win. Only win is important," Dariusz sputtered.

"We *were* winning. Big," I said, holding him in the spray.

"Gary, you listen," he said, water falling on his serious expression. "This is Poland. Win is never sure."

Earl Wasserman, Johns Hopkins, Baseball and Me

Eric Solomon

THE STRANGEST ASPECT of the year I spent at Johns Hopkins was not the Baltimore row house filled with nude oil paintings, not the paranoia my presence awakened in the English department, not even the odd circumstances that led to my becoming an Honorary Fellow and thus an alumnus. My relationship with Professor Earl Wasserman, one of the strong men in a strong English department in the 1963–64 academic year, still fills me with a sense of wonder.

The first encounter between Wasserman and myself occurred in the spring of 1963 when he gave a lecture in his specialty of Romantic poetics at Ohio State, where I was a young, recently tenured assistant professor of English. Since my wife had just received a research fellowship to work with Robert Blizzard at the Hopkins medical school, I was particularly eager to make contact with someone in my field in Baltimore. And at the ritual postlecture cocktail party, I made a special effort to ingratiate myself with Professor Wasserman who, I had learned, was not only a distinguished scholar but also the department chairman.

A compact, solidly built man with a shy smile and hooded eyes, Wasserman seemed warm and charming—even thrilled at the thought of my entering his bailiwick for a year. "That will be wonderful," he told me. "I'll get you an office to work in, make you a member of the faculty club so you can have lunch with the department. We eat lunch together every day, you know, and we really need some new blood." He went on to promise to find a house for me, my wife, and our three-year-old daughter. So genial, I thought. So friendly. I'm going to be very well received at Hopkins.

Later, after his friend Roy Harvey Pearce, a Johns Hopkins alumnus, had assured Wasserman of my economic probity, he expanded into specifics. "I'll get you Jack Cope's house to rent while he's on leave in England. My, it will be a pleasure to have you in the department. Make sure you come to see me the moment you arrive, so I can arrange everything."

The house he did arrange. After a long exchange of letters with Mrs. Jackson Cope—so many that the woman I've never yet met was signing herself "Jamie"—we had sublet their brick house on Tudor Arms Avenue across from Wyman Park. She reassured us that it would be fully appointed, and our only restriction was that we must not read in bed, *their* bed, a priceless brass bed that should not be bruised.

Actually, we fit snugly into the narrow row house. There was almost no furniture, true, and nearly all the dishes had been hidden, but there was Cope's marvelous library of eighteenth-century and James Joyce first editions, and many oil paintings of a variety of nude women, including a full-length "Eve" in the living room, rendered in what I called a neorealistic manner. I once remarked to Don Cameron Allen, the wry equal of Wasserman in the running for Hopkins's most distinguished scholar of literature, that the painting embarrassed me, especially when we were employing a young baby-sitter; yet I didn't see fit to remove it or turn it to the wall. "Shave it," growled Allen and turned to more important matters of Miltonic imagery. Until our son was born, we had a tiny guest room; we inherited a truly charming cleaning lady who later handled our childcare (and fixed everything from plumbing to furnaces); and I respected the brass bed.

Fitting into the neighborhood was easy, since I'm a porch-sitter, as were all Tudor Arms Avenue dwellers, from the Steuarts next door, who advised us about old Baltimore customs, to the Baldwins a few porches down, who explained the workings of Johns Hopkins itself from the vantage point of a medieval historian. Particularly nice for me, an inveterate baseball fan, was being within walking distance of where the Baltimore Orioles played my beloved Red Sox—a special joy after six years of exile watching the execrable minor-league Columbus Jets.

Thus it was with a light heart that I set forth early one July morning to be welcomed by Earl (as I now thought of him) and the Hopkins English department. Following John Baldwin's directions, I crossed over a bit of park, down into a ravine where during the 1930s hoboes used to camp by the B.&O. railroad tracks, over a stream by way of the sole remaining girder of a bridge—which Cope, I was told, was accustomed to run across, and across which I uneasily edged my careful path—up a hill, through the woods, and not to grandmother's house (though just as naively as Red Riding Hood) but to Gilman Hall. I arrived and knocked at Earl's door. And knocked.

Eventually, grudgingly, the door opened, and Earl Wasserman stood there. I had not before noticed the overwhelming quality of his crinkly, graying hair, wrinkled brow, heavy eyebrows; now he stared at me, uncomprehendingly, looking like a hairy owl.

"Hi, Earl, I'm Eric Solomon," I said, brightly. He continued to stare. "You remember, from Ohio State. I'm here for the year, and you're going to give me an office and make me a member of the faculty club, lunch . . ." He made a distinct effort. "Right. Solomon. Well, we have no office space. None at all. I'll have to look into the faculty club business." He seemed remarkably dour, but then he brightened. "What I *can* do is find you a nice place in the library stacks. In the *English* section of the stacks!"

Beaming at this solution, he led me to the library. "I want Professor Solomon, from Ohio State, to be given every privilege. I want you to find him a seat in the *English* part of the stacks," he announced to the woman guarding the stack entrance. "Certainly, Dr. Wasserman"—she sounded puzzled—"he can have any place he wants; the whole section is empty." Oblivious to this denigration of his munificence, Earl Wasserman gave me a quick smile, a quicker handshake, and rumbled away. There was no further mention of an office, of a faculty club, of lunch.

Undaunted, I made my way back along the corridor of English department offices, glancing at the impressive names, Don Cameron Allen, Charles Anderson, Richard Green, Jackson Cope, until I came to the one I wanted: J. Hillis Miller, my old pal from Harvard graduate school days. Once more I knocked. Once more no response. A wait. Another knock.

Finally, the door opened, just as in Wasserman's office, and Hillis stood in the doorway. He hadn't quite mastered the art of looming, but he certainly could imitate his chairman's quizzical look. "What are *you* doing here?" was his warm greeting. Again I explained my presence, and we gossiped a bit about our youthful gambols in Harvard Yard, but nostalgia had insufficient power to lead him to ask me to sit down. So we completed our little talk while standing, and I departed to the firm sound of a door closing.

Not until I had befriended one of the more nervous faculty members did I learn that I had broken a hallowed custom. No one disturbed a professor of the English department while he was writing in his office. They met for coffee twice a day in the Levering cafeteria; they gathered around a special table for lunch. Otherwise, except for classes and rare office hours, they were incommunicado—except to each other. "They"—meaning Earl, Don, and Hillis—"have a secret knock, you see; that lets them talk to each other without fear of encountering a student."

And the lunches? "Well, one doesn't *have* to eat lunch with the English department," John Baldwin informed me. "After two years I managed to get their medievalist to sit down at lunch with me. But he kept glancing over to the English table, got more and more nervous, and before dessert, he couldn't stand it any more; he excused himself and rushed over there." Clearly I was on my own.

In an odd way, however, I made a real place for myself in those library stacks. Partly because the English faculty seemed obsessed with their own scholarly production, partly because the newly arrived graduate students who joined me in the dank stacks were working from the start with compulsive terror—I found literary research more attractive than I had for years. And since some of the Hopkins faculty productivity came from their studied avoidance of graduate students, I became a kind of coach, along with some of the third-year students and a somewhat older recruit from Oklahoma, Homer Brown. Because we did know some basics about bibliography and research, we became, despite age differences, part of a team.

Thus I settled into my own Johns Hopkins rhythm. Each morning my wife and daughter went off to the hospital and nursery school respectively, and I went to the Homewood campus. There I would read, take notes, and talk with my (fellow) students—all male—in the Gilman stacks. Most mornings, I would join the English faculty coffee gatherings in Levering, always at 10:30; ditto at 2:30. Lunch was never to be considered, but coffee seemed acceptable. In the autumn, I drove to Washington a couple of times a week to use the Library of Congress—I was working on the idea of parody in the fiction of Stephen Crane. And once a week I had lunch, always oysters, beer, and cheese, with a genuine Hopkins faculty member, Tom Fulton, a physics professor whose wife had roomed with my wife in college.

The graduate students were a marvelous group. They seemed much amused by my presence in their ranks and often discussed my work in very helpful ways. And one, whose wife worked in the library receiving department, saw to it that I got first crack at any new book relevant to my research. When late in that November of 1963 we were all shaken by the John Kennedy assassination, we gathered around a radio in the stacks to deal with the immediate shock. I suppose that the faculty also stopped work long enough to seek some group support, but I was now in another world.

The two worlds occasionally crossed, of course. When we had dinner at the Fultons, Hillis Miller appeared. And I discovered, to my delight, a former Brooklyn taxi driver turned brilliantly erudite professor of the history of science, Harry Woolf, who also bridged the worlds of scholarly commitment and (why not?) Jewish funkiness. Indeed, he and the philosopher Maurice Mandelbaum, along with Fulton and Baldwin, tried to explain the special mandarin quality of the English faculty; their theory was that the past great giants of history of ideas — such as Raymond Havens, A. O. Lovejoy, George Boas — loomed over the Wassermans and Allens, filling them with what Harold Bloom now calls the anxiety of influence.

Whatever, my first six months at Johns Hopkins University were comfortable, rewarding, stimulating, and virtually untouched by any genuine relationship with the cold, formal, and highly intellectualized department that had originally seemed to promise warm hospitality. Despite some breakdowns in discipline — we dined with the Greens, for example, and learned of his uneasiness with the scholarly compulsiveness, spent evenings with the Millers, and, eventually, with the Allens — I was in no way a part of the department.

And yet. They seemed to do nothing but read, write, and discuss what they wrote. So I read, voraciously, wrote every day, and talked to the graduate students about what I was writing. Lo, when January arrived, I had completed a manuscript, a new child was ready to take over the study in Cope's house, and Bruce Franklin arrived to clear up some of the mysteries.

Now, Bruce Franklin, author of a respectable book on Herman Melville and an assistant professor of American literature at Stanford, was not yet the stormy revolutionary of the late 1960s whose behavior so enraged his Stanford colleagues as to lead them to revoke his tenure. Yet when he came to Hopkins to present a talk to the graduate students (me included!), he handled Charles Anderson's effusive introduction with cool casualness. "Dr. Franklin will give us new material from his latest research since the publication of his book," cooed Anderson. "No," stated Franklin, "this is all material from the book."

Not following Hopkins custom, the audience was extremely respectful. I asked the only vaguely hostile question. Later, Harry Woolf explained to me that Anderson was insisting on Franklin's being offered a junior faculty position. And, continued Woolf, the department was convinced that I had learned earlier that they were going to make an appointment in American literature—and, that I had come to Baltimore to be on the spot and attempt to wiggle into the job.

Filled with righteous innocence, I exploded: "Why don't they believe I came here because my wife had a fellowship at the medical school?" Harry nodded in his best rabbinical manner and sweetly explained, "Because that just doesn't fit their experience. When an English professor gets a leave, he goes to England. Maybe to Cambridge, Mass. Not to Baltimore. Never to Baltimore. Unless he has an ulterior motive."

That mystery explained, the curtain of paranoia lifted. Franklin accepted the Hopkins offer, I (to do the Hopkins English department some justice—for even paranoids have real enemies) was offered and accepted a position as associate professor at San Francisco State College, and everyone seemed mightily relieved. I even had an office. It arrived appropriately, for I had a first draft ready to type, and benign and friendly as the stacks were, typing in such a setting was implausible.

Leon Madansky, the head of the physics department, was amused by my tales of tenuous relations with his English colleagues, and he scoffed at my exile to the stacks. The next day I found myself ensconced in a large physics office, with not one but two desks (and a blackboard, on which, alas, I had no formulae to inscribe). For the rest of my Hopkins year, I pecked industriously away in the physics ambience. Indeed, I became a kind of Visiting Fellow from the humanities, as physics faculty members took to dropping by and questioning my research methods. Right, like Dr. Johnson, I *am* clubbable, and the physics people provided me the collegiality I had not found among the English faculty and had improvised among the graduate students.

When in 1966 the time came for me to write the acknowledgments for the Harvard University Press edition of my book, I worded it very carefully: "My appreciation goes to the Library of Congress and to the Johns Hopkins Library for their resources, to the hospitality of the English Department of Johns Hopkins University, and particularly to the Hopkins Physics Department and its Chairman, Leon Madansky, who kindly provided me with an office in which to write this book."

Still, the reference to the English department was not entirely ironic. There did exist an *intellectual* hospitality, and I reflected their remarkable work habits. Work was in the ambience, so I worked hard too, in order not to seem churlish. Then, too, hospitality arrived along with the spring and baseball season.

I truly love baseball. Since I was twelve, I focused my most intense scholarly abilities on box scores, sports pages, batting averages; *Who's Who in Baseball* was my *PMLA Bibliography,* the *Sporting News* my *New York Review.* Baseball I knew, just as Earl Wasserman knew Keats and Shelley. Imagine my wonder, then, when I sat down to coffee at Levering one sunny April morning, to hear Earl asking Hillis Miller, "Do you know who caught a baseball thrown from the Washington Monument?" "Gabby Street," I replied to the stunned silence around the table. "Wilbert Robinson tried also. Uncle Robby. Dodgers manager later."

Wasserman looked at me. At that moment, as I gazed back into his hooded eyes, I realized that he had never looked at me, directly at me, in eight months. "Was there ever a ballplayer who fell down rounding third base in a World Series game?" "Sure. Chuck Hostetler of Detroit in 1945. That was called the worst Series ever played. Against the Cubs. One writer said both teams were so bad, neither could win. Hank Greenberg had just come out of the Army . . ."

I don't know from what recess of my brain I had dredged that particular item. Like all baseball buffs, I recalled best the players of my youth. Chuck Hostetler was enshrined with such trivial wartime players as Sig Jackucki and Dick Wakefield. But Earl Wasserman wasn't staring at me now; he was scribbling hastily in a notebook. He stopped. Again he looked directly at me. "How do you know these things?" "I just know them," I responded, "but there *are* books and histories, you know."

"Of *baseball?*" Earl Wasserman, one of the world's leading scholars, gasped astounded. Then he spoke the magic words. "Let's have lunch tomorrow. I want to talk to you about this."

We had lunch. A number of lunches. At the faculty club. Carefully, Earl Wasserman explained his problem to me. He had been asked to give a paper at Cornell. But at Cornell lurked Meyer Abrams, Wasserman's only peer as America's greatest Romantic scholar. So Earl was going to fool them all and give a talk on a completely unexpected subject: a Jungian reading of Bernard Malamud's baseball novel, *The Natural.* Yet, while Malamud's book was rich in Jungian archetypes, animas, Arthurian myths, the work was also full of baseball folklore. Earl Wasserman knew Carl Jung but not Carl Hubbell. This is where I came into the picture.

We studied the novel, we visited the stacks to discover the sports section, we even went to an Orioles game. I was of some help, tracing more baseball references than Wasserman actually employed in his paper, but certainly preparing him for any queries he might encounter from a baseball fanatic. We discussed the Black Sox scandal, Ted Williams, the shooting of Eddie Waitkus, many Babe Ruth stories, Shoeless Joe Jackson, the House of David team, spring phenoms such as Clint Hartung, old rookies like Jim Turner, pitchers turned out-fielders like Johnny Lindell, bonehead plays like that of Fred Merkle, Casey Stengel releasing a bird from his cap, the rookie Floyd Giebel beating the great Bob Feller in the last game of a season to win the pennant, Judge Emil Fuchs, the corrupt Braves owner—and much, much more, from Pepper Martin's wild base running to Pete Reiser's penchant for crashing into outfield fences, from Ruth's stomachache or calling his home run shot to Joe Medwick's bad ball hitting.

I enjoyed our talks, and Earl became increasingly amused and fascinated by the near-Talmudic way I unraveled my baseball worship. The long-term results of our discussions were his talk—later published as "*The Natural:* Malamud's World Ceres" (the pun was all his) in the *Centennial Review* —and my own "Jews, Baseball, and the American Novel," an MLA paper and part of a book I'm now writing.

Another result was my admission to the Hopkins Club (sound of trumpets and flourishes). Actually, it wasn't easy. In order to attain guest privileges for me at the faculty club, Earl Wasserman had to get me official Johns Hopkins status. This only came about after he appointed me to a Graduate Fellowship (without stipend) in the English department. The story might end neatly here, with perhaps an ironic twist from the fact that I only used that club once myself, to feed a nervous high school friend just before his Baltimore wedding to the daughter of London Fog raincoats. But baseball talk opened up—as it often does—a flood of Earl Wasserman revelations to me.

When he reminisced about his career, his Navy years, his scholarship, especially his start in the profession as the youngest graduate student of English in Hopkins history (he went, I believe, directly into the graduate program from his freshman year), I discovered a very differ-ent Earl Wasserman from the tough autocrat of the seminar table.

While we sat alone musing over coffee, he revealed a vulnerable, rather sweet persona.

Why was he nervous about his upcoming talk at Cornell? "You see, Mike Abrams and I were among the first Jewish professors of English literature in this country, and I think he'll be looking to catch me out. We're sort of rivals." I expressed wonderment that in the late 1930s there were so few Jewish faculty. Wasserman laughed: "I'm not talking about places like Yeshiva or even CCNY—they took care of their own. But there was only Lionel Trilling at Columbia, Ludwig Lewisohn had lost his job, Harry Levin was a Junior Fellow at Harvard . . . Abrams and I. Let me tell you about my first job."

As his story unfolded, I, from my protected situation of a later time when it seemed every English department in the country was brimming over with Jewish professors and students, could start to perceive some of the reasons for his self-protective shell. At age 20, Ph.D. in hand, he applied for a number of teaching slots and received not a single offer. So he took a job teaching composition in a Baltimore business school.

When the next year he still received no responses, he got up his courage to ask his thesis advisor to reveal the letter of recommendation he had prepared. "It was a good letter," Earl Wasserman recalled, "full of praise for my energy, youth, promise, scholarship. Then it closed with quite a final sentence: 'Unfortunately, Mr. Wasserman is a Jew.'" "What did you do?" "Oh, I asked him if he would mind removing the last sentence. He was perfectly nice about it, even though he didn't quite see why. Then I got a job at Illinois . . . "

He went on talking about his war service, about more insecurity as to whether he would get a teaching post after the war. And as I realized some of the doubts that even the most successful scholarly young Jewish graduate student in our field must have faced during the Depression, I felt much more warmly towards Earl. In a way, we became friends.

There are two twists to this tale, after all, lest it seem too neat. Before I left for the West Coast, I tried to play an avuncular Wasserman-type role with the newly arrived Bruce Franklin, to explain the odd nature of the Johns Hopkins English department so that he would avoid some of my errors. He scoffed at their lunch traditions and remarked that he would spend little time on campus anyway, since he intended to find a home in Baltimore's black slums, to live among the people. Somehow, the thought of this committed political radical as the protégé of the genteel, aristocratic Southerner Charles Anderson made me chortle. Fortunately for Hopkins, Bruce Franklin returned to Stanford in time to join the revolution.

Oh, I saw Earl Wasserman a few more times, at meetings, and we exchanged a couple of letters, but I like to remember my last encounter with him, for I appreciate stories that come full circle. A few years after my Hopkins stay, I went to Boston, in all innocence, to visit my parents, as I did every summer. Following my invariable custom, I spent a day at Harvard, wandering through the Square, the bookstores, visiting old haunts and mentors. I strolled through the Yard, and coming down the steps of Widener Library was Earl; he was teaching summer school at Harvard. He took a long look at me, bridled with suspicion, and growled, "What are *you* doing here?"

VI

FANS

From *Blue Highways*

William Least Heat Moon

I WALKED DOWN to the bakery, the one with flour sacks for sale in the front window and bowling trophies above the apple turnovers. The people of the northern midlands—the Swedes and Norgies and Danes—apparently hadn't heard about the demise of independent, small-town bakeries; most of their towns had at least one.

With a bag of blueberry tarts, I went up Main to a tin-sided, false-front tavern called Michel's, just down the street from the Cease Funeral Home. The interior was log siding and yellowed knotty pine. In the backroom the Junior Chamber of Commerce talked about potatoes, pulpwood, dairy products, and somebody's broken fishing rod. I sat at the bar. Behind me a pronghorn antelope head hung on the wall, and beside it a televised baseball game cast a cool light like a phosphorescent fungus.

"Hear that?" a dwindled man asked. He was from the time when boys drew "Kilroy-Was-Here" faces on alley fences. "Did you hear the announcer?"

"I wasn't listening."

"He said 'velocity.'"

"Velocity?"

"He's talking about a fastball. A minute ago he said a runner had 'good acceleration.' This is a baseball game, not a NASA shot. And another thing: I haven't heard anybody mention a 'Texas leaguer' in years."

"It's a 'bloop double' now, I think."

"And the 'banjo hitter'—where's he? And what happened to the 'slowball'?"

"It's a 'change-up.' "

The man got me interested in the game. We watched and drank Grain Belt. He had taught high school civics in Minneapolis for thirty-two years, but his dream had been to become a sports announcer.

"They put a radar gun on the kid's fastball a few minutes ago," he said. "Ninety-three point four miles per hour. That's how they tell you speed now. They don't try to show it to you: 'smoke,' 'hummer,' 'the high hard one.' I miss the old clichés. They had life. Who wants to hit a fastball with a decimal point when he can tie into somebody's 'heat'? And that's another thing: nobody 'tattoos' or 'blisters' the ball anymore. These TV boys are ruining a good game because they think if you can see it they're free to sit back and psychoanalyze the team. Ask and I'll tell you what I think of it."

"What do you think of it?"

"Beans. And that's another thing too."

"Beans?"

"Names. Used to be players named Butterbean and Big Potato, Little Potato. Big Poison, Little Poison. Dizzy and Daffy. Icehouse, Shoeless Joe, Suitcase, The Lip. Now we've got the likes of Rickie and Richie and Reggie. With names like that, I think I'm watching a third-grade scrub team."

The announcer said the pitcher had "good location."

"Great God in hemlock! He means 'nibble the corners.' But which of these throwing clowns nibbles corners? They're obsessed with speed. Satchel Paige—there's a name for you—old Satch could fire the pill a hundred and five miles an hour. He didn't throw it that fast very often because he couldn't make the ball cut up at that speed. And, sure as spitting, his pitching arm lasted just about his whole life."

The man took a long smacking pull on his Grain Belt. "Damn shame," he said. "There's a word for what television's turned this game into."

"What's the word?"

"Beans," he said. "Nothing but beans and hot air."

Three New Twins Join Club in Spring

Garrison Keillor

My TEAM WON the World Series. You thought we couldn't but we knew we would and we did, and what did your team do? Not much. Now we're heading down to spring training looking even better than before, and your team that looked pitiful then looks even less hot now. Your hometown paper doesn't say so, but your leadoff guy had a bad ear infection in January and now he gets dizzy at the first sign of stress and falls down in a heap. Sad. Your cleanup guy spent the winter cleaning his plate. He had to buy new clothes in a size they don't sell at regular stores. Your great relief guy, his life has been changed by the Rama Lama Ding Dong, and he is now serenely throwing the ball from a place deep within himself, near his gallbladder. What a shame. Your rookie outfielder set a world record for throwing a frozen chicken, at a promotional appearance for Grandma Fanny's Farm Foods. Something snapped in his armpit and now he can't even throw a pair of dice. Tough beans. Your big left-hander tried hypnosis to stop smoking and while in a trancelike state discovered he hated his mother for tying his tiny right hand behind his back and making him eat and draw and tinkle with his left. So he's right-handed now, a little awkward but gradually learning to point with it and wave goodbye. That's what your whole team'll be doing by early May.

Meanwhile, my team, the world-champion Minnesota Twins, are top dogs who look like a lead-pipe cinch to take all the marbles in a slow walk. My guys had a good winter doing youth work. Last October they pooled their Series pay to purchase a farm, Twin Acres, north of Willmar, where they could stay in shape doing chores in the off-season, and they loved it so much they stayed through Thanksgiving and

Christmas (celebrating them the good old-fashioned Midwestern way), and raised a new barn, bought a powerful new seed drill to plant winter wheat with, built up the flock of purebred Leghorns, chopped wood, carried water, etc., along with their guests—delinquent boys and girls from St. Louis and Detroit who needed to get out of those sick destructive environments and learn personal values such as honesty and personal cleanliness. Meanwhile, back in Minneapolis, the Twins front office wasn't asleep on its laurels but through shrewd deals made mostly before 8:15 A.M. added to what they had while giving up nothing in return. They did so great, it seems unfair.

Other Teams Gnash Teeth or Sulk

It's considered impossible to obtain *three top premium players* without paying a red cent, but the Twins:

• Traded away some useless air rights and obtained Chuck Johnson (23, 187 lbs., 6'1", bats left, throws left), a native of Little Falls, Minnesota. Maybe that's why the scouts who work the Finger Lakes League ignored his phenomenal season with the Seneca Falls Susans. They figured, "Minnesota? Forget it!" But how can you forget thirty-eight doubles, twenty-two triples, and twenty-nine round-trippers—and in spacious Elizabeth Cady Stanton Stadium! That's a lot of power for a lifelong liberal like Chuck. And what's more, he *never struck out.* Not once. Plays all positions cheerfully.

• Sent a couple in their midforties to the San Diego Padres in exchange for Duane (Madman) Mueller (29, 280 lbs., 6'2", right/right, a.k.a. Mule, Hired Hand, The Barber). Duane is a big secret because after he was suspended by the Texas League for throwing too hard he played Nicaraguan winter ball for three years and then spent two more doing humanitarian stuff, so scouts forgot how, back when he was with the Amarillo Compadres, nobody wanted to be behind the plate, Duane threw so hard. His own team kept yelling, "Not so *hard,* man!" If that sounds dumb, then you never saw him throw: he threw *hard.* A devoted Lutheran, he never ever hit a batter, but in one game a pitch of his nicked the bill of an opponent's batting helmet and spun it so hard it burned off the man's eyebrows. No serious injury, but big Duane took himself out of organized ball until he could learn an off-speed pitch. He's from Brainerd, Minnesota, where he lives across the street from his folks. His mom played kittenball in the fifties and had a good arm but not like her son's. She thinks he got it from delivering papers and whipping cake mix. "I'd sure hate to have to bat against him," she says.

• Gave up a dingy two-bedroom house in St. Paul (it needs more than just a paint job and a new roof, and it's near a rendering plant) to acquire and activate Bob Berg (24, 112 lbs., 5'3", right/left), the fastest man on the basepaths today (we *think*), but he sat out last year and the year before last and the year before *that* because he didn't have shoes. Reason: he's so fast he runs the shoes right off his feet. Now athletic foot specialists have studied his film clips (sad to see: three lightning strides, a look of dismay on Bob's face, and down he goes with his loose laces like a lasso round his ankles) and come up with a new pair of pigskin shoes with barbed cleats that stick in the turf and slow him down. Born and raised in Eveleth, Minnesota, he is probably the nicest fast man in baseball. Nicknamed The Hulk ("berg" means "mountain" in Norwegian). He used those three years on the bench to earn a B.A. in history, by the way.

That's Not All

• Joining the team later will be Wally Gunderson (17, 191 lbs., 6'4", left/right), who dons a Twins uniform June 8, the day after he graduates from West High in Minneapolis. The Twins have saved him a number, 18, and assigned him a locker and paid him a bonus, twelve hundred dollars, which was all he would accept. He's thrilled just to be on the team. A big lanky loose-jointed kid with long wavy blond hair and a goofy grin, he throws a screwball that comes in and up, a slider that suddenly jumps, a curve that drops off the table, and a stinkball that hangs in the air so long some batters swing twice. You don't expect so much junk from an Eagle Scout, but Wally's got one more: a fastball that decelerates rapidly halfway to the plate — a braking pitch. Some he learned from his dad and the rest he invented for a science fair project. "Pitching is physics, that's all," he says, looking down at his size-13 shoes, uneasy at all the acclaim.

Detroit and St. Louis offered the lad millions in cash, land, jewelry, servants, tax abatements, but he wasn't listening. "I want to play my ball where my roots are," he says quietly.

Twinsville wasn't one bit surprised. Personal character and loyalty and dedication are what got us where we are right now, and that's on top. We're No. 1. We knew it first and now you know it, too. You thought we were quiet and modest in the Midwest but that's because you're dumb, as dumb as a stump, dumber than dirt.

You're so dumb you don't know that we're on top and you're below. Our team wins and your team loses; we need your team to amuse us. Minnesota soybeans, corn, and barley; we're the best, so beat it, Charley, or we'll shell ya like a pea pod, dunk ya like a doughnut — sure be nice when the game's over, won't it — take ya to the cleaners for a brand-new hairdo. We can beat ya anytime we care to. Shave and a haircut, two bits.

From *The Dodgers Move West*

Neil J. Sullivan

W HEN THE YEARS of disappointment finally ended in the championship season of 1955, the borough-wide elation revealed how frustrating the earlier defeats had been to Brooklyn. A fan interviewed by Peter Golenbock, author of *Bums*, an oral history of the Brooklyn Dodgers, recalled that he had been a Marine corporal stationed in Maryland when the Dodgers finally beat the Yankees. "I called my sister on the phone, and here I was in the brig guarding prisoners, and I said 'Ronnie, what is it like in Brooklyn?' And she said, 'Listen to this,' and she stuck the phone out the window, and I could hear the roar of the crowd, the screaming. And I wanted so badly to be there, I just started to cry, and the prisoners, a couple of sailors, they started laughing when they saw me. Here I am, a big marine, and I'm crying, tears rolling down my face. Those were great days. The greatest in the world."

Donald Honig told Golenbock, "It was almost as though you were finding your manhood at stake. You rooted for this team, and every October it would die. And when you put the win in the context of a small neighborhood, where your personal relationships were very tight, it became even more important. The Yankee fans and Giant fans were always ribbing you, saying that you choked. Dodger fans very well knew the sentiments of the mythical Man on the Street. He knew that it was said that the Dodgers choked every October, and what the hell were you going to say? They did lose every October.

"I know all this sounds so superficial—your team won, so what? A nonfan could not conceive of how important it was. But baseball was an important factor in my neighborhood. For twelve months a year, it was baseball and little else. Everyone knew who you rooted for before they knew your religion or nationality. It was important to you that your team did well. Baseball was very important, and rooting for the Brooklyn Dodgers was something special."

In their emotional intensity, the Dodgers' fans often forgot the pressures threatening the team's continued presence in Brooklyn. When the prospect of losing the Dodgers became a public issue, residents wrote to Mayor Robert Wagner. Some of their arguments raised basic questions about the role of government, but many were simple appeals to keep the team in Brooklyn. One such plea, from a Mrs. Tyree Smith, began, "I am writting [sic] this letter as a loyal Brooklynite, New Yorker and Democrat. (I am putting them all together because they go together like coffee and cream with sugar). . . . If we lose the Dodgers and the Giants because you think they are bluffing, I will give you something to think about." Another woman wrote: "You won't get my vote in the coming election, if you do decide to run again, if the Sports Center for the Dodgers isn't built so they will stay in Brooklyn." Still another voter, Mr. R. Cucco, put the matter more directly. "I am a man of very few words so I will come straight to the point. I voted for you. I pay your salary. I WANT THE DODGERS IN BROOKLYN. I don't want any excuses from you or any of your men there at City Hall. I WANT THE DODGERS IN BROOKLYN, and you can do it by building that Sports Center. You had better get it built or you'll not get a vote from me."

Even theology and sociology were invoked to influence Wagner's decisions. Gloria Cerrato wrote, "I am a young girl of 16 and enjoy baseball to great extents [sic]. If the Dodgers move to Los Angeles I will no longer enjoy this right given to me by my Creator. Please keep them here. Baseball keeps a lot of us teen-agers off the streets and prevents J[uvenile] D[elinquency]."

"Let's keep the Bums in Brooklyn forever and ever, by building them their stadium. It won't only be for them. Remember."

Another letter took a more dispassionate approach: "I cannot impress upon you too much how important it is to keep the Dodgers in Brooklyn. It keeps the children off the streets during the day, it gives them someone to look up to, someone to imitate. Instead of acting like 'tough guys,' they try to imitate Duke Snider, Pee Wee Reese, Roy Campanella, etc. It also gives them a feeling for 'fair play.' And the Dodgers, being composed of Negroes, Spanish, and Whites, are a good example of how good you can get if everyone works together regardless of race or color."

The Dodgers were more than a business, more even than a sports franchise. They represented a cultural totem, a tangible symbol of the community and its values. Baseball and the Dodgers were a pastime that lured young people away from the inducement of crime and indolence. During the summer months, when young people were not constrained by school, the Dodgers served as a kind of baby-sitter. From our perspective, these people's trust in baseball's saving grace may strike us as naive; but our culture had barely been introduced to rock music let alone the other distractions that would follow. Brooklyn was undergoing many changes, and the Dodgers were one of the few means for getting one's bearings.

The Dodgers also played a role in improving race relations. Like the Giants, the Dodgers aggressively pursued black athletes as an untapped market of talent. This might seem a natural occurrence in a multiracial city such as New York, but the Yankees didn't sign a black player until Elston Howard joined the team in 1955.

This team would have attracted a following in Brooklyn solely on the basis of its many exasperating failures to win championships, but much more than their performances on the field bound the Dodgers to Brooklyn. The itch to escape the tag of bumpkin, the possibility of racial harmony, and, perhaps most importantly, the futile hope that borough life would return to familiar patterns—all these sentiments bound the Dodgers to Brooklyn, and made their presence essential.

Even as the Dodgers and Brooklyn carried on their romance, the business of baseball was unobtrusively adapting to new conditions. The impact of television, the mass exodus to the suburbs, the popularity of the automobile, and population shifts to the South and West affected the financial stability of most teams. No one had a keener sense of these changes than Walter O'Malley, for whom sentimentality about the Dodgers' past would not be sufficient to keep the team in Brooklyn.

Confessions from Left Field

Raymond Mungo

IT WASN'T THE BEST DAY to visit Candlestick Park in San Francisco. The Giants had lost the first two games of the series and were facing the Braves in the final game under cloudy skies and light drizzle, a noon start on June 6. In all, they'd lost seven in a row and were mired in last place in the N.L. West, owners of the worst record in baseball. Nobody could explain it, least of all manager Frank Robinson, who the day before had received a death threat and was told not to venture out of the dugout by league officials.

We drove up from Monterey, two and a half hours on the Blood Alley strip of Highway 101, increasingly despoiled by the San Jose sprawl. I poured vodka grapefruits into plastic cups from a thermos in the backseat of the station wagon, and our little group of four was in fine spirits by the time the old 'Stick came into view. Rain fell intermittently and fierce, cold winds swirled around the park. We wore down parkas and gloves, carried umbrellas. New York was in a heat wave.

I wanted to see the Braves, not the Giants. My gurus are Monsignor Murphy and Professor Perez and I miss Knucksy Niekro a tone and wish him well in Bronx. Ted Turner is constructing a bronze, life-sized statue of Niekro to be unveiled at Atlanta Fulton County Stadium this August, in an astonishing display of sentiment for a guy he sent packing last fall. Too bad the statue can't pitch. The inside skinny was that Manager Joe Torre supposedly felt threatened by Niekro's leadership role, a role the Yankees were glad to have around.

Anyway, the Braves on June 6 were in first place and on an eight-game winning streak, all on the road. Even the loss of Bob Horner hadn't hurt their hitting, and the pitching was remarkably all right, with Steve Bedrosian in the bullpen (4-0, 0.57 ERA) to slam the door in the late innings.

We took our seats in the upper deck behind home plate. The game started off badly for the Giants, with a Joel Youngblood error setting up a gift run driven in by Murphy on a sacrifice. Second inning, another Atlanta run, this time without the benefit of a hit — and again driven in by Murph. (What a man, fans.) But in the bottom of the third, Giant catcher, Bob Brenly, hit a towering grand slam to deep center field, and for a shining moment some 4,000 wet, cold fans went bananas. The sun even peeked out from behind the ever-blackening clouds.

The score remained 4-2 for the hometown heroes until the ninth inning, when a combination of errors and what seemed bad managing gave the Braves two to tie it. The guy sitting behind me, who'd been drinking beer continuously through the game and getting more and more angry and abusive toward the Giants, went into a complete rage. "Fuckin' Robinson, get the fuck out of there! You don't know shit! Minton, you get your fuckin' paycheck. You worthless fuck!" (Robinson had brought in Minton to set up a righty-lefty switch and the Braves successfully countered by pinch-hitting Bob Watson, who smacked a double. The Giants blew a two-run lead with two outs and nobody on in the ninth.)

In the tenth inning, with the rain now pouring down, we shivered and wished it would end. There hadn't been much fireworks from the Braves, but the Giants found every way to beat themselves. The drunk behind me was still ordering beers and inventing new obscenities to scream at the Giants. Our group looked at each other, rolled our eyes, snickered. "Wow, that guy is really out there." "You can't blame him. He's a frustrated Giants fan." He was about 30, bearded, with long hair, a grungy one from the Mission District perhaps.

In the eleventh, Robinson made another pitching change, to Lavelle I guess it was, and then another to one of his rookie pitchers from AAA. The Braves scored the go-ahead run on a walk to Chris Chambliss, and the irate fan went totally berserk. In the bottom of the eleventh, Bedrosian blew the Giants away, the ballgame was over, and the Black Day at Candlestick Park had come to an end. Nearly.

My companion Dwight, an orchid grower from Carmel, was saying that the Giants had lost 12 of the 13 games he'd been to see in person. We bundled up soggy programs and "Sporting News" and hardly noticed that Crazy Fan had staggered down to the upper-deck railing below us. He was still screaming at various Giants in the most obscene terms, leaning over the rail, rocking on it.

In less time than it takes to tell, he fell and crashed to his bloody death below, shattering a chair and injuring a bystander. It was the first such death at a baseball game in Candlestick Park. We decided to take the coast route and rode home in silence, oblivious to the majestic ocean, crashing waves, muted green scenery, wild birds. You root for the home team and if they don't win it's a shame. But enough is enough.

A Note on the Editor

Jerry Klinkowitz is the executive director of the Waterloo Diamonds, a San Diego Padres Class A affiliate. He is also a professor of English and University Distinguished Scholar at the University of Northern Iowa and has published extensively on American literature.